Photo by Don H. Evavold

respect to neglected or abused children —
this book's revealing message speaks to
psychologists, psychiatrists, and social
workers, as well as to the more conscientious
practitioners of family law, pastoral
counseling, education, and parenthood.

John Joseph Evoy is the author or co-author
of four previous books relating to human
personality. While serving as professor of
psychology at Gonzaga University he
conducted a clinical practice for more than
thirty years. The recipient of degrees in
philosophy and theology from Gonzaga and
Saint Louis Universities, he was awarded a
Ph.D. in psychology by Loyola University,
Chicago.

The Rejected

The Rejected:
Psychological Consequences
of Parental Rejection

John Joseph Evoy

Emeritus Professor, Psychology
Gonzaga University
Spokane

The Pennsylvania State University Press
University Park and London

Library of Congress Cataloging in Publication Data

Evoy, John J.
  The rejected.

  Includes bibliography and index
  1. Parental rejection.   2.   Psychology, Pathological.
I. Title. [DNLM: 1. Parent-child relations. 2. Rejection
(Psychology)   3.   Personality disorders—Etiology. WM 190
E93r]
RC455.4.F3E96   155.9′24   81-47172
ISBN 0-271-00285-9   AACR2

The right to affection, love and understanding.

The right to adequate nutrition and medical care.

The right to free education.

The right to full opportunity for play and recreation.

The right to a name and nationality.

The right to special care, if handicapped.

*The right to be among the first to receive relief in
times of disaster.*

*The right to be a useful member of society and to
develop individual abilities.*

*The right to be brought up in a spirit of peace and
universal brotherhood.*

*The right to enjoy these rights, regardless of race, color,
sex, religion, national or social origin.*

—U.N. Declaration of the Rights of the Child

Contents

Acknowledgments

My grateful expressions of appreciation are extended to:

—the thousands of men and women who, during the course of some thirty years, confided their most intimate thoughts and experiences to me.

—the client who generously proposed that I record his counseling sessions for use in any way I might choose. Two of these sessions have been transcribed and reproduced in the appendix.

—my four brothers (Gerard, Matty, Larry, and Bob), for their constant love and support.

—Dr. David P. Ausubel, for his ongoing professional inspiration.

—Dr. Michael Brown and Dr. R. Steven Heaps (my colleagues in the Psychology Department at Gonzaga University), for their critiques and suggestions.

—Dr. Maureen O'Keefe, S.S.N.D., for her unwavering support and encouragement.

—so many S.S.M.O.'s (especially in Beaverton, Oregon), for their continuous reinforcement.

—Mrs. Russ (Billie) Davis, for her assistance with editing and grammatical structure.

—Mrs. Charles (Alice) Tietgen and Mrs. Lawrence (Ginny) Moeller, for their endless hours of typing.

—Nancy Safford, for her always cheerful clerical help.

—other friends and colleagues, too numerous to mention, for their confidence and reinforcement.

Introduction

Every book presumably is intended for a specific reading audience. Some psychological expositions have been written exclusively for professional colleagues. Others, making no claim to being professional in nature, have been popularized with the view of appealing to the greatest possible number of readers. This book was written with the hope that psychologists, psychiatrists, sociologists, social workers, and other professional persons might find something of value in its pages. Yet, because its contents are of such general concern, nontechnical language has been used so that its subject matter will be within the grasp of interested laymen.

Almost six years ago, I looked back on twenty-five years of professional psychological counseling with thousands of people and asked myself, "What have I learned from these people that could be beneficially passed on to others?" By a process of elimination, I decided it should be the psychology of the rejected. Two considerations particularly influenced me in reaching this conclusion. First, the experiences and behaviors of the rejected stood out so clearly in my memory that they seemed to be the most frequently reported clinical phenomena; and second, it was my impression that a comprehensive work on the psychological aftermaths of rejection had not yet been written. Subsequent research in the literature confirmed this impression.

My primary purpose was to present, as clearly as possible, the commonly reported feelings and behaviors of the rejected. This important area of pathology constitutes legitimate subject matter for scientific investigation. A large number of the rejected had become aware of their rejection by one or both parents, while others had not recognized their rejection. To say that those clients who reported all these phenomena were rejected by their parents is one thing. To maintain that any *one* of these experiences and behaviors is to be found *only* in those who have been hurt by parental rejection is quite another (127). This position would in no way be warranted by my clinical findings, even though the *full array* of these experiences and behaviors was observed by me *only* in the rejected.

Let me clarify the preceding statement. Nowhere in these pages has the assumption been made that any of the individual experiences and behaviors presented is to be found exclusively in the rejected. Neither has it been assumed that every person in whom one of these feelings or behaviors has been found would therefore be considered rejected. What is being said is that the *integral panoply* of feelings and behaviors presented in this book was reported to me only by the rejected. The entire array appeared to be characteristic only of those who felt they were rejected.

In my own clinical experience, I encountered persons who clearly manifested one or another unwholesome experience or behavior depicted in this volume—for example, jealousy—but who nevertheless gave no evidence of parental rejection. Though I have not stressed it in this volume, at least the occasional experience of intense jealousy was reported almost universally by the rejected. On the other hand, I encountered intensely jealous people who made no mention of rejection and, moreover, did not appear to have been rejected.

Some of the experiences and behaviors described in this book were reported by persons who were not *conscious* that they had been rejected by their parents. They gave me clear indications, however, that even though still unrecognized by them, such hurtful parental relationships were nevertheless denoted in their clinical pictures. The identity of these "clinical indications" will be disclosed later in the exposition of the psychological defenses the rejected frequently had unknowingly employed to protect themselves from the painful recognition of the true nature of such hurtful parent-child relationships.

My secondary purpose in writing this book was to offer some explanations for these commonly experienced feelings and behaviors. Certain of them had baffled the rejected. Their external behaviors, especially, seldom adequately carried their own meanings. The meaning of observed behavior implies some interpretation of the corresponding nonobserved (internal) behavior. This refers to the intention or purpose underlying that observed behavior. The meaning, for example, of the observed behavior of a man counting money into a woman's hand depends ultimately on his intention. It might be payment to a prostitute, disbursement for groceries, payoff of a bet, payment of blackmail, or any of the myriad reasons that money exchanges hands. The meaning of this man's external, observed behavior could not be adequately comprehended without reference to his intention or purpose.

Accordingly, I have endeavored to make some of the reported *behaviors* more meaningful by offering explanations for them. Such explanations—especially those presented to account for the more unusual behaviors—are, without question, tentative. A number of them have been proposed by other authors. Some of the behaviors, together with their suggested explanations, have not to my knowledge been presented elsewhere. Only further research can substantiate or refute their validity. This also holds true for a number of the *experiences*. Fears, jealousies, hurts, guilts, depressions, angers, and so on, at least occasionally did not carry their own meanings. The rejected were simply unable to explain why these experiences were present. Often these people reported that they felt a certain way, but were unable to explain why even to themselves.

It frequently happened that the rejected initially confessed bewilderment at certain of their experiences and behaviors. Many of them said that the more they had striven by themselves to understand these happenings, the more confused they had become. As they continued in counseling, however, a great number discovered explanations for many of their previously baffling experiences and behaviors. Such explanations were not suggested to them by me, either within or outside of therapy. Often, they occurred to them while they were talking in counseling. Less frequently, they occurred outside of the therapy sessions.

Such explanations at times revealed to them an aspect of their own psychological integration of which they had, until that time, been unaware. For instance, some had come to understand that their persistent tendencies to play down or even deny the accomplishments of other persons became meaningful in view of their poor self-concepts. They saw that the achievements of others who could in any way be compared to them by contrast highlighted their own feelings of worthlessness. Thus they felt threatened by the successes of those others. They understood why they kept putting the others down. They came to understand that their negative reactions to the success of others had been defense reactions against anxiety on their part.

While some of the symptoms which these people experienced could be classified as neurotic, I have not so labeled them. Professional readers need no such classification. For other readers, the classification of experiences and behaviors as neurotic or even psychotic does not seem to be an appropriate means for increasing their understanding of these phenomena. Such labeling, on the contrary, could readily induce readers to fit these occurrences into preconceived categories in such a way as to increase the difficulty of further understanding them.

Regardless of labeling, the area of explanations opens up consideration of a question: Are such hurtful experiences and behaviors *caused* by parental rejection, or are they rather the result of *many* causal factors of which rejection would presumably be one? At this time, the argument cannot be definitively won. There were numerous other kinds of parental impacts, as well, which were reported by the rejected—for instance, a father's view of woman and her place in society that downgrades her in the eyes of her children. Further research from other investigators can furnish data strengthening one side or the other of the argument. Meanwhile, since the full array of reported pathological experiences and behaviors was observed by me *only* in the rejected, I favor the position that such experiences and behaviors were *caused* by rejection.

The book is not meant to be an ethical treatise, and it therefore should not be expected to ascertain the moral accountability of the rejected. Moral accountability is neither denied nor affirmed in these pages. The book refrains from considerations which rightfully belong in the domain of ethicians and concerns itself with those that belong in the domain of psychologists. Yet, inasmuch as it is a psychological treatise, it necessarily treats of causation.

Does this reopen the nature-nurture controversy? Though psychologists have long since shelved this argument, they are well aware that it is not dead. Because both heredity and environment have an effect on every human experience and behavior, perhaps the curiosity to find out which of the two has the greater impact on a specific psychological happening will always be with us. In this book, such curiosity is not operative. Because the reports of clients centered largely on the impact of environment, that aspect is given more attention in the book, but there is no intention to demean the importance of heredity nor to reopen the nature-nurture controversy. In fact, many research studies have resulted in an increasing number of hypotheses concerning the importance of the role the genes play in accounting for human experience and behavior (24, 72).

In nonscientific terms, what seems to be going on here is that people's genes account for their typically human response-themes, such as their being characteristically nervous, apathetic, hyperactive, and so on. In the rejected, learning might explain a number of their characteristic experiences and behaviors as having been superimposed on their basic, genetically determined patterns. In this way environment and heredity would both have fashioned the kinds of responses they gave to the recognition of their rejection. Whatever the truth of the matter, I am presenting response-themes which were usually reported as having been learned by the rejected. These themes maintained themselves alongside whatever had been determined by these persons' genetic endowments.

The mention of such psychological themes calls for a further description of the contents of this volume. In what way have the experiences and behaviors of the rejected been presented? Nowhere in this volume have I attempted to completely separate internal experiences from externally observable behaviors. While behaviors and experiences were not wholly identified by my clients, the two were nevertheless almost inseparably linked. Every significant behavior appeared to have a corresponding experiential component, and every salient experience a tendency to express itself in some externally observable manner.

Under separate headings I have gathered together those experiences and behaviors that, in my judgment, pertain to the same psychological themes. It was an exacting task to tease out of the reported phenomena only those experiences and behaviors which belonged to such psychological themes as anxiety or damaged self-esteem. Undoubtedly, in my efforts to do so, I have included under one theme contents which another psychologist might well regard as more fittingly placed under a different one. In following such a procedure, I have of necessity lifted the reported experiences and behaviors out of context. Consequently, I am aware that they are peculiarly open to my own biases. To minimize such errors, I have tried to relate faithfully the exact information the rejected clients reported to me. The perfect fitting of human experiences and behaviors into any category is, in my judgment, an impossible undertaking. Nevertheless, the categorizing of the experiences and behaviors of the rejected, no matter how imperfect, had to be attempted because the very nature of our finite attention span requires us to study such contents piecemeal, in some understandable structure, rather than globally. The questions of methodological approach and accuracy in reporting clinical observations are discussed more fully in the final chapter.

Two points which are well recognized in the general body of personality studies permeated these reports by the rejected. First, patterns of human experiences and behaviors tended to persist, although a number had been changed with professional help. Of these, it could have been predicted that some would change only with professional help. Such patterns had been learned and subsequently reinforced to the point where they remained highly resistant to change. Persons who had suffered from chronic anxiety tended to remain anxious, and those who had been hostile and aggressive for years did not readily become docile persons.

Second, many experiences and behaviors were closely integrated. This meant that psychologically, as well as logically, they went together in meaningful patterns. People, for example, who suffered periodically from severe bouts of jealousy could be expected also to have poor self-concepts, experience frequent hostility (whether or not it surfaced in overt aggression), suffer from affection-hunger, be highly competitive, be self-preoccupied, and so forth.

These two points—the persistence and the integration of human experiences and behaviors—also furnished bases for predictions. Given sufficient knowledge of some of these people, certain of their future experiences and behaviors were in good part predictable.

The feelings and behaviors reported by the rejected included many variables, a point I tried never to lose sight of. At the same time, I strove to remain open to what appeared to emerge as *kinds* or commonalities of psychological contents reported by many, if not all, of the rejected. Only further research can supply ample grounds for accepting or rejecting the presence of such seemingly common experiences and behaviors.

This book does not set out to blame parents—it is not a matter of blaming anyone—but, rather, is intended to "tell it like it is." I think the findings reported in these pages point out the almost unbelievable importance of being loved and accepted from infancy by one's parents. As one woman summed it up: "Thank God we are a kissing family. It's so essential that people know parental love." When a recent radio report mentioned a fifty percent increase in American adolescent suicides for 1978 over the preceding year, a psychiatrist was quoted as offering the explanation that "they felt their parents didn't love them." While presumably he would be hard pressed to substantiate that explanation, I think many clinicians, including myself, would suspect that he was very close to the truth.

Some effects of parental rejection on a child have been treated in the literature. Both Becker and Brown discovered that the child who has warm, wholesome, maternal experiences will feel basically secure and not be subject to morbid fears of loss of support, of annihilation, and so on. By contrast, they found maternal rejection to be devastating (15, 29). Rheingold's position is that the experience of annihilation anxiety is not natural to a child but is engendered by bad experiences with a depriving mother (156). Several times in his writings Freud said, in effect, that children feel themselves to be inferior when they perceive that they are not loved. The profound impact of parental rejection appeared to work its deleterious effects not only on the rejected children, but also (through them) on their children and (through their children) on their grandchildren (87, 142, 212). Rejection appeared to establish a predisposition to repeat these hurts down through the generations (20).

The main source of the data presented in this volume was the experiences and behaviors reported to me orally over a thirty-year period by thousands of people in the wake of their rejection by one or both parents. The personal letters written to me over the same period by rejected persons were an additional source, from which I have selected appropriate excerpts. There was a distinct advantage in being able to quote from the letters: inasmuch as the writers had described their experiences *in their own words,* distortions were much less likely. For this reason, I have quoted passages from their letters wherever possible to exemplify experiences and behaviors, as well as explanations. I have also tried to retain clients' actual words in the transcriptions of oral remarks, in order to give a more accurate presentation of what they were reporting. At the same time, I have taken every reasonable precaution to safeguard their identities. My anticipation is that my clients alone will recognize themselves in these pages.

In this book there are no references to animal studies. This should not convey the impression that such findings are to be viewed as valueless. A number of studies of animal behaviors, besides being valuable in their own right, appear to be dealing with behaviors analogous to those in their human counterparts. For this reason, I was at first inclined to include in my references findings such as resulted from Harlow's studies on rejecting monkey mothers and their rejected offspring. However, animal behaviors are also vastly different from human behaviors (simply stated, because animals lack a symbolic identity and the self-consciousness associated with it), and therefore great caution must be used in extrapolating behavioral findings from animals to humans.

What was my precise role in collecting the data reported in this volume? To clarify the nature of that *role,* it may be helpful to quote here a few pertinent paragraphs from the final chapter of this book:

> My role . . . was to strive, as far as possible, to *see* and *understand* the behaviors and experiences being described to me by each client and their meanings as he came to interpret and then report them to me. I functioned most efficiently in that role if and when a psychological climate spontaneously occurred in which a person felt sufficiently safe to share with me his desires, disappointments, anxieties, fears, beliefs, personal meanings, goals, thoughts, convictions—in effect, the entire gamut of experiences which he chose to reveal.
>
> My continuing effort was to understand these experiences and behaviors *from the point of view* of the person who was relating them to me. My remarks were intended to verify whether I was understanding what he was telling me and, if so, to indicate that to him. When I was not clear

about what the person was telling me, I would ask what he meant. I endeavored to focus my attention on discerning as clearly as possible what he was describing to me.

I tried to leave each person wholly free to speak or remain silent and, when he chose to speak, to tell me only what he wanted. In no way did I seek to guide or direct the conversation or to interrupt, comfort, reassure, or enlighten the client. I was satisfied just to try to grasp, as fully as possible, what the person was relating.

Some of my clients told me later in therapy that they would never have trusted me enough to confide in me had I not been a Jesuit priest as well as a psychologist. Unfortunately, following counseling with other therapists, some had picked up in gossip revelations of what had originally been told in professional confidence. Although such incidents were rare, these clients had become skeptical of professional persons.

I did not make the assumption that there was never any freedom in the rejected to choose their *behaviors*, even though many said that they possessed very little, if any, control over their *feelings*. In addition, in making important behavioral choices, some clients recognized that they were never aware of all the psychological factors, conscious and unconscious, that were involved. Such a lack of awareness of some of the factors operative in their options, however, did not inevitably preclude their ability to choose among them.

At times clients proudly reported that, in the face of their clearly recognized, strong negative inclinations, they had with great difficulty curbed these urges. Some of them viewed the restraining of these tendencies as personal victories. Their awareness of having courageously controlled them was an immediate datum of their experience.

For many months I pondered the problem of what would be the most effective organization of the contents of this book. A strictly academic, textbook approach to the presentation and explanation of perplexing human experiences and behaviors offered the distinct advantage of facilitating a systematic and orderly arrangement. Its shortcoming was that it would necessitate stripping such phenomena away from real people. The findings it presented would not be actual experiences and behaviors, but common denominators abstracted from reported behaviors and experiences. Any similarity of such experiences and behaviors to those of living persons would appear to be almost coincidental.

It seems well to note, however, that this shortcoming of the academic approach is encountered only in the presentations of *human* phenomena. An academic presentation of *animal* behaviors offers no such problem to psychologists, since they are dealing with *behaviors* only and need not be seriously concerned with either the identity of a particular animal or with that animal's experiential characteristics.

In contrast to the academic textbook approach, a casebook approach would avoid the abstract presentation of human experiences and behaviors. In fact, that type of format is calculated to depict flesh-and-blood occurrences. It would fail, however, on another score. Because of its very nature, it would not readily lend itself to a *systematic* presentation of meaningful human experiences and behaviors.

My major endeavor in writing this book has been to combine the best features of both the academic textbook and the casebook approaches, while attempting to avoid the shortcomings of both. Accordingly, I have tried to make a systematic presentation of the often puzzling experiences and behaviors reported by the rejected and then immediately to flesh them out by relating them to the actual experiences reported by those who confided in me.

Now, a few words about the use of the masculine and feminine forms of pronouns in this book: The English language, unfortunately, is clearly unwieldy in this matter. Rather than writing *he(she)/she(he)* or *him(her)/her(him)* whenever the sex of the pronoun is unspecified, I have chosen to avoid verbal clumsiness by employing the masculine form throughout. It should be understood that each time the reader encounters the pronouns *he, him,* or *his,* unless otherwise indicated, the pronouns *she, her,* or *her* could just as correctly be employed.

I remain deeply indebted to the rejected men and women with whom I worked—they taught me a great deal. It seems to me that the best way to repay that debt is to endeavor to share with others, in a beneficial way, some of what I learned from them.

Finally, my hopes for the book are that it will become a means through which:

—professional counselors will find further insights into the motivations of these suffering people;

—lay readers will gain a sympathetic understanding of the rejected;

—readers who have been rejected will be helped toward a more meaningful perspective regarding their psychological hurts and some of them will be encouraged to seriously consider seeking professional help;

—rejected readers who find themselves facing parenthood will be enlightened and supported in their determination to avoid rejecting their own children.

I hope, as well, that the *therapy* for the rejected will be presented by someone else in another book.

1
Parental Rejection

About sixteen months after I began work on this book, I happened across some words of one of the characters in John Steinbeck's novel *East of Eden*. Speaking of the story of Cain and Abel, he says: "I think this is the best known story in the world because it is everybody's story. I think it is the symbol story of the human soul. The greatest terror a child can have is that he is not loved, and rejection is the hell he fears. I think everyone in the world to a large or small extent has felt rejection. And with rejection comes anger, and with anger some kind of crime in revenge for the rejection, and with the crime guilt—and there is the story of mankind."

These observations from a novelist make no claim to supporting scientific data, of course; but, in my judgment, they are nonetheless insightful ones. Steinbeck's character seems to be saying that at least some parental rejection is *everybody's* story. If this inference is correct, then I must take issue with his position. On the basis of my findings, I cannot agree that it is everybody's story—though I do think it is the story of many, and I appreciate his propensity to generalize in this way. However, just as a marriage counselor needs to resist the temptation to conclude that there is no such thing as a happy marriage, so must a clinician withstand the temptation to universalize the evidences of parental rejection which have been reported to him.

A number of those people who came to me over the years to discuss personal problems gave no clear indications that they had feelings of parental rejection. On the other hand, a great many acknowledged openly that they had such feelings, or they clearly demonstrated symptoms which, though still unidentified as such by them, revealed that they had been rejected.

Why has the area of human rejection and its psychological after-maths gone begging for attention for so long? Perhaps the situation is largely attributable to the delay in recognizing its importance in human feelings and behaviors.[1] In 1929, the term "rejection" was introduced in an article by Levy (103) and a book by Lee and Kenworthy (101). Subsequent studies of parental rejection have focused on the behaviors or attitudes of the parents or on those of the child. In each of these areas, investigators have searched for the meaning of parental rejection. Endeavors to verify rejection on the part of the parents have been replete with difficulties (67, 148). First of all, what is the norm for *parentally rejecting behavior*? Operational definitions which describe measurable or concrete activities or processes that accompany the "abstract quality" of the emotion of rejection have proven unsatisfactory. For example, maternal deprivation very early in the child's life has been regarded as a kind of rejection that produces separation-anxiety.

"Maternal deprivation" has been operationally defined as the absence of a positive and continuous relationship between infant and mother or mother surrogate (149). Since 1952, when Bowlby summarized the published findings in this area up to that time (23), it has received a good deal of attention. Bowlby, in conjunction with his associates at London's Tavistock Institute, has been the foremost researcher in this area. However, he has not always adhered strictly to operational definitions of "maternal separation." He pointed out, for instance, that maternal deprivation is a state of affairs in which "the child lacks that *warm, intimate* and continuous relationship with his mother (or permanent mother-substitute) in which both find *satisfaction* and *enjoyment*" (23, p. 67). The introduction of these affective tones goes well beyond an operational definition. In later publications, Bowlby wrote solely of "early mother-child separation" (24) or of "being removed from mother figures" (25) as the stimulus which gave rise to later acute conflicts in love relations.

Ainsworth, Bowlby's colleague, omitted nonoperational aspects in her definition of maternal deprivation. She mentioned only "absence of maternal care" and "early mother-child separation".[2] Numerous criti-

---

[1]It appears that much of the blame for the long delay in recognizing the salience of human rejection must be laid at the door of Sigmund Freud. His insistence that parental behavior was to be viewed almost solely in terms of its impact on the child's psychosexual development was at fault. As a result, psychoanalytically oriented psychologists mainly tended to disregard parental attitudes in their concern with the impact of parental behaviors on the child's oral, anal, phallic, and genital fixations and growth sequences. In fact, the word "rejection" is not found in the General Index of any of the twenty-three volumes of *The Complete Psychological Works of Sigmund Freud* (62). Volumes 4 and 15, of course, do not have a General Index.

[2]Readers familiar with the well-known study of "separation anxiety" done by the Mayo Clinic and the Mayo Foundation should reflect that, although this study utilized the same term ("separation anxiety") used by Bowlby, it referred to the study of a neurosis found in school-age children (51) and so is not related to this area.

cisms have been marshalled against an operational approach such as Ainsworth's. The definition has been characterized by Rabin as vague, complex, and lacking in precision (149). Unresolved problems in using such a definition have been many. For instance, would the absence of the opportunity for the child to form an attachment to a mother figure have to be complete or only partial? Why? On what basis was the study confined solely to those absences occurring in children from twelve to forty-eight months of age (23)? How long a period of time would be needed for such a deprivation to occur? How would the specific length of this period be determined?

What about situations in which there is a change from one mother figure to another, as when intermittent mothering takes place? In an experiment at Iowa State College, each infant (starting at less than one month of age) was cared for by as many as sixteen different mother figures during a three-month period (144). Would this be maternal deprivation? Or what of the pattern of "mothering" in a kibbutz? What of "distorted mothering" or, as it is also termed, "masked depriva-tion," where a physically present mother figure is actively or passively rejecting the child (137)?

Moving away from an operational definition, what case can be made for using *parental feelings* or *attitudes* of rejection towards the child as the norm? Symonds defined the rejected child as one who is unwanted by either father or mother (196). But what is the norm for determining who is unwanted? Symonds himself acknowledged that in all but the most extreme cases of rejection the parents' attitude toward the child is covered over with a coating of ostensible affection and pleasant rela-tions (196). Newell defined maternal rejection as that situation where the birth of the child was unwelcome to the mother (138). Again, what criteria are to be used to define "unwelcome"?

Mussen and his colleagues attempted to evaluate fathers' attitudes and feelings toward their sons on the basis of the testimony of their wives (135). Inasmuch as this required one parent to testify about how the other parent regarded the children, it posed serious verification problems. Porter asked parents to rate themselves on a self-inventory type of questionnaire regarding their actions and feelings toward their six- to nine-year-old children (148). Obviously, this also raised ques-tions about validity. Witmer defined the rejecting mother as one whose behavior towards her child indicates a strong dislike for him (211). Again, who's to determine the criteria to be used in such evaluations?

Finally, in any endeavor to validate the norm for parental rejection when it is believed to be situated in the parents, something else should be noted. It now seems unmistakable that the specific practices to which parents resort do not appear to be as crucial as their characteristic attitudes toward their children (40).

A few authors have searched for norms of rejection in the *behavior of the children*. Bowlby's studies of "separation anxiety" attend to the *behavioral* criteria of the child's protests and detachment. Soddy made the surprising observation that the one inescapable criterion of whether children are wanted or not is the child mortality rate (186). His primary references for this remark, however, were to other cultures, and it is doubtful that he would seriously try to apply it to ours.

What is to be said of focusing on the *child's own feelings* as a criterion of his rejection? A great deal, I think, even though it poses its own problems. It is interesting that, as early as 1914, Freud declared that a person's emotional attitudes toward other people have already been established by the time he is six years of age (62). This would seem to imply that by the age of six the rejected child has already sensed and been damaged by his rejection.

My position is consonant with Hawkes' insistence that, in order to understand what human subjects see, researchers must learn to see through the eyes of their subjects (76). It simply does not follow that, because a mother fondles her child, the child must experience this as a sign that his mother loves him (105). Hawkes maintains that it is not the physical nature of a stimulus but rather the way in which that stimulus is interpreted by the individual stimulated (76). It is the *meaning* of the relationship, or of its lack, that is the important factor for the subject (105). I also agree with Hawkes that the crux of parent-child relations as far as the child in the family is concerned appears to be in the area of children's perceptions of what they, the parents, are, rather than in very definite and specific characteristics of home life (76). My choice, then, is a phenomenological norm of parental rejection. This views rejection as it is experienced *by the rejected person*.

Some people would be sorely pressed to answer with any degree of confidence the question, "Did your parents love you?" Presumably, such perceived parental attitudes would be distributed along a continuum. At one end would cluster those who felt certain of their parents' love. There would be a middle ground of those who were not really sure of their parents' love. Huddled near the other end would be those who, at some psychological level, knew their parents did not love them.

The clients whose reports furnished the substance of these pages would have been clustered at or near the rejection end of that continuum. In fact, many of these persons stated without qualification that they had indeed been rejected by one or both parents. Some of them had been confronted with indisputable evidence that they were rejected. Such findings have also been reported by other researchers. Pemberton and Benady found that a group of children (averaging about nine years of age) whose parents consciously rejected them had also been physically assaulted by their parents (145). Such parental behaviors would leave very little room for nonrejecting interpretations.

I am prescinding entirely from the question of whether the parents of these persons who felt rejected had actually rejected their offspring. My concentration here is exclusively on those persons who, at some psychological level, *felt* they had been rejected, regardless of the extent to which such feelings did or did not correspond to parental attitudes (73). Indeed, were it possible for parents to reject a child and for that child never to know, at any psychological level, of that fact, then theoretically it could be anticipated that no damaging aftermath would result. However, this would have to remain a questionable possibility for me. In my experience, all parental rejection seemed to have been felt in some damaging way by the child. Would it be possible, on the other hand, for a child to experience parental rejection where, in reality, there was none (141)? Perhaps, but it seems the baseless feeling itself would be as damaging as if the parents had actually rejected the child.

In terms, then, of the phenomenological norm I am using, what is rejection? It is a reported, subjective *experience*. As such, it is not capable of exact definition nor of an operational definition. Therefore, I have not endeavored to give "operational definitions" to any of the other phenomena treated in this book. Instead, I have presented these experiences by striving to accurately *describe* them as they had earlier been communicated to me by clients. Some readers may regard such a descriptive presentation of phenomena as inexact and imprecise. I wish there were more scientifically suitable methods at hand. Indeed, it is my hope that other researchers will contribute additional findings from similar and other empirical sources, and thereby be able to give "operational definitions" (200) to some of the variables associated with the experience of rejection.

As clients *described* the phenomenon of rejection, what was it? It was *their emotionally toned knowledge that they were not loved and wanted—for themselves—by one or both parents*. How clear was this experience of being rejected? Feelings ran almost the entire gamut among rejected people. In some of the rejected, there was an open recognition (with an associated full complement of exceedingly painful feelings) that they were not wanted and not loved. In other rejected, there was a knowledge that they had experienced phenomena actually rooted in rejection (92) but, as yet, had failed to identify rejection as the source of these phenomena.

In my clinical findings, very few rejected entertained any serious *doubts* about whether they had been rejected. An exceptional few *thought* they had been rejected but were not entirely sure of it. The reader will appreciate that this occasionally encountered questioning of their rejection might have been one form of defense against the necessity of recognizing it.

Did their clear, open recognition of rejection permit them to sense *degrees* of rejection on the part of their parents? Rejection did indeed appear to admit of such degrees. The awareness that they had been rejected ranged all the way from the agonizing view that they were hated and/or regarded as worthless by their parents to the feeling that their parents thought they loved them or at least wished they loved them but were incapable of doing so. Ausubel noted such differences in degree of parental rejection by categorizing it as "malignant" or "benign" (10). To date, I have not discovered any substantial differences of hurtful experiential and/or behavioral characteristics in the rejected that appeared to be directly associated with their perceptions of different degrees of rejection by their parents.

A closely related consideration here is that there is a great deal of evidence to show that little children normally see their parents as "ten-feet-high" giants (62) who are both omniscient and omnipotent (134). Accordingly, almost without exception, small children do not question the *correctness* of perceived parental evaluations and attitudes toward them, no matter how much they might dislike, resent, or be hurt by them. This correctness exists both at the child's intellectual and emotional levels.

Rejection, as considered here, was not something these individuals happened to feel when they were depressed or otherwise out of sorts and which later disappeared when their spirits picked up. Rather, once they openly came to recognize the very painful feeling that they were rejected, it remained constant for them. Even when they happened not to be aware of it, the feeling of rejection did not go away. When not in the focus of their attention, it receded to the periphery of their awareness. Even successful psychotherapy did not phase out the hurts flowing from the experiences of rejection (168). It did, however, help the rejected to understand their rejection and cope more effectively with it.

As they perceived it, the rejection by their parents had characteristically taken either an *active* or *passive* expression toward them (105). The rejected felt their parents had tended to express their rejection either by the things they did and said, or by exaggerated neglect of and indifference toward them. Rejection taking the more passive form was perceived as having been prolonged and rather constant parental disinterest and neglect. The children had come to feel that either or both parents simply were not concerned and did not really care what happened to them. On the other hand, children's experiences of active rejection usually lay concealed in their deeply hurt feelings which were the aftermaths of parental actions. These included the feelings that they were not loved and/or wanted for themselves.

Some rejected had experienced both active and passive expressions of parental rejection. A boy still in his teens recalled that, even as a small child, he had been physically attacked by his mother when she happened to be in a rage. Times without number since infancy she had grabbed him by an arm, yanked him up off his feet, and thrown him across the room—often up against a wall. A few of these incidents resulted in severe injuries. For the most part, however, both of his parents simply paid a minimum amount of attention to him.

Because his parents both worked, there was no one home after school. From the time he started to school, he would tag along with older boys in the neighborhood until late into the night, and so would not be at home for supper. At first, his mother would leave something for him in the warming oven. Later, she discontinued this practice; when he came in, he would have to look around for something to eat. In general, as long as he did not cause them trouble or serious inconvenience, his parents left him alone. The boy's account of the relationship with his parents was later independently confirmed for me by a long-time neighbor.

My clinical findings agree with those of Ausubel and Koch in indicating that, if and when they were given a choice, the rejected chose the active expression of rejection as being emotionally less painful (11, 96). They chose to have their parents hurt them rather than ignore them. A boy who was still in the elementary grades was brought to me for help because of his behavior. He had misbehaved in school to the point where his teacher had to carry out her threat that it would be necessary to speak to his father about his conduct. The father's response had been to instruct the teacher that any time the boy misbehaved she was to send a note home with him. He assured her that each time the child received such a note he would be punished.

The father's job required him to be out of town about half of the time. What baffled both the parents and the teacher was the fact that whenever his father was out of town the boy's behavior in school presented no problem. When his father was at home, however, he inevitably misbehaved in school until a note was sent home with him.

Each time he brought a note home, his father punished him severely. The boy had discovered, it later became clear, that the only way he could get his father's attention was to misbehave. Then, his father was forced to take time from what he was doing to punish him. He had obviously opted for being punished by his father rather than being ignored by him.

Beyond the active and passive, are there yet other expressions of rejection? One other might conceivably be implicit in the interpretations of certain parental behaviors that were not in themselves clearly expressing rejection. Levy suggests that the experience of receiving unrelieved manifestations of parental affection has been associated with underlying parental feelings of rejection (105).

Any adequate treatment of parental rejection, it seems to me, must also take note of another area—one that appears to be a kind of parental acceptance—namely, "extrinsic valuation." In this sort of relationship, children feel they are valued, not for themselves, but valued for what their parents can gain from or through them. Hence, it seems to them that they are wanted only to the extent they show promise of fulfilling frustrated parental ambitions or desires. Some of my clients reported that, at times, they were the recipients of warm parental affection when they had achieved in significant ways. While I prefer not to designate such acceptance as love, occasionally it had been of an ardent nature. Again, this is interpreting a situation from the viewpoint of how these parental valuations were experienced by the recipients; but some of these experiences of extrinsic valuation have indeed been proved to have had a solid foundation in reality.

Vogel's study found that one of the determinants in the emergence of emotional disturbance in children appeared to be that the children were being used as a means of preserving their parents' marriage (204). Had these children been rejected? As yet I am not wholly satisfied that the experience of being extrinsically evaluated is identical with that of being rejected. A common denominator in the study, however, was that in both cases the children had felt they were not wanted and loved for themselves.

The way the children had experienced it was the factor determining the presence of extrinsic valuation. No profound insight is required to recognize that, included among the ambitions many parents cherish for their children, there are elements of self-seeking. But how did the *children* see these manifested parental ambitions?

There was a vast difference in perceived parental evaluation, for instance, between two pre-med students. One said: "I am glad that I am going to be a doctor, and it will make dad very happy, too, because

he has wanted it as much as I. In fact, I am aware that, because dad
has always wanted the M.D., this will be his dream come true." The
other said: "Dad has lived for my going to med school. He will finally
get his damned M.D. by extension in this, his offspring, when I earn it.
He's lived for that day. Were it not for that, I wouldn't stick out this
lousy field another day. I loathe medicine, but he would never accept it
if I dropped out; so somehow I'll tough it out." Both students were
manifesting their awareness that this M.D. degree would be very
pleasing to their fathers. The second was also implying that his father's
acceptance of him was based on the fact that he was a means to that
end. The first did not appear to experience his father's acceptance as
extrinsic valuation.

The acceptance a number of individuals had received from their parents was conditional on their being able to fulfill certain specific, frustrated, parental ambitions or desires (129). They were rewarded with
warm acceptance in direct proportion to the success they achieved in
fulfilling such parental longings. In effect, such terms offered them the
best rewards possible in view of the impossibility of getting what they
really hungered for.

Almost without exception, those who were given the option chose,
with considerable resentment, to fulfill the dictated parental terms,
rather than to go without rewarding responses. Moreover, these terms
were eventually adopted by the extrinsically valued themselves as the
unquestioned yardstick of their own personal acceptance. As far back
as one man can remember, his father had repeatedly told him, "You'll
never amount to anything." The stamp of paternal blessing had been
reserved solely for his son's success. The son now feels that his only
hope of getting personal acceptance is to achieve visible successes. It
seems never to have seriously occurred to him to question the correctness of the position that his worth as a person should rise or fall on the
basis of these successes. In some vague way, he senses that he is still
proving to himself and to his father (long since dead) that his father
was wrong. In spite of his father's judgment to the contrary, he insists
that he will someday amount to something. Implicitly, he seems to be
saying that he will then merit his father's acceptance and also his
self-acceptance.

In some instances, parental terms were spelled out only in a *general*
way. Their children came to feel that rewards were to be earned by
constantly striving to fulfill the entire range of expectations the parents
held for them. All through his early years, one man felt he had to
accomplish everything his parents wanted; otherwise, they would have
been hurt and disappointed. Consequently, failure for him became

simply unthinkable. He lived in fear of letting them down. Now, he experiences intense fear of failing whenever he undertakes any task that is "in the public eye."

Others learned from their parents that they had to earn *all* acceptance and affection. As unmerited parental acceptance had been a fiction, so was undeserved personal acceptance from others. There was a price tag on all such desired responses. One man had received acceptance and affection from his parents only by being a "good boy"—a pattern which they had spelled out for him in great detail. Now, he feels he can get acceptance and affection from others only when they are earned. This holds for his relationship with God, as well. God's love and acceptance, he feels sure, will be his only when and if he really earns them by his prayers, penances, and sacrifices. If and when he is not performing in ways pleasing to God, he feels that God really doesn't have time for him. At present, his concern is mainly with his physical appearance—he has a serious weight problem. Even though he has largely displaced his anxiety to his physical appearance, he still cannot bring himself to do something in the presence of others that he might do poorly. He feels strongly that any hope of his own acceptance of himself is to be sought principally in terms of how he appears to other people.

The parental acceptance of some depended, not on their achieving a specific thing, but rather on their *refraining* from one or more specific behaviors forbidden by their parents. All during the years of his childhood, one man never felt free to make any noise or commotion at home, regardless of the circumstances. Noise was simply forbidden. When his pals came into his home, he was embarrassed because they were noisy and loud in the presence of his parents. He now experiences no real peace or relaxation and is always on edge. He has interpreted the parental prohibition against making noise in the house as a manifestation that he was not appreciated at home. He added that he was never appreciated by his parents nor by other important persons in his life. Even his athletic coaches during his school years invariably let him know, in one way or another, that he was "not good enough yet." This feeling that he is "not good enough yet" continues to persist.

Still other clients had been forced to *search out* behaviors to which their parents would warmly respond with acceptance and/or affection; otherwise, these responses were absent. A woman whose father was not present during her entire girlhood had found her mother so self-preoccupied in her loneliness that she paid very little attention to her. Every attempt to win warm responses from her mother had frustratingly failed until the day she happened to tell her mother a humorous story which she had completely made up. Her mother listened and laughed. From that point on, almost every night—in something of her personal version of the *Tales of Arabian Nights*—she held her mother nearly spellbound with a serial-like whirl of stories, spun entirely out of her fantasy. She prepared these stories carefully during the day, and each evening she narrated them to an enraptured audience of one, her mother. She not only enjoyed telling them but also felt they were helping her mother.

She now finds herself repeatedly telling similar, wholly fabricated stories to her peers, who listen attentively and take them for the truth. Having acknowledged that sometime she will be found out and thoroughly discredited, she continues anyway, relishing the attention. She also mentioned her unusually strong tendency to pick up any "scoop" or gossip; then she can't wait to become the center of attention as she spreads it to others.

Parental acceptance of some offspring required that they play *specific roles*. While the father of one man had, as much as possible, ignored him, his mother had never made any secret of the fact that she had wanted a daughter when he was born. With no hope of positive paternal response, he learned very early in life that any acceptance from his mother would be based solely on the extent to which he would play the role of the girl she had wanted. When he did play that role, she lavished affection on him; whenever he dropped the role, she had no time for him.

His mother always insisted on very high ideals for women, and he has come to believe that women are far superior to men. He firmly holds that women do not go to the bathroom—in fact, that they do not even possess an elimination tract. Women, he insists, are above such bodily needs. He knows this is foolish, and says it is foolish, but nevertheless still believes it. He insists that this womanly characteristic of not going to the bathroom is not found in "pick-ups" and "street-walkers," because to him they aren't really women. He sees his wife, whom he considers very much a woman, going to the bathroom and can't explain it.

He resents deeply having to play a feminine role with his mother, and also reacts with fury to any question raised about his masculinity. He said he is "just killed" by being called names such as "softy," "sissy," "fairy," "daisy," "gay," or "queer"—all of which he has, in fact, been called.

Among the most commonly reported specific roles demanded by parents were the following: to become a college graduate, an outstanding athlete in a designated sport, a member of a specific profession (such as a priest, minister, rabbi, doctor, or lawyer), or to marry someone socially prominent and wealthy.

Some persons sensed that they needed to *identify* as completely as possible with a parent as the price for receiving warm parental acceptance. A man who had been completely rejected by his father found he could get acceptance from his mother only insofar as he modeled himself after her. Deeply attached to his mother, he said he is very like her in almost every way. Like her, he explained, he is nervous and hypochondriacal, cherishes a love for the better things of life, and values highly cultural and refined things, as well as education and wealth. Like her, he feels sorrow and even contempt for the poor and ignorant. All his life his foremost motive has been his desire to be like her and to be everything he felt his mother wanted him to be, so that she would not be disappointed in him.

For others, parental acceptance depended on *specific accomplishments* which had been designated by their parents. A recollection that has never left one man is that, during his childhood, whenever company came (irrespective of the hour of the day or night), he was permitted to remain with the guests solely on the condition that he would flawlessly play the piano for them. If he made mistakes or was unwilling to play, he was sent to his room until the visitors left the house. Now, he feels he is accepted or rejected by others in terms of how he *appears* before them.

Finally, aside from the fact that they had to *earn* the most rewarding parental responses they could get, those reporting parental extrinsic valuation appeared to have experienced hurtful psychological patterns which did not differ substantially from those reported by the rejected.

What *percentage* of the American public should rightly be classified as rejected? Readers who have known only warm, parental love may find it difficult to believe that a considerable number of people have felt rejected. In fact, parental rejection of a child may appear to them so gross as to be actually found only by way of cruel exception. In support of this feeling, Gallagher holds that most parents have genuine affection for their children (67). Ostow takes the position that there is normally an instinctual need to love and protect one's children and to inhibit aggressiveness toward them (142). Within this context, is it not at least conceivable that some people who were actually loved by their parents later came to believe that their parents had rejected them? While this remains a possibility, it appears highly unlikely that it could have been a frequent occurrence.

A number of research studies report psychological findings that by no means support the assertion that all parents want or love their

Why did rejection happen? I will indicate briefly some of the motives for parental rejection as they were revealed to me, either by the rejected themselves or by some of their parents. Any serious endeavor to establish actual motivation for parental rejection of a child must necessarily include both the situational and psychological factors involved in such rejection.

As Toffler has acutely observed in his book *Future Shock,* all of us are—to a far greater extent than we suspect—creatures of our time and culture. We live in a "throw-away," changing environment in which our relationships to things and places increasingly tend to be fragile and temporary. Impermanence is the touchstone of our society (198).

One important aspect of this impermanence is the increasingly seen reluctance of younger American men and women to commit themselves *for life* to anything or anyone, including a marriage partner. In any such long-range commitment, they see their own personal fulfillment and happiness in life threatened with unknown and unforeseeable variables. People have always known that the risk cannot be taken out of living; but for many of today's younger people, to lock themselves irrevocably into any situation is experienced as a violation of their "selves." Any permanent, irreversible commitment which might preclude other possibilities of personal development is seen as constituting an unwarranted restriction of growth potential. Hence, it sometimes happens that children are resented for the reason that they threaten to deprive the parents of their freedom to be able to terminate their marriage relationship.

Realistically, motivation for rejection of children was very seldom based on the parents' depravity or consciously sadistic behavior. Rather, by actively rejecting the child, their strong psychological needs had been receiving, often unconsciously, some satisfaction; or a preoccupation with their personal psychological needs had resulted in passively ignoring the child (110, 140). In either case, when admitted, it required abundant psychological strength to acknowledge that they had rejected their child. Why? They did not want to feel that they were bad persons; and to see themselves as rejecting parents was, at least to some extent, to see themselves in that light.

A number of parents disclosed to me that they deeply disliked—and a few even despised—their child. For the most part, they held the child himself responsible for their negative feelings; for example, the child's conduct, personality, or appearance was irritating or disgusting and antagonized the parent. Some referred to the small child's very frustrating—and, as Bowlby has shown, characteristic—reaction to a lengthy separation from his mother (24). At first, the child would give absolutely no response to her; then later would convert this indifference into an intense possessiveness and whining "mummishness." The child would not let his mother love him.

Some parents questioned whether their "reasons" for rejecting the child were the true ones. Occasionally, they admitted being completely baffled by their negative feelings for the child, and readily acknowledged that their motivations were not all that clear to them. The literature supports this lack of clarity of motives in the minds of some rejecting parents—for instance, Coopersmith found that mothers with low self-esteem tend to express only limited affection for their children and are not likely to have close relationships with them (40). On the other hand, a few parents did recognize and were able to spell out their actual motives for rejecting their children. Whatever the underlying motives may have been and whether or not they were recognized, many parents clearly expressed their negative feelings toward their children.

The following specific motives for rejecting children were either reported to or observed by me. Since it is understood that parents who are struggling with serious mental illness can reject their children (137), this motive for rejection will not be treated in the discussion.

First, let's consider those motives which were found in *either* parent. Maladjusted marriages frequently were fonts for child rejection, as witnessed by me and other clinicians and confirmed by nonclinical research. Porter found that marital adjustment was positively related to parental acceptance of children. On the negative side, this finding showed that, the less the marital adjustment, the less acceptance there was of the children (148).

Sometimes children who seemed initially to be the recipients of parental love felt rejected later, perhaps as the result of the arrival of a more attractive sibling or because of a deeply disappointing I.Q. test score. The parents felt they could not cope with either ugliness or intellectual inferiority in their children.

Infants were rejected if they very closely resembled a self-loathing parent and, as such, were seen as concrete expressions of the parent's own despicable traits (66).

Children who resembled the "other side" of the family fell heir to a reservoir of hostility which had been built up by one parent, not necessarily against the other parent, but against the other parent's family (212). Such hostility sometimes appeared to have an understandable basis. Hurtful, unjust treatment had been meted out to one parent by the other parent's family. At times, this resentment continued to exist in a parent alongside his acceptance of the spouse whose family was deeply resented.

Aside from considerations of health, untimely pregnancies were resented by parents (142). This often was the case with children born out of wedlock. A child who arrived when parents were not ready, but for whom they did not want an abortion, was regarded as an unwanted and unjust imposition. There were also some mothers who had repeatedly attempted abortion—but without success. According to Newell, one mother who had seven children stated that she had attempted abortion with each one (138).

Another motive for rejection was characterized by a particular pattern of affection: A child gradually sensed something wrong with the affection being received from one or both parents. Eventually, he came to recognize that the affection was being lavished on him, not in his own right, but precisely because he was a stand-in for the other parent. Parental affection had safely been given to him as an infant, when he could neither spurn it nor reject the affection-giver. Moreover, as an infant, he had made some return of affection. With the passing of the years, however, this picture changed. As an older child, he was no longer so safe a recipient of love. No longer was he a secure replacement for the other parent. Hence, there developed in the parent a growing reluctance to lavish on him the affection which rightly belonged to the other parent. The child eventually became unmistakably aware that he had never been loved for himself by this affection-giving parent.

Perhaps some unconscious motivations are present in every parental rejection. My clinical findings, in agreement with those of Block (20), have led me to conclude that, in many instances, the main motives for parental rejection are well concealed below the conscious level—as, for example, in cases where parents were unknowingly taking revenge upon the wrong generation (20). The latent hostility toward their rejecting parents was now being unconsciously displaced onto their own children (66). This doesn't seem logical, because it was aimed at the wrong generation; psychologically, however, it somehow felt fitting to retaliate for hurts *received* in a parent-child relationship with hurts *meted out* in a parent-child relationship. That the generations were now reversed did not appear to alter its psychological suitability.

Through such displacement, moreover, the rejected not only felt they were somehow getting back at their own parents, but they also employed richly symbolic patterns in these reprisals (197). They retaliated in a way which tangibly corrected the rejection pattern of their parents. The rejected who had been told by their parents what to do and what not to do in everything to the point that they had felt manipulated and deprived of basic human freedom employed the very opposite pattern toward their own children. They followed a hands-off policy to the point of neglect. On the other hand, a number of those who had felt largely disregarded by their parents reported, in effect, that they now overdominated their own children.

The rejected, who in turn were rejecting their own children, for the most part found great difficulty in acknowledging that they were doing so. Yet often they experienced no reluctance whatever in repeatedly pointing out that, in dealing with their children, they were rectifying what had been wrong with the way their parents had treated them. They made remarks, for instance, such as, "My dad was way too strict with us; I leave my kids strictly alone," or "My folks turned me loose to do as I liked. That's wrong. Believe me, my kids don't do anything unless I tell them to."

What were the motives underlying the rejection of children by their *mothers?* One motive was the result of the mother's immediate identification of her child with the child's father. Years ago, I was asked if I would talk with a young, unwed woman in a hospital maternity ward. The problem was that she refused to even look at the baby to whom she had recently given birth. "The nurses," she told me, "keep telling me what a beautiful baby girl I have. They don't understand. If they only knew her father. He's an animal. I will never lay eyes on his child. I'm determined to put her up for adoption. Nothing can change that." Was not this infant a person in her own right, to be accepted for herself, regardless of who her father and mother happened to be? Not to her mother. In her eyes, this baby *was* that father. To the extent that she hated the man, his baby was hateful. As far as her mother was concerned, this child's identity had been clouded over by her loathing for the child's father.

This reaction becomes more comprehensible when we recognize that the same kind of father-child identification is found when the child's mother deeply loves the father. When such a mother gazes upon her baby, she sees the infant as their fleshed-out, mutual, marital love. For her this baby *is* that loved man, the baby's father. Accordingly, when she tenderly and lovingly ministers to the baby, regardless of the infant's sex, she is expressing her love not only *for* the baby's father, but also *to* him.

Some mothers simply could not afford the emotional risk involved in loving a child. One woman had given her heart to her first child, only to suffer the excruciating agony of losing that child. With regard to her other children, she said: "I resolved 'Never again!' I would be a dutiful mother but no one of them would be mine. I felt terribly guilty, but I simply could not possess another one of my children."

Children were rejected by their mothers precisely because they came to be viewed as anchoring them to marriages which, on one score or another, had become insupportable for them (57, 138, 145).

Some women had regarded the men they married as the most acceptable mates then available. This did not, in their minds, preclude the possibility of the later appearance and availability of someone much closer to their ideal man. Consequently, they experienced animosity toward their child as the one tying them firmly to their present mate when an available, more attractive man had appeared on the scene.

Others had discovered that the men they married fell seriously short of their anticipations and expectations. Their husbands had revealed an unsuspected brutal streak (which soon placed the women in the ranks of battered wives) or had manifested previously well-concealed weaknesses, such as cowardliness, dishonesty, or alcoholism. Meanwhile, the mothers came more and more to reject their children as binding them to these offensive men.

Still other women had become increasingly dissatisfied with their husbands' earning performances. No matter how much they had urged their men up the ladder of financial income, the husbands had fallen notably short. Income held so prominent a place in these women's priorities that what they had come to regard as eking out an existence in continued poverty made their marriages insupportable. The children caught the brunt of their increasing frustrations.

Some children had been wanted very much and had been needed by their mothers as, hopefully, the means of salvaging shaky marriages. To the extent that these children continued to give promise of being able to cement together the marriage partners, they were desired and valued. If and when they no longer gave promise of serving as the human glue that held such tottering marriages together, they lost the conditional acceptance they had been receiving.

Because some divorced women felt tied down by their children or held them responsible for the discord and subsequent disintegration of their marriages, they felt deeply resentful toward them (96). Another cause of resentment for children was maternal health. Some mothers viewed their babies primarily as grave health burdens, both during their pregnancy and afterwards.

Maternal jealousy of children was also grounds for rejecting them. The following pattern was reported by a number of women who had themselves been rejected. Each had come to resent her child as an intruder with whom she felt she was being forced to share her husband. Because she needed all her husband's love, she bristled at this competitor for his attention and affection. Some rejected women reported having felt jealous of a daughter, even when the daughter had been very young. Occasionally, they reported having had similar feelings of jealousy toward their sons.

There appeared to be one family situation which was typically productive of such a jealous response. A man who was married to a rejected woman had, with time, discovered that she was not the warm, understanding, dependably affectionate woman he thought he had married. The birth of a daughter presented him with another feminine person of his own flesh and blood to whom he could spontaneously relate affectionately. His wife sensed this immediately, and their daughter soon felt the stings of her jealousy.

One such wife felt certain that her little girl, instinctively employing her feminine wiles, was designedly playing the part of the other woman in her husband's life. What seemed to be happening here—as in many such instances—was that the daughter, receiving no love from her mother, was forced to seek parental love exclusively from her father. The more hungrily she approached him, the more warmly he responded, and the more jealousy her mother experienced. It is really something of a vicious circle.

As another rejected woman waits for her husband's return home each evening, she knows her five-year-old daughter is also waiting. Inevitably, as soon as the front door opens, the little girl darts around her to jump with delighted squeals into his arms. His wife, seething with jealousy, watches him respond affectionately to her tiny rival for perhaps a minute before he manages to greet her with a perfunctory embrace, lasting but seconds. Her green-eyed resentment of this competitor for her husband's love grows daily.

In the late 1970s women increasingly began reporting another kind of experience—the strong feeling that their offspring had deprived them either of the job they had come to enjoy or one they would like to have had. As a result, kept from the world of men and women associates whose company they had relished or felt they would have relished, their feeling became one of enslavement. They came to resent being forced to remain at home just to care for their child. This feeling of resentment was repeatedly reinforced by what they read and heard from other women. With the experience of this loss of freedom—even though they had looked forward to and wanted their baby—came the frustration of feeling imprisoned within the walls of their house by their offspring. They approached the point of almost hating the child who thus held them captive there (138).

Within this context should be mentioned those mothers who felt that their baby had interrupted their professional, social, or athletic activities (138). Even those mothers who did not consciously dislike housework found it nonfulfilling and, at best, insufficient to occupy their time in any satisfactory way. To their surprise, they had begun to feel resentful toward the child they held responsible for their being thus forcibly confined.

Some women who reported having had sexual relationships with a number of partners before marriage seemed to have developed a need for a variety of sexual partners. Apparently, below their conscious level, a need had developed which raised the question of whether they could ever again be satisfied with a single sexual partner. (Clinical evidence for the existence of such a need includes the self-reported, not-understood restlessness and general frustration of a number of women with such a history.) Some of these women were married to partners whom they felt they loved and with whom they were unable to find serious fault. Nonetheless, they experienced periodic, baffling, intense feelings of being tied down and of deep resentment toward the children who were perceived to be the cause. From time to time, they were aware of intense and persisting feelings of mounting restlessness and discontent which they felt were making them nervous wrecks.

What were characteristic and distinctive motives for child rejection that were found in *fathers?* Some motives, of course, were much the same as those experienced by mothers—a maladjusted marriage, a physically or psychologically unattractive child, an untimely pregnancy, a close resemblance to their loathed selves or to their mate's despised relatives, jealousy, an inability to love, and an unconscious repayment of their own parents.

In addition, the feeling of personal inadequacy on the part of some fathers was distinctly evident. The new responsibilities as breadwinner and head of a family had only too clearly been spelled out for them by the birth of children. Fatherhood was very threatening. In this light, the children had come to be viewed as exceedingly burdensome.

A large number of men who had had sexual relations with numerous partners before marriage had promised, and said they sincerely intended, to love only one woman after marriage. Within a short period of time, they had concluded that they could not be wholly satisfied with only one sexual partner. However, they told themselves that their subsequent sexual relationships with other women were not really infidelities, because they were giving to none of these other sexual partners any of the love they had promised their wives. In fact, they felt they were giving these other partners practically nothing—they were taking, not giving. They were not even particularly concerned about their casual partner's sexual satisfaction, except insofar as they felt it would enhance their own. While they had no serious intention of discontinuing these other relationships, it seemed to some of the men that their wives were unreasonable in insisting on labeling such relationships as infidelities since they really didn't mean that much. Their anger at their "temperamental" wives was, at times, vented on their children.

Another group of men had begun to question—now that they had really gotten to know their wives—whether they were the right marriage partners for them. Some had even found themselves wondering whether a man can ever really be sure of getting the right woman. As a result, they had seriously been considering whether a less-binding, live-in arrangement, which would leave both parties important areas of personal freedom and yet provide affection and a meaningful bond, might not be preferable. In such cases, even those children who at one time had been wanted came to be regarded as human balls and chains, enslaving the fathers in their marriages.

When did the rejected come to the clear, open recognition that they had been rejected? If the parental rejection was unmistakably evidenced to them while they were still little children, many had no choice but to recognize it, since they could neither disregard it nor explain it as something less painful than rejection. However, a number of cases are recorded in the literature of young children who, when forced to acknowledge unmistakable parental rejection, manifested psychotic or even autistic behavior. Many early-childhood victims of the now familiar battered-child syndrome were clearly forced to recognize parental rejection. Nonetheless, there have been instances when even battered children appeared to have somehow explained to themselves that the hurtful behavior of their parents was something less painful than rejection (66). The literature appears to support the finding regarding a child's ability to interpret injurious parental behavior as expressing something other than rejection. Pemberton and Benady found also that measurable, prolonged, emotional deprivation by parents did not invariably produce the feeling of rejection in early-school-aged children (145).

In my clinical experience, instances of children being forced to face openly their parental rejection constituted the exceptions. The overall reported picture was that those who had been rejected had succeeded in avoiding the clear recognition of that fact for years. While I have found little research in support of this finding, Coopersmith reported that prior to adolescence children find it difficult to face even the possibility of parental rejection (40).

In my findings there were also indications of sex differences regarding the time when rejection had been openly experienced. In general, women testified that they had come to realize clearly that they were rejected as early as their middle teens. For the most part, however, it was unusual for men to have been vividly aware of their rejection before they had reached their twenties, and such an awareness frequently occurred even considerably later.

A particularly rugged individual in his late thirties remarked during a counseling session that his father did not love him. No sooner were the words out than he began to cry bitterly, and he continued to do so for about an hour. Later he explained that he had never actually faced his father's rejection until he finally said the words out loud. Some men managed to avoid this recognition even longer. During his first counseling session, a man well into his fifties paused for some time and then said, "My father hit me," and began to sob. Only later did he mention that his father had been dead almost twenty years. Nonetheless, he explained, on that day he had for the first time interpreted this action as the undeniable expression of his father's rejection.

Though I am unable to recall finding this phenomenon in even one woman, there were middle-aged and older men who, though their rejection was clinically manifested, utterly failed to recognize it. A man in his fifties, who evidenced a number of behavioral symptoms associated with rejection, would become so furious at anyone who questioned any mother's love that he was just not responsible for what he did. From time to time, his praise of the unique love of his own mother for all her children appeared to be extravagant. He never tired of insisting that every mother loves her children. He gave no indication that he recognized his own maternal rejection, though he hesitatingly volunteered the information that, because of her many pressing obligations, his mother never had been able to give any notable amount of time to him or to any of the other children.

If this sex difference regarding the age at which open recognition of rejection occurs should be substantiated by future research, how could it be explained? I would suggest that part of the explanation might be found, in our culture, in the seemingly greater attention of most women to their interpersonal relationships and in women's more acute awareness of their needs for affection than is evidenced by most men. However, any attempt at this time to formulate a hypothesis that would account for the reported sex difference regarding the age at which rejection was clearly recognized would be premature. To my knowledge, this sex difference has not been mentioned in the literature; hence, further research findings would be needed to confirm whether or not such a sex difference can be verified.

The phenomenon of the *suddenness* of the open recognition of rejection raises a related question. Though the open awareness of rejection came as a shocking surprise to nearly all of the rejected, did they earlier have any knowledge whatever that they were being rejected? Many of them, looking back, testified to some kind of not-attended-to recognition of rejection. One man wrote: " . . . The third important point was simply the realization that Mom never loved me (or any of the kids, with the possible exception of my brother in [name of city]) and was simply using us as part of her defense reaction against her own problems. I unconsciously knew this (as well as many of the things listed in the previous paragraph), reacted very strongly, and completely repressed the reaction."

All of the rejected testified that painful feelings had accumulated in their relationships with their parents. A reservoir of hurts from parental behaviors and attitudes had remained unexplained or inadequately explained. It was only later that the evidence of these painful experiences was revealed, in the light of this new awareness, to be a factual body of happenings reinforcing the correctness of their newly found interpretation of parental rejection.

Some rejected, after they had openly faced their rejection, reported that they had much earlier had ongoing, but only dimly conscious, knowledge of the correct interpretation of hurtful parental behaviors. While such knowledge had not yet clearly surfaced in their awareness, it was almost as if they knew it was there; but because they had not yet looked at it, they had not seen it.

In summary, then—according to my findings, the rejected usually managed somehow to delay the clear, open recognition of parental rejection for years. They universally reported that, when such recognition finally occurred, it was both a surprising and exceedingly painful experience—in fact, some reported it as catastrophic.

Nonetheless, it seems at least probable that, as children, all the rejected had had painful feelings that something was seriously wrong in their relationships with their parents and that they had sensed at least some rejection in these relationships. At the same time, presumably because a lucid recognition would have been so painful, they spontaneously but unknowingly had striven, in a psychologically self-protective way, to interpret the hurtful behaviors as experiences less painful than rejection.

Consequently, initial recognitions of rejection were pushed, and safely maintained, below the conscious level. There they remained until such time as these persons had acquired the psychological strength to cope consciously with them. Accordingly, when the unconsciously self-protective custody of these feelings below the level of awareness was no longer psychologically needed, they spontaneously surfaced in consciousness.

To my knowledge, there is no reliable method for testing such a presumption. However, it seems reasonable to me to assume the likelihood of some early, if only partial, experienced rejection which, at some level, had been recognized by all the rejected.

No matter how obscure the explanations of just how they had eventually come to know they were rejected, one point seemed indisputable. A substantial number of the rejected reported that, after they had finally recognized their rejection, for years they unknowingly employed one or more psychological devices to protect themselves from the unlovely realization that they had been rejected. These psychological, rejection-concealing devices were "defense mechanisms," which involved no aspect whatever of conscious deception or pretending. Rather, they were psychological tricks that these people had automatically and unconsciously used in order to shield themselves from the exceedingly distressing experience of rejection.

There is nothing new or remarkable about the use of defense mechanisms. Their importance in human behavior has long been appreciated. Since the time of Sigmund Freud, it has been generally maintained that such psychological stratagems unconsciously played on oneself are aimed at blotting out or attenuating painful anxiety. Freud indicated, in fact, that all of the defense mechanisms, with the exception of "isolation" and "undoing," are but so many channels of *repression* (62). He saw repression as functioning to automatically maintain below the level of awareness those painful experiences which a person is not psychologically prepared to face. Essentially, repression is a spontaneous, unconsciously motivated kind of forgetting. It is well to remember, as Freud pointed out, that a person may use more than one defense mechanism and that, at times, it is difficult to be certain about the correct classification of the defense mechanism being employed. Freud's daughter Anna, picking up where her father left off, has made *the* classical contribution on the subject of defense mechanisms (59).

While I have not found the specific use of defense mechanisms to avoid recognition of rejection mentioned in the literature, the conclusion reached as a result of my clinical experience is that the rejected had unwittingly employed defense mechanisms to protect themselves against such specific knowledge. They were being utilized to conceal, not anxiety, but rather one of its principal sources, namely, the knowledge of their own rejection.

Such self-protective psychological operations in the rejected were not, of course, ascribable to intentional self-deceiving. Could the automatic, self-protective loss of consciousness that occurs when physical pain becomes unendurable be said to be deliberately chosen? Obviously, the individual in extreme pain does not deliberately choose to lose consciousness, and an individual's particular defense mechanism is just as automatic. Moreover, if it does not succeed in really deceiving him to the extent that he remains blind to what it is hiding from him, then it fails to provide him with the psychological protection he needs.

Thus, these psychological tricks the rejected played on themselves gave protection primarily against the naked recognition of their having been rejected. Indeed, such defenses marshalled directly against the clear awareness of their rejection were so frequently reported that they appeared to be universal in the rejected.

The following defense mechanisms either had been used or were still unconsciously being used by the rejected to guard against the recognition of their rejection.

Repression was the mental process by which perceptions, ideas, and other painful experiences that might indicate to them the truth that they had been rejected were unknowingly forced below their awareness and maintained there. These rejected experiences remained below the conscious level, not in a passive, static state, but in a highly dynamic one. While remaining hidden from the rejected themselves, their feelings of being rejected unknowingly continued to motivate much of their behavior. In addition to concealing from them the fact of their parental rejection, repression often blotted out from their consciousness, as well, a number of other experiences associated with rejection. One well-educated man, who had moved to another part of the country and there continued in therapy with a psychiatrist, wrote:

> . . . To retrace a bit: I had a whole galaxy of symptoms as a kid, obsessions and compulsions, each of which I got rid of by realizing that it was ridiculous—but, of course, something else always popped up. Other childhood symptoms: severe nervous asthma, constant guilt feeling (still largely present), and the constant habit of repressing, controlling, and hiding every inclination, emotion, and reaction. I showed nothing of what I felt, attached myself to no one, had no affective life, communicated freely with no one, faced my own problems, sought my own information in devious, indirect ways, and, I think, came to identify affection with sex. (Incidentally, both parents were basically unconscious Puritans and our upbringing shows it constantly—although

we've all become aware of it and fought to overcome it.) Until therapy
brought it back, I had completely forgotten how completely miserable
my whole childhood was, and how terribly lonely. (I don't really feel
very tragic and dramatic about it at this point—I'm just trying to be
clear.) . . .

At times repression was only partial. It spontaneously blotted out of
consciousness, not the clear knowledge of rejection, but only some
hurtful aspect of that knowledge—for instance, the distressful *feelings*
connected with the naked viewing of rejection. One woman casually
remarked, "I doubt if my mom ever cared anything at all about me, let
alone loved me, but I could care less how she felt about me." In several
subsequent therapy sessions, she nonchalantly repeated substantially
this same remark. During a much later session, she broke down and
cried almost hysterically. The realization that her mother did not love
her, she afterwards explained, must have been so painful that she
simply could not bear it. Now she realized that unconsciously she had
been denying to herself that it mattered, and somehow she had really
convinced herself that it didn't. Lately, she had become aware of how
terribly important it was to her, and her mother's rejection hurt her
very deeply.

A considerable number of clients followed this pattern of cavalierly
acknowledging parental rejection, only to discover during the course of
psychological counseling how painful that rejection really was. In fact,
I do not recall a single client who began therapy with such expressed
indifference toward his recognized rejection who did not eventually
experience such painful awareness.

There were other aspects associated with this partial repression. It
had been extended to feelings about all humans—but *only* humans.
The ability to retain feelings about nonhuman living things had, at the
same time, remained intact. A girl in her late teens explained that it did
not even concern her, let alone pain her, that her parents did not love
her. She repeatedly remarked that she simply had no feelings about it,
one way or the other. They couldn't hurt her in this or, for that matter,
any other way, because she simply had no feelings whatever about
people. In an effort to demonstrate how true this was, she gave me this
illustration: "I could line up a dozen people and with a rusty saw-
edged sword, slowly cut their heads off one at a time without the
slightest feeling about it."

On the other hand, she admitted that she cried at the suffering of
animals. To see especially a young animal in pain broke her heart. She
expressed her longing to go out by herself into the wilderness and live

there all alone, " . . . where there would be only the wild animals, so nothing to fear." I do not know whether this young woman's deeply painful feelings that were linked with her parental rejection surfaced later in her consciousness. Shortly after she told me about her total lack of feelings for people, she left the area; and I did not hear from her again. Incidentally, though she was an unusually bright student, she gave not the slightest hint of seeing that her remark, " . . . where there would be only the wild animals, so nothing to fear," was logically inconsistent with her assertion that she had no feelings whatever about people.

The rejected used the mental process of *rationalization* to unconsciously manufacture ostensible reasons in order to justify interpretations of hurtful actions and experiences as something other than rejection. Some rejected rationalized, with only limited success, the hurtful behavior coming from their parents with explanations not as personally unacceptable to them as rejection. One man was certain his parents had always loved him; it was just that they never *needed* him. As therapy continued, he was beginning to experience some doubts about their love. Whenever such doubts arose, he immediately pushed them into the back of his mind. Nevertheless, these doubts had lately been surging more frequently and distressingly into his consciousness.

Others appeared to have more success in using rationalization. One man explained that, though he was sure his parents loved him, he had suffered intensely because they were always too *busy* to spend any time with him. His financially well-off parents had traveled a great deal. Invariably, when they returned from a trip, they had brought him costly toys. "By the time I was fourteen," he said, "I had toys that would fill the corner of this room right up to the ceiling. Yet I would gladly have dumped the entire lot of them into the Spokane River if, in exchange, either of my parents would have spent just fifteen undistracted minutes with me. But they were always too busy." He then requested that I never inform his parents, since he felt sure that they had never suspected how deeply hurt he had been feeling all these years. Because they loved him, he added, they would have dropped everything to spend time with him had they known and he was sure they could not afford that time.

Children, especially, characteristically used this mechanism to protect themselves very effectively from the unlovely realization of their parents' rejection. A twelve-year-old girl, an only child, whose alcoholic parents had for some years been receiving just enough government income to enable them to remain generally under the influence of alcohol, had the following history:

When she was seven years of age, the neighbors became concerned that she was not getting sufficient food. They finally talked with the girl's parents about it. The parents did not see that there was any problem; in fact, they said, it was beneficial for their daughter to learn early in life to be self-reliant. Shortly afterwards, the neighbors (somewhat shocked by her parents' response) informed the girl that they had made arrangements at a neighborhood grocery store, where she could go at any time and "charge" food. She did this regularly for years thereafter. Her diet during these years consisted mainly of candy and soft drinks. By the time a social worker referred her to me, in her thirteenth year, she had already lost all of her permanent teeth. As she talked to me, she repeatedly introduced the subject of her parents' "illness" and invariably added that, though they both loved her very much, they were too sick to do anything for her.

My anticipation was that she would have openly recognized her parents' rejection of her, at least by the time she reached her late teens. This, however, remains speculation, based on what I witnessed in somewhat comparable situations, since I was not in contact with her during these late-teen years.

Again and again, adults reported their utter astonishment at discovering they had been effectively using rationalization to hide from themselves their parental rejection. Throughout her childhood a young woman had been unable to question her parents' love for her, but she very early had discovered that the older child in the family was *preferred* to her. There were repeated confirmations of this preference. Terribly hurt by it, she frequently would go off into the hills with her pet animal and, in tears, would tell this animal about how her parents were breaking her heart. Though she could pour out her secrets to her pet, she could confide them to no person. Eventually, when the older child left home, her parents turned their attention and affection to her; but it was too late. She could not force herself to respond warmly; she remained cold and stiff around them.

Years later, in the course of counseling, she came to recognize openly that her parents had rejected her. Then, she expressed amazement at the rationalization she had so efficaciously, but unknowingly, employed over the years. During all that time, she had kept telling herself that the behavior of her parents evidenced a preference for her sibling and nothing more. She had continued to remind herself that, though they loved both of them, they preferred her sibling to her. In fact, she had not even been able to admit to herself that they loved her less, though she deeply resented having this sibling preferred to her.

Regression in the rejected was the mental and/or physical action of returning to patterns of living which belonged to earlier, less mature, periods of life. This mechanism unconsciously served to delay the open recognition of rejection by lessening the evidences of that rejection. An unmarried woman in her early thirties had long felt that her mother had never been pleased with her. Nonetheless, she seemed to have not clearly perceived her mother's rejection of her. Her mother's displeasure was undeniable when she got a job and moved into her own apartment. For some reason, after the inception of her new-found independence, her relationship with her mother had become increasingly unpleasant.

Recently, however, her mother expressed delight when her daughter mentioned to her that she was thinking of giving up the apartment and moving back home. She has since moved home and, while she has not been comfortable there because of her mother's dominating possessiveness of her, she has found her mother less vexed at her. Recently, her mother mentioned to her that there was really no need for her to work, assuring her, "I can still take care of my little girl at home." She is now seriously thinking of quitting her job. She said that the loss of her independence is not too high a price to pay for peace.

In employing the defense mechanism of *insulation*, the rejected unknowingly managed to set themselves apart from the pain of rejection. It had taken one man years to learn the lesson of survival in this hurtful world. He felt that what had helped him most was the advice he had read in a book. It was that, in order to cope successfully with life, one must learn to encapsulate oneself in time. According to this formula, once he had completely phased out his past life, he then had to avoid assiduously every temptation to look ahead. The secret was to live completely enclosed in the present. He had to persuade himself that today is all that matters and all that he will let matter. For him, the result of constantly following this advice was that he had succeeded in shutting out almost everything painful in his life, including what would strongly appear to have been rejection by his parents.

In utilizing the defense mechanism of *reaction formation*, the externally observable behavior of some rejected contradicted and so refuted the unacceptable feeling of rejection, which was thus held safely beneath the level of their awareness. One man has been almost consumed with the need to repay his parents for all they have done for him. His greatest longing in life, he remarked, has been to care for his parents in every way. Repeatedly, he has told his brothers and sisters that they should leave it to him to take care of the folks. In passing, he mentioned that each of them seemed not only willing but almost relieved; and it baffled him that not one of them had volunteered to do something for the folks.

His wife has not been able to understand, nor has he been able to explain to her, why he must put the welfare of his parents ahead of the welfare of his own family. Repeatedly he has told her that it's something he simply has to do. His parents have appeared to be pleased with what he has thus far been able to provide for them. They seemed especially glad when he told them that he was going to see to it that they would live better than his own family. Such a manifest behavior pattern of gratitude and love for his parents serves to completely deny any unrecognized feelings of rejection and counterrejection which may be present below the conscious level.

Following are a few less frequently reported defense mechanisms that were employed by some of the rejected against the painful recognition of their rejection.

In employing *compensation*, the rejected indulged in pleasurable activities which, because they were highly gratifying, tended to counterbalance the excruciating pain of their rejection. A young woman shunned every kind of intimacy with others—even shaking hands with people bothered her. However, she did not dread the repetition of rejection, since she had never openly faced her rejection because of her repeated use of compensation. Whenever she began to feel depressed, she immediately slipped into daydreams in which she fantasized herself relating sexually, in every conceivable manner, to imagined men. Then her rich imagination, fueled by her erotic arousal, furnished her with ongoing, intensely pleasurable, passionate experiences that outweighed any tendency to feel depressed. At the same time, she was filled with guilt and thought increasingly less of herself for thus gratifying herself. This pattern of compensation which she reported is by no means an exceptional one. In fact, almost every rejected individual who acknowledged having put himself on such a social-starvation diet eventually reported that he also repeatedly indulged himself sexually in his fantasy life.

Withdrawal enabled the rejected to move either physically or psychologically away from the awareness of their rejection. A chronically unemployed rejected man spontaneously went to bed and slept at any time during the day whenever anything upset him or in any way bothered him. At such times, he would automatically go into a sound sleep. All he now recognizes is that certain distressing thoughts make him very tired and sleepy.

The self-deception termed *displacement* involves mistaken identification. Through it the rejected unconsciously attributed their own rejection to one or more others or ascribed its source to people other than their parents. One rejected woman has never been able to understand why God could have allowed what has happened to her. No matter where she went to school she was always certain that at least one teacher deeply disliked her, even though that teacher tried to hide it. She is presently stunned at the deep resentment her daughter-in-law feels toward her. The insidious part, she explained, is that the latter has never verbalized her resentment nor shown it by any overt behavior. She can feel, nevertheless, the almost unbelievable intensity of that dislike, for which she has never given this daughter-in-law the slightest grounds.

In yet another aspect of displacement, some rejected openly faced their parental rejection but unknowingly displaced the basis for it to something other than their own unlovableness. They were thus able to stake out their own grounds for their parents' rejection of them. The basis of their selection was invariably something less hurtful to them than the feeling of having been rejected precisely because they were unlovable. Almost without exception, the alleged grounds for rejection in these displacements were such that these rejected could have removed or changed them if they had so chosen. Had they done so, however, they would thereby have put to the test the correctness of their explanation for their parental rejection. For the most part, they simply had not done this. In fact, it apparently had not even occurred to most of them to do so.

One woman felt certain that the reason her parents rejected her was because she had always been so obese. From the time she was in the sixth grade, she also knew that her unpopularity with the other kids was because she was so fat. She was convinced that her parents and others did not even want her around because they were embarrassed by her excessive corpulence.

At the same time, she remained puzzled by the fact that she regularly engaged in eating sprees during which she gorged herself, especially with sweets. Her behavior evidenced that this was not merely compensation. Once when she found out that one of the foods she craved was only slightly fattening, to her great surprise she immediately lost all desire for it. This still baffled her when she told me about it. She had particularly craved these fattening foods immediately after she had been hurt by someone. At such times she had even stolen money in order to buy large amounts of such food, on which she then glutted herself.

It had not crossed her mind that the agony of her rejection by her parents, which she could no longer deny, was in this way being effectively attenuated. It was as though—deprived of her first line of psychological defense, which was to keep the rejection concealed from her awareness—she had unknowingly retreated to the second line of defense, that of reducing the pain of the rejection by displacing its grounds.

Since the reports of the rejected generally testified to an unconscious arraying of their psychological powers against at least some aspects of parental rejection, what had caused the breakthrough? What kinds of events or situations had possessed the requisite strength to penetrate the protective psychological armor of the rejected so as to reveal to them their rejection?

I prescind from those exceedingly regrettable and extreme instances already mentioned in which very young children were personally violated by parents to the point that their rejection had become undeniable (207). The behaviors that were reported to have occasioned the naked viewing of rejection usually followed a pattern: Some very early experiences furnished incontrovertible evidence of parental rejection, but were recognized only later when the child had come of intellectual and emotional age and other parental behaviors triggered open and unmistakable awareness of rejection. The first-mentioned experiences laid the foundation for rejection waiting-to-be-realized; the second occasioned its recognition. Often it was difficult, if not impossible, to ascertain exactly where the first left off and the second began.

Infrequently, a single parental behavior triggered the naked consciousness of rejection, but there invariably had been a history of hurtful parent-child relations. In either case, the parental behaviors involved could have been *actions* or *omissions*.

Children were deeply hurt by one or more parental *actions* other than remarks (24, 168). At times, the predisposing element was a single action so gross in nature as to later appear to be unquestionable rejection. A woman vividly recalled that, as a child, she had been sexually initiated by her father. At the time, she had not understood what was transpiring, but remembered only that he insisted she tell no one about it. Not until she reached her teens, and with revulsion recalled the incident, did she clearly realize the rejection that had been implicit in that paternal action so early in her life.

Often, a number of early parental behaviors furnished the basis for later-recognized rejection. One woman had been sent away to boarding school when she was in first grade. Months later, her mother came to the school for a visit with her and her brother, who was also a boarder. As she had fearfully anticipated, her mother—after a leisurely visit with her brother—managed to spend just a few distracted moments with her. At the end of the school year, she returned home only to discover that her mother had left home shortly after returning from her visit to the school. In shock, she understood that the school visit had been her mother's good-bye. Then and there, something in her died. Years later, she identified this experience as rejection. Thereafter, she told everyone her mother was dead and lived in fear that her friends would detect her lie. She now knows where her mother lives but is not interested in contacting her, because this woman—she says—is just another stranger to her.

The type and severity, rather than the frequency, of punishment were later recognized as evidence of undeniable parental rejection (40). It is almost incredible, in view of the nature and severity of their punishments, that some children were able to postpone the recognition of their parental rejection until considerably later. They had been burned with cigarettes and cigars, scalded, half-drowned, suffocated, and beaten with heavy metallic instruments. Their flesh had been laid open; their bones had been fractured; they had received concussions (94).

The punishments meted out by rejecting parents were "justified" by those parents. They were given a veneer of being both reasonable and suitable. A man who happened to have his six-year-old daughter along with him during a counseling session told her at one point to stop fidgeting and sit still. Not satisfied with her response, he asked her sharply, "Do you want daddy to help you?" She immediately stiffened and remained rigid.

Noting my surprise at her reaction, he explained: "This kid was precocious; she started to walk at eleven months." He went on to narrate that, when she was about eighteen months old, he was sitting on his front porch one afternoon keeping an eye on her as she toddled about in front of the house. She had just walked with short, uncertain steps across the parking strip and was standing at the curb looking down into the street.

> At that point I hollered at her, "Don't step into the street." She hesitated, looking first at me and then down into the street, so I added, "If you step into the street, daddy will help you." Father, it's pretty much the same principle as training a horse. You have to let them know immediately who's boss. Still looking at me to see if I meant it, she defiantly stepped over the curb. I was off that porch like a flash, and around to the back of the house, where I grabbed the switch I had already prepared and hidden there. I ran back around the front and caught her as she was heading at full steam for the front steps and her mother. She knew what she had coming to her.
>
> You understand that I *had* to let her know I meant business. I switched her legs and bottom as she fell and crawled screaming up the

walk, and I continued to switch as she scrambled up the front steps on all fours and onto the porch. Her legs were bleeding when she made her escape through the front door, but there was no other way—and, believe me, it worked. Now, any time she misbehaves, all I have to do is ask her, "Do you want daddy to help you?" She knows only too well what that means. Father, some people are naturally strong personalities and born disciplinarians, and some are just weaklings.

Parental behavior that *triggered* open awareness of rejection was usually of a crude nature; infrequently, it was but a single action. One woman will never forget something which happened to her when she was still in her teens. It was winter and, because the furnace had broken down, the house was very cold. She complained to her mother, the only other person at home, about how cold she was. Her mother's response was, with no warning, to slap her very hard across the face and stare at her "with naked hatred in her eyes." This response of her mother had chilled her completely. In fact, she will never forget the horror of it. Until that moment, she had never *openly* acknowledged to herself that her mother did not love her. After this occurrence, she felt certain that she could no longer believe that her mother loved her. To this day, she has never entertained the slightest doubt about her mother's rejection of her.

Multiple actions rather than a single one more frequently tripped the clear awareness of parental rejection. As an adolescent, a woman had been sexually assaulted repeatedly by her father. She even discovered that her mother knew of it but said nothing. She could no longer hold to the thin hope that her parents loved her.

Parental *remarks* at times were experienced as lethal. In fact, some of them appeared to have been every bit as deadly as the severely hurtful, physical actions of parents. Such incidents inevitably occurred within an uncomfortable and somehow wanting parent-child relationship. For the most part, the element of surprise seemed to have been even greater in damaging parental remarks than in their injurious behaviors. Some rejected reported that their parents had never had anything good to say about them. Never had they said they were proud of them. Instead, they had repeatedly battered them with harsh, biting criticism. The parents had focused on the failures, inadequacies, and disappointments they found in their children. Often the resulting pain and anxiety was so great that their children could not even recall the remarks.

Remarks made by parents under the influence of anger, alcohol, emotional stress, and so forth, had devastatingly communicated rejection. Later parental assurances that they really didn't mean what they said had changed nothing. A man in his twenties acknowledged that, though the whole family had long known his father had a terrible temper, they were thankful that he seldom lost it. This man will never forget the one occasion when his father, exceedingly angry, glared at him and in cold, measured words stunned him with the remark, "I could kill you." In view of his awareness that his father had never given him any expression of love or affection, he could no longer deny his father's rejection of him. A woman vividly recalled with chills the time in her childhood when her father, referring to her, shouted angrily at her mother, "And I doubt that that kid is mine."

While one woman was still in her teens, her mother, who had been drinking heavily, confronted her with the words: "We never planned on having you and we didn't want you." As she listened, utterly stunned, her mother continued to pour out the explanation that she and her husband not only had not planned on having her, but both had developed grave doubts that she was really their child. They had become so disappointed in this "bad" child that they had gradually concluded that a mistake must have been made in the hospital where she was born. As a result, they believed they had unknowingly brought home someone else's baby.

One man recalled most vividly that, when the brother closest to him in years was killed in an accident, his mother—under severe emotional stress—suddenly turned on him with: "Why couldn't it have been you?" Nothing further needed to be said.

Several times, such damaging remarks made under one of these conditions had been followed by apologies, but it was too late. The damage had been done. The recipients of these devastating utterances experienced incontestable rejection.

Occasionally, injurious remarks made by those to whom the rejected were not related by blood seemed to fit into this same pattern of devastating rejection. Such persons were very important in the lives of those reporting the remarks. When a man had been in grade school, he was highly active in various sports and activities around school. Then came the unforgettable day when he lined up with the other kids to try out for a class play. The teacher, whom he secretly idolized, looked at him and said coldly, "You should not be here with the others; you are rotten." He was utterly stunned by this shattering verbal blow. Right then and there, he began to build a "cloud" about himself. He added: "My mother liked me, so I could come out of the cloud at home." When he got to be a senior in high school, he finally found one friend with whom he could come out of his cloud. "In the cloud," he said, "I daydreamed all the time." Over a period of many months of counseling, he never mentioned his father. He had remarked more than once that his mother liked him but said nothing about whether she loved him. The fact that he could emerge from his cloud in her presence seemed to indicate that he did not clearly experience rejection from her.

This and similar reported experiences raised the question of whether devastating rejection could also originate from nonparents who were "significant others." In this instance, it was not clear that rejection proceeded from the parents, and it seemed likely that the rejection which was so destructive had come from another important individual in the person's life.

This type of rejection from people other than parents was frequently experienced as a result of remarks made by parent surrogates. One woman wrote: "I was told I would never amount to anything, that I was just like my mother—and, in the eyes of the person talking, my mother was no good. This person who was taking care of me when I was a little girl said she was going to send me to reform school, but would not tell me for what. She never had one decent thing to say to me. She accused me of being out with some boy—that's the way it was all the time."

This rejected woman gave no indication of feeling that her mother had rejected her, and said so little about her father that I was uncertain how she felt about him. Her feelings about her surrogate mother, on the other hand, were unmistakable. That cruel woman, who was also an incredibly crude individual, had repeatedly made such remarks to this girl and her sister as, "You're nothing but two cheap slits." Neither girl could begin to guess at the meaning of such remarks, but nonetheless were deeply hurt by the way they were said. The surrogate mother (whom the girl felt hated her) nevertheless remained the most important person in her early life. She knows she has been hurt psychologically and feels that the damage came principally from the woman's injurious words during those early years.[4]

Parental remarks, in order to be deeply damaging, did not need to be made to the rejected themselves. Remarks of rejecting parents that had been directed to others but were overheard by the rejected also triggered the clear awareness of rejection. At times a single overheard remark had sufficed. A woman who was an only child happened to eavesdrop when her mother was talking to a friend. She was horrified

[4]In addition to the reported impact of parental surrogates, it should be noted that certain rejections experienced later in life (such as being abandoned by a spouse or betrayed by a loved one) have appeared to parallel both the experience described above and its psychological aftermaths. Also, a few persons with very poor self-concepts told me that they had been rejected by their schoolmates until they had become nonpersonalities or nonpersons.

to hear her mother confide to the other person that she now regretted not having gone ahead with the abortion she had originally planned.

In some instances, such remarks blamed the rejection, not on the parent, but on the rejected person. A man in his twenties happened to overhear his mother (who was talking to a woman friend about him) say: "His birth spoiled a perfect love affair, something for which I can never forgive him."

Remarks capable of causing rejection to emerge in consciousness also included those made by the rejecting parents to others that were later reported back to the rejected. A girl in her late teens had always found it very frustrating that her father never responded with any affection to her daughterly approaches. Later, she was told in confidence by a girl friend that her father, in talking about her, had said: "I wish she would just go away—anyplace, and stay away—for good." She was afraid to ask her father if he had actually said this, but, subsequently, she received the numbing confirmation that he had. No longer could she force herself to believe that he loved her.

Finally, remarks written by parents to the rejected brought about the open recognition of their rejection. Near the end of her junior year at a boarding school, a girl received a letter from her mother which devastated her. It informed her that they would not be up as usual at the end of this school year to take her home. Her mother imparted to her the information that they had already scheduled their vacation for that time. The letter went on to instruct her to look diligently for a summer job just as soon as she got home. It added that they would probably see her in a couple of weeks when they got back.

When she came to see me, letter in hand, she was despondent. She had already purchased the means to take her life. She had also been thinking seriously of yielding to insanity as a way out. Certain she could not go home, she acknowledged that she had no place else to go. Some weeks later she came to tell me that now she could go home, "because I made a deal with God that I would take this, providing he would get me the guy I love."

Obviously, this change of plan did not mean that she had lost her feeling of having been rejected by her parents. What she was saying was that she felt, in bargaining thus with God, that the indescribable hurt from her rejection would be somewhat compensated for by a very rewarding experience.

Parental *omissions* expressed rejection, even though they were not recognized as such by the parents manifesting them. This kind of rejection took the form of absences: absence of devotion to the child's interests, absence of sensitivity to his needs and desires, absence of affection and approval (40). It was often difficult for the rejected themselves to determine just when they had come to identify these absences as conveying clear-cut parental rejection. Nonetheless, their feeling responses to such omissions had manifested some awareness of it being a painful experience. Moreover, though they had not yet identified their emotional hurt as rejection, they knew that it was somehow associated with these parental neglects.

In any serious consideration of psychologically hurtful parental omissions, attention must be paid to Bowlby's studies of the effects on a very young child of lengthy physical absences of the mother. Inasmuch as it has been impossible to ascertain with certainty whether such maternal absences are experienced by little children precisely as actions of abandonment or simply as omissions of physical presence, I have arbitrarily decided to treat them here as the latter.

Bowlby employed naturalistic observation in his study of infants who were physically separated from their mothers for lengthy periods. He and his fellow researchers were struck by the intensity and universality of the resulting "separation anxiety" (25). Bowlby's analysis indicated that separation-anxiety can be divided into three stages according to the length of time the mother was away. He found that during an absence of from a few hours to more than a week, the child cried distressfully, shook the crib, and carefully scrutinized every person who came near. After a certain time he appeared to lapse into "despair," "hopelessness," and "mourning." Finally, he moved into a pattern of detachment which persisted. In other words, the child passed successively through the stages of protest, despair, and detachment (25). In this last stage, he gave the superficial appearance of being more social than he had been in the previous two stages, but avoided attaching himself to any person and became primarily occupied with things (25, 168). Prolonged absences of the mother from a child have been found to have grave consequences, including a notable slowing down of the motor, intellectual, and language development of the child (60, 189, 190, 191, 192, 193).

What were the *long-range* effects of such maternal separation? Bowlby noted "the acute exacerbation of separation anxiety after the child's return home" (26), but did not indicate how long this exacerbation lasted. Elsewhere he remarked that "statements implying that children who experience institutionalization and similar forms of severe privation and deprivation in early life *commonly* develop psychopathic affectionless characters are incorrect" (26). This appears to be a rather sweeping generalization for which he listed no specific substantiating findings.

Did any of my findings offer observations on the *long-range* impact of maternal separations? A number of the rejected recalled that very early physical separations from parents, particularly mothers, had been deeply hurtful to them, irrespective of motive. They had later come to identify this experience as the feeling that they had been rejected. In addition, where the separation was prolonged—even if it included periodic visits by the mother—there was a counterrejection of the mother by the child.

When a girl in her teens had been an infant, her mother, with no source of income, decided that she would have to work to support herself and her baby. In order to do so, she had to place her baby in the care of someone else. During those years she visited her baby regularly and paid for her entire support. Recently this daughter gave birth to a child out of wedlock. When her mother became aware of this, she pleaded to be privileged to provide her grandchild with a good home. Her daughter adamantly refused. Her reply to her mother was: "If you wanted a child, why didn't you keep me?"

No matter how reasonable the grounds for the parents' absence, it appears that the separation was almost invariably experienced—at some level of knowing—as rejection, although it had not yet been identified as such. One woman had been only three years old when her mother became so mentally ill that she had to be taken to the hospital, where she was to remain for many years. She will never forget the actual departure of her mother. As she desperately clung to her mother, she was gently but firmly pushed aside. In absolute panic she watched them take her mother away.

It was her mother's manner of leaving her that she later felt as the evidence of her mother's rejection, even though she did not recognize it as such at the time. Now she readily acknowledges that her mother was too sick to be at fault and so was not in any way to blame for leaving her. Nevertheless, even though it doesn't make sense to her, she still *feels* this "abandonment" as the unshakable evidence of her mother's rejection of her. Another woman, who was unable to justify such feelings of her own, summarized it this way: "I know it isn't fair, but I can't help it. It's the way I feel."

Some people who were unable to logically support strong feelings of parental culpability for their early "abandonment" reported that they carried a heavy burden of guilt for harboring such feelings of rejection. As an infant, a man had been so seriously crippled with polio that he had to be institutionalized. He was not brought home to live with his parents until he was eleven years old. Now he feels that this long separation is the confirmation that his parents did not want him and did not love him. At the same time, he has been tortured with guilt. He readily acknowledges the truth of his parents' assertion that the excellent physical therapy and medical care he received during those years at the institution would not have been available to him at home. In addition, during all those years his parents very frequently visited him, though they lived a considerable distance from the institution. Hence in his own thinking he has been unable to justify his feeling that this separation from his parents unquestionably spelled out their rejection of him. The feeling has persisted, however, and he continues to bear the resulting burden of guilt.

Another parental omission that invariably produced intense suffering—later identified as rejection—was the psychological absence of physically present parents. The memory that haunts one woman is that of herself, as a mere tot, endlessly tugging at her mother's dress, usually to be ignored and only occasionally to receive the response: "Don't bother mommy. She's busy." She remembers that much of the time her mother was just standing or sitting and appeared to be doing nothing. While she can only guess at her mother's motives for such behavior, she cannot bring herself to believe that her mother loved her.

Another type of experience occurred that was somewhat puzzling. It was the feeling produced, not by the parent who expressed rejection through omissions, but by the other parent who went along with those omissions. One man's parents always took care of their own needs first. Anything that happened to be left over went to the children. Even when the youngest child had not yet started school, their mother informed the children that she and her husband owed it to themselves to spend a month alone each summer at a beach resort. She directed that the older children were to shop, cook, and generally take care of the younger ones. The strict orders she left made it crystal clear to the children that, aside from an extreme emergency, the parents were not to be contacted during this time. Even if one of the children had to be hospitalized, their vacation was not to be interrupted unless there was actual danger of death. She said that when they returned they would give some thought to vacations for the children if they could afford them.

This man added that all the children agreed that this and other such incidents were omissions of their mother and not of their father. He now feels that he is not certain he can identify as rejection their father's obsequious compliance in these and other very hurtful omissions.

Certain parental omissions would have transparently expressed rejection if examined by almost anyone other than the persons being rejected. Nevertheless, they simply were not identified as such by the recipients of this behavior until after a number of years had passed (37). When one man and his brothers and sisters were very small, their father would never eat with them "because it made him ill," so he ate in a different room. Later, their father insisted he could not eat at the same time as his children, even though they made very little noise. This client eventually came to recognize these behaviors as clear evidences of his father's rejection. When he was much older, his mother told him his father had repeatedly told her through the years that he did not want any more babies. In fact, when she was about five months pregnant with each baby, he had become increasingly disturbed and even had talked of killing himself. She added that his father had always been a very immature, spoiled person.

Other parental omissions eventually were unveiled as rejection only when further experiences of the rejected person had provided a meaningful framework for such an identification. One man first started to sense that something important was missing in his relationship with his parents when he visited a friend's home and became aware of the parents' love and affection for their son. After a great deal of reflection, he was forced to contrast this behavior with his own parents' characteristic coldness and so face their rejection of him.

Some persons finally were forced to view their parental omissions as clearly spelling out rejection when, over a considerable period of time, they had simply exhausted all other explanations. As a high school boy, one man had been kept at home by his parents in order to do the chores on the farm and, for a time, was the envy of the other kids. As this went on year after year, however, he finally had to recognize that his parents were not only postponing his further education but were interested solely in having an extra nonsalaried "hand" on the farm. In fact, it became increasingly clear to him that they were openly opposed to making any notable sacrifice whatever for his education. At that point, he could no longer deny to himself that their primary interest in him was only as cheap labor. It became undeniable that they did not love him.

Still other persons were unwilling to interpret the hurtful omissions of their parents as unmistakably manifesting rejection until they had first gone through a lengthy process in which every other interpretation finally fell short of offering a satisfactory explanation. A man's parents had been aware that as a child he had longed for years for a particular gift at Christmas, one which even then he knew they could afford. Each year he waited expectantly, but in vain. This waiting for his Christmas gift became crucial in his life. He came to look on it as the acid test of whether his parents loved him. Eventually the day dawned when he no longer desired this Christmas gift; only then did he acknowledge to himself that they did not love him.

What appeared to be blends of parental actions and omissions were exceedingly hurtful, but the people being hurt could not afford to test them to see if they were really spelling out rejection. As a young boy, one man had been sent away to boarding school. No one suspected he was so homesick and hurt by this that he thought he would die. He couldn't dream of letting his parents or his older brothers and sisters know how he longed to stay home. If they knew and sent him back anyway, it would have been a personal catastrophe. When he arrived home for vacations, with stiff upper lip he would regale the members of the family with tales of his "successes" at school, how great it was, and so on. He was afraid that, even as he held their complete attention, his eyes were betraying his lie. No matter how broadly he smiled, he feared they would see that his eyes were beseeching them to let him remain at home. Each night, on the verge of panic, he prayed that they would not let him go back. At the end of each home visit, as he waited, suitcase in hand, at the front door for his father to drive him to the train, he fought back the tears. To this day, he feels deeply that "they didn't want me."

Occasionally, it was reported that some surprising, late development had triggered the realization of rejection. In his late thirties, a well-educated man had returned to the home of his mother in another city for her last illness. As her only child, he had the duty of going through her personal effects. While doing so, he was dumbfounded to discover adoption papers for himself, together with the names and address of his real parents. A thunderbolt! He said he felt that all these years she had deceived him and had lied to him even about his nationality. His real parents, he reflected, could not have given him away for adoption had they really cared about him. He had to conclude that the woman who had adopted him—as well as his real parents—had rejected him.

Finally, the releasing mechanism which would have permitted the clear recognition of rejection had remained wholly *unknown* to a few of the rejected for a long period of time. It seemed that protective psychological operations had been at work here, so that these persons simply did not see what was most painful for them to face until they were capable of facing it. This does not imply that they were later able to handle it easily. It means only that openly coping with it was no longer beyond their strength. Whatever the factors which entered into their unexplained, open recognition of parental rejection, that awareness had been excruciatingly painful. Yet, for the most part, they were not crushed by it. It might be assumed that the moment of their preparedness had arrived by the very fact that the recognition had occurred.

Such rejection appeared to have revealed itself spontaneously, without any perceived stimulus. Frequently, this occurred during counseling sessions. For some, it happened outside the counseling room (but during the period of counseling); and for others it happened entirely apart from any such professional relationship. A woman who was not at the time in counseling wrote:

> I suddenly realized that I had to go back a good many years in order to set things straight. I went back to the time when my parents were separated and, though I have never seen or acknowledged this before, I see now the attitudes I took regarding persons, places, and circumstances. I built a real wall around myself, inside which no one entered. As the rejected child, I sought and obtained recognition because of talents and abilities. This attitude has been fostered over the years without my realizing it.

I have found that rejection is no respecter of creed, sex, social class, intelligence, education, race, or any other such consideration. It is a tragic fact in the lives of many. Disregarding it does not make it go away. It is a deeply destructive human experience. Underlying the individual variations in their responses to it, the rejected reported certain discernible, unwholesome, psychological themes. These themes or generalizations, which appeared as impaired psychological patterns left in the trail of parental rejection, will be treated in the following chapters.

2
Damaged Self-Esteem
and Some of Its Ramifications

The experiences of damage to the self-esteem of the rejected conversely would seem to imply that parental love and acceptance is the source of people's self-esteem. Such may well be the case. Nonetheless, other sources of self-esteem have been identified. According to Becker, these sources include the infant's elemental physical experience from which he draws his sense of confident narcissism and his experience of invulnerability, dependable maternal support, a strong paternal figure with whom the child can identify, and the secure possession of his own body (15). The point at issue here is that the rejected—regardless of the source of their self-esteem—had, in fact, suffered the experience of its being notably impaired.

The personal destruction observed in the trail of rejection has been almost unbelievable. A number of researchers have concluded that such personal psychological damage not only was present in the rejected but was stimulated in them by their rejection (45, 119, 129, 151, 212, 215, 216). One notable sphere of such psychic injury is that of impaired self-esteem, together with its ramifications within the person himself and in his relationships to others (15, 40, 45, 151). Following are some specific research findings that have been found to be associated with damaged self-esteem in the rejected. While these findings are not always directly concerned with damaged self-esteem, they do bear some relationship to it. They are given here in order to help the reader appreciate the range of hurtful experiences that has been uncovered in the path of parental rejection, and especially the parental attitudes and behaviors found to be related to these experiences.

According to Symonds, the rejected have pronounced feelings of inferiority and inadequacy (196). Becker et al. reported that inferior-feeling children showed no association whatever with the behavior and attitudes of the mother. However, they did show a close relationship with maladjusted and child-thwarting fathers (16). In a study by Rosenberg, it was found that children who reported only punitive parental responses tended to have lower self-esteem than those who reported only supportive parental responses, and the children who reported indifferent parental responses had still lower self-esteem than the first-mentioned group. Extreme parental indifference was associated with very low self-esteem in the children (165). This finding, of course, is consonant with the previously mentioned finding that passive parental rejection was more injurious than active.

Gecas et al. found that a child's self-concept is more closely related to the parents' perceptions of him than to his parents' self-conceptions (68). Rogers and Dymond disclosed that ten-year-old children's perceptions of parental acceptance and their own feelings of self-esteem were highly correlated (164). According to a study by Jourard and Remy, a subject's self-appraisals correlate with his perceptions or beliefs about his parents' appraisals of him. A subject's negative self-appraisal and his perceived negative parental appraisals of him correlated with his psychological insecurity (88). Gardner Murphy noted that the tendency to value rather than disvalue self was correlated with one's parental approval (133).

Serot and Teevan ascertained that, whereas the well-adjusted child perceived his parent-child relationship as relatively happy and close to the theoretical ideal, the maladjusted child's perception of his relationship was far from ideal (180). Parents of disturbed children were reported by McDonald to be more self-rejecting than parents of "normal" children; they more frequently described their children as distrustful, self-effacing, and dependent than did parents of normal children; they more frequently failed to identify with their children when compared with parents of normal children; and they devaluated the personalities of their children more frequently than did parents of normal children (123). Goodstein and Rowley, as well as Liverant, noted that parents who sought aid for their children in psychiatric clinics were more disturbed than were parents in the general population (71, 108).

While to my knowledge there have been no contradictory findings, not every study has clearly confirmed the intimate relationship between parental rejection and impaired self-esteem in the rejected. Helper found only a slight tendency toward similarity between parents' evaluations of their children and the self-evaluations of their children (81). Burchinal and others reported no statistically significant correlation between the scores for parental acceptance and the adjustment of their children. They explained that either no such relationship was present or that their negative findings were principally due to inadequate measurement (31).

Some who readily grant that certain people have deep feelings of inferiority explain them as having had causes other than rejection. Alfred Adler's well-known contention is that they are rooted in the infant's experience of helplessness. Otto Rank takes issue with Adler's explanation as well as with that presented in these pages. Rank's position, in fact, is much closer to that of the existentialist philosophers.[1] As he sees it, these deep feelings of inferiority well up within the religious man when he is no longer able to sustain any illusions about his importance. Then, the growing awareness of truth about himself leaves him with feelings of utter powerlessness and inferiority (152).

Nonetheless, since most studies have revealed deeply damaged self-esteem in the wake of parental rejection, some questions arise. First, how stable are these hurtful aftermaths of parental rejection? My findings, confirmed by those of other researchers, indicate that these experiential residues tend strongly to remain through the years. Christie and Jahoda, in partial confirmation, found that at some time preceding middle childhood an individual forms a general appraisal of his personal worth that is relatively stable over a period of several years (38).

Second, can notable damage to self-esteem be correctly universalized to all the rejected? Even though this question cannot presently be answered with anything approximating finality, I think it should be raised. I am unable to recall a single rejected person coming to me professionally over a lengthy period of time who did not sooner or later indicate at least the symptoms of considerably damaged self-esteem.

A further question in regard to the converse of this discussion should be raised. Has every person with damaged self-esteem been rejected? Any such conclusion, as I have already indicated, would be unwarranted by my findings, and I would seriously question that such would be the case. People who have experienced psychotic (particularly schizophrenic) episodes, for instance, have often been thought to have low self-esteem. To my knowledge, however, it has not been seriously maintained that all such episodes have been the result of parental rejection. Moreover, some professional people favor the position that even the "functional" psychoses, for which no organic pathology has been found, have a still-undisclosed, underlying, organic causation. As such they cannot be primarily the result of rejection or any other experience. While this position is highly controversial, it ought not to be summarily dismissed.

---

[1]Kierkegaard saw angst (anxiety) as arising from the very nature of man's finite existence. Sartre ascribed the sources of these feelings to man's realization that the world's and his own existence are meaningless. Heidegger insisted that, because man becomes aware that his life is inescapably oriented toward death, he feels deeply anxious and inferior.

In any treatment of damage to *self-esteem,* clarification of terms is necessary. What do I mean by "esteem"? I am employing it according to the meaning in Webster's dictionary: to value highly; have great regard for or favorable opinion of; prize; respect. Accordingly, it refers to an individual *placing value on himself as a person,* estimating highly his personal worth, approving of and respecting himself, liking and holding himself in high regard (39, 40). This meaning appears to approximate closely Carl Rogers' "self-acceptance," i.e., being self aware, open, perceiving self as a person rather than as an object (159).

To say, without further qualification, that a person has self-esteem means that he respects himself and feels good about himself *as a person,* or that he has a good self-concept. This latter should not, however, be confused with a person's feeling good about some things he either can do or has done. It has direct reference not to his competencies but to his personal adequacy. The two are not necessarily related (210). Self-esteem is measurable and has, in fact, been measured.[2] A relationship between creativity and self-esteem has also been confirmed by Kris (99). To say, then, that a person has damaged self-esteem means that he has a poor self-concept, or that he has experienced self-devaluation. What has been the nature of the damage to self-esteem in the rejected? My clinical findings invariably revealed a deep, personal hurt present in them. A debased self-concept was universally experienced. Its most frequent expression was that the rejected did not like themselves, nor did they find themselves worthy of respect or approval. Some hated, loathed, despised themselves.

Did such damage to the self-esteem of the rejected imply a serious *questioning* of their personal worth? At one time I thought so. For years it appeared to me that the rejected gravely doubted their value as persons. This since appears to have been an oversimplification. The clearly rejected had entertained no doubts whatever about their low evaluations of personal worth. This appeared to hold true even for those whose outstanding abilities were bolstered by notable accomplishments and who were held in high regard by others. The rejected

---

[2]Some of the instruments which have been employed to measure self-esteem are: Coopersmith's Self-Esteem Inventory and his Behavior Rating Form (40); the Rogers and Dymond Scale (164); and batteries of clinical tests, including the Wechsler Intelligence Scale for Children, the Rorschach, the Thematic Apperception Test (T.A.T., selected cards), and Figure Drawing and Sentence Completion Tests. In addition, there have been experiments designed to measure behaviors presumably related to self-esteem, tasks to measure levels of aspiration, variations of the perceptual defense experiment involving presentation of high- and low-affect stimuli, recall and repetition of both success and failure experiences, susceptibility to conformity pressures, and measurement of the motor and perceptual reactions to stress (40). Interviewer ratings have also been utilized (6, 38).

simply did not value themselves highly. In fact, they felt the very opposite of self-esteem.

The foundations for their low self-evaluations were unmistakably evident to them. A woman wrote:

> I know I am nothing but the scum of the earth. I only wish I could be clean and decent like some. I hate myself because I am not. I would like to make others think I am, but I know with all I have said to you that you don't think any different, and it's only natural, because it is the truth. That is one reason why, when I work with other people, I feel terrible because I am not like others, and I always feel inferior to them. I wouldn't ever be any different. That is why I hung on to the bad companions so long. They are my own class. I feel odd when I am with others.

Regardless of how they verbalized it, the rejected had an undeniable lack of personal value, seeing themselves as anything but admirable, worthy of respect, interesting, and acceptable persons. Instead, feelings of personal emptiness, insufficiency, inadequacy, low evaluation of self, bankruptcy of self-esteem, or not-enoughness as persons had inevitably surfaced.

What had the rejected regarded as proofs of their personal lack of worth? So often they appeared to be reasoning from cause to effect in arriving at their low self-evaluations. They seemed to feel lacking in worth *because of* the contemptible things they had done. Examination of my clinical findings, however, clearly showed something quite different. They had actually *begun* with what to them was the irrefutable fact of their personal unacceptability. Their undesirable behaviors had then appeared as manifestations of that fact. As they viewed it, they were not despicable because their conduct had been despicable; their conduct simply showed them for what they were. Some of them who were not clearly manifesting their unacceptability, at least to themselves, had experienced a powerful urge to go searching for such manifestations. They sought behavioral evidences which would demonstrate how they really were.

Anyone who may have endeavored to show a rejected person that his failure did not "prove" his personal inadequacy has very likely found such reasoning futile. Logically enough, he assumed that the rejected person had erroneously concluded that his failures proved his worthlessness. Quite the opposite. It was rather that he *knew* he was worthless. His failures had simply *revealed* this sorry fact to anyone who happened to witness them.

The position taken by the rejected regarding their self-evaluation was a nonnegotiable one. That is why the best-intentioned efforts to dissuade them from making such an erroneous judgment simply missed the point. Moreover, it remains doubtful that anyone could ever convince them that their failures did not exhibit how they really were—worthless. This underlying conviction that their every fault or blunder inevitably revealed their personal worthlessness appears to be at least implicit in many of their remarks quoted in this volume. At the same time, I am fully aware that I have not seen this explicit point anywhere in print: that their every failure had revealed their personal inadequacy. It stands in need of further research.

Battered self-esteem was experienced by some rejected as expressly associated with guilt. In others, it had not been tied to guilt feelings. To mix these, it seems to me, would be at least to risk the error of forcing such experiences into invalid groupings. Accordingly, I have chosen to treat the two separately.

First, there was the damaged self-esteem *without any clear reference to guilt*. How did these rejected describe such experiences? They conveyed their deep feelings that *as persons* they were of little or no worth by such expressions of self-reference as, "I'm a nobody," "deficient," "wanting," "lacking," "impoverished," and so forth. One woman wrote:

> I wanted to prove to so many that I was someone and that I would amount to somebody. My religion—that should mean everything to me—well, it doesn't have too much bearing. Everything is fine for a while; then I get discouraged and don't care. I often wished myself dead. I am so tired of trying to prove to people that I am something.

She went on to describe a very human failure and then added:

> Nothing ever hurt so bad. I had failed again. I guess I just want to be someone big and know I never will be. Well, I'm sure not much in many respects. It's funny, though; just because I have known you and for what you stand for I do want to do the right thing. I never cared about anyone enough to do anything before, but I want really to show someone that I am not all bad. I know it is silly to tell you all my defects and vices and then say I want to do all right.
>
> I haven't been always on the up and up, but I will from now on. I guess I couldn't be before because you wouldn't have understood. I told you so many times how I was told I was no good and how I thought that I was good. Well, I wanted to think that, and have others think it, too, but down deep I knew I wasn't; and that is why I did let

go of myself. Then when I would try to break away, I didn't have what it took. You are always miserable, unhappy, and always afraid—suspicious, too.

Frequently, in addition to these convictions of personal worthlessness, the rejected were certain of the transparency of their worthlessness. It could not but be evident to anyone who happened to get close enough to begin to know them. A girl in her late teens, who is sure she is no good, predicted that her boyfriend will walk out on her for good just as soon as he sees through her.

This adamantly clung to, low self-esteem, however, existed in many rejected along with their acceptance by others. Some of the rejected—women particularly—maintained that they had been almost continuously sought after, but never for themselves. They had been pursued for what others could hope to get from them. So they persisted in the certainty that the only acceptance available to them must be based on extrinsic valuations. In response to the interest and concern I showed, a number of persons—particularly young women—repeatedly asked, "What's your angle?" They insisted that there had to be an angle, especially after they felt I had come to know them well and would not take a fee. Each, in her own words, repeated this same conviction.

I recall an unusually bright young woman insisting: "There's got to be an angle, and I'll find it. I know by now that you're not out to make me or get your ego-kicks by slumming with one of society's rejected, but I'll find it. . . . Aha! I know what it is. You're getting material to write a book. That's it. That has to be it." Now I wonder (with a smile) if that is where the idea to write this book—which I did not then entertain—actually originated.

Closely paralleling these findings on low self-esteem were observations by some young college men and women who were engaged, under my direction, in a practicum course with institutionalized delinquent girls. They reported back to me, after they had come to know the girls well, that they had been repeatedly confronted with such remarks as: "What do you want from us? You have to want something. No one could possibly be interested in any of us just *as people.*" These college students became convinced that the girls' lack of personal worth was so self-evident that they felt that anyone who would really get to know them could not possibly miss it.

Since they felt that their personal debasement would be unmistakable to any person who succeeded in establishing any sort of personal, intimate relationship with them, what was the point in trying? One woman who felt such acting was preposterous, summed it up this way:

"Because I feel so hateful, I feel sure that others see me as hateful—so I act hatefully. I'm irritable, sharp, sarcastic, and downright cruel to those who really are helpless to do anything about it."

Had those who carried this degraded self-concept and were convinced that they were nothings agreed that the only kind of acceptance they could possibly hope for would be that of extrinsic valuations? Had they lost all desire to be accepted just for themselves? In no way. A woman wrote: "I guess because I feel so low myself, I think everyone else thinks so, too. If there is anything I ever wanted more in life, it was to have someone like me because I was me and not because of what I pretended to be. But how stupid that is! How could I expect such a favor!?" After she had described an accident which was really not her fault and for which she knew she was not responsible, she concluded, "because of it, I hate myself."

The rejected went on *longing* to be loved and accepted just for themselves, especially by the important people in their lives. In the face of their certainty that such was impossible, did they gradually *move toward* actually seeking such intrinsic acceptance? So deep and unshakable was their conviction of personal worthlessness that they had attempted no such thing. Instead they continued to live on with the unutterably frustrating experience that this, their deepest yearning, was not being fulfilled. Thus, while they went on craving authentic love every day of their lives, though simultaneously denying its possibility, they had not so much as approximated it. A woman wrote:

> . . . Not a very nice story is it, Father? Don't worry. I'm not happy about it either. In fact, I don't accept it. Now I know my parents were right when they kept saying I was no good. Only God knows how right they were and are. Mother and Daddy were right, too, when they said I'd never be a Ph.D. They're right again. I might as well face it now. I'm not going to kid myself any longer. I just haven't got what it takes. I have nothing. Forgive me, Father, if you can—if not, I'll understand.

This self-devaluation was not merely deep discouragement. The very fact that so often a discouraged person can realistically be encouraged to go on despite set-backs presupposes the existence in him of a requisite ability needing only to be properly motivated. Moreover, his discouragement centers on lack of achievements.

The feelings of the rejected, however, were those of personal bankruptcy. In the case of the woman from whose letter the excerpt was just quoted, the rug had been pulled out from beneath her self-esteem. She was following the characteristic pattern of the rejected. Her every lack of achievement was an unmistakable exhibition of her unquestionable personal deficiency. Because she was sure she was no good, she remained convinced that she didn't have whatever would be required to do anything that really mattered.

A number of the rejected who had experienced personal worthlessness held tenaciously to an intense self-hatred. Not all of these, however, possessed grounds justifying their self-hatred. They were sure that they were hateful, though they were not sure why. Some of them had gone searching for such grounds. Where they failed to find them they had, at times, created them. One rejected man has always deeply disliked himself. He feels he has done so much compulsive running because he simply could not stand to live with his profoundly disliked self. At the same time, he has needed somehow to substantiate that self-loathing. Therefore, he has done just what his parents did, namely, expressed hostility toward others. His compulsion has been to be hateful toward others because he is certain he is hateful. He has repeatedly said, "I am a nobody, no good, not much." Besides, he knew he was fooling others whenever they thought highly of him, as, in fact, he has been told a number of times. This has resulted in his feeling that he is a hypocrite, as well.

The fact that at least some rejected felt sure they were simply fooling others who happened to think well of them implied their deeply felt conviction that others did not really know them. They remained sure that, if others were to see them as they really were, such responses would simply have been out of the question. Whenever one rejected man received praise, recognition, and especially expressions of friendship from others, he wasn't able to accept any of them seriously "because," he explained, "I know *emotionally* that I'm not a big guy, but just a very little guy."

How did the rejected explain the fact that relatives or therapists, who thought they had come to know them, said that they respected and accepted them for themselves? Many just did not bother to try. Why strain to explain the nonsensical?

For those who attempted to explain it to me, the invariable clincher justifying their cavalier dismissal of all such reassurances was the reference to their self-evident personal worthlessness. These kindly, well-meaning persons were simply mistaken. Nevertheless, a few rejected attempted a further explanation of their inability to accept such commendations from others. Over the years, a woman had been told by a number of people, in one way or another, that she was really a fine person. None of these people, however, had even begun to shake her conviction that she lacked personal value. She summed up her interpretation of their personal compliments this way:

When they have tried to tell me that I am somebody fine, their assurances can be explained in one of three ways. Some were stringing me
along, giving me a line, out of kindness or pity to make me feel good,
which just nauseates me. Others may have been leveling with me, but
didn't really know me. One or two, perhaps, were on the level and
maybe even had gotten to know me a bit but, nonetheless, their compliments just rolled off me like water off a duck.

This exemplifies the point made earlier that the rejected, instead of
having suffered grave doubts about their personal worth, were absolutely sure of their serious deficiency of it. As they viewed the matter,
all the charitable intentions and complimentary opinions of others were
not able to dislodge the one contradictory fact which remained crystal
clear to them. In their eyes, they were zeros, and no matter how you
multiply, add, or modify a zero, it remains a zero.

A particularly hurtful aspect of damaged self-esteem in some rejected
was the feeling of their having, in effect, been *emotionally eviscerated.*
Some had expressed it, in substance, as having the feeling that emotionally they were hollowed-out shells. A woman who had recently given
birth to a child felt exceedingly guilty. She identified the source of her
guilt: "My baby is crying in the next room. I don't go to her. She needs
me, but I can't—I can't go to her. I don't have enough for myself." She
was referring, of course, to the fact that her baby needed not just her
physical help, but her love and affection. She couldn't give these. Why?
She sensed that in giving her love and affection to her baby she would
be giving away something of herself. Had she possessed adequate self-
esteem, there would have been no possibility of feeling that, in loving
another, she was giving away something of herself and so becoming still
more a zero. In fact, quite the opposite would have been the case.
Sharing her love would have enriched her. Indeed, there seems to be
something of a parallel here between love and knowledge. One who
gives knowledge to another loses nothing but instead gains, at least
insofar as having the rewarding experience of knowing the other is
thereby intellectually enriched. In giving love, one who has enough
self-esteem not only relishes seeing the other personally enriched, but
frequently enjoys a return of love, as well. This presupposes, however,
that he already possesses adequate self-esteem.

By contrast, this woman was implicitly expressing the experience of
the rejected that they have been emotionally emptied, drained, or eviscerated, and so have nothing left of themselves to give (145). How
could they give love to others when they hadn't enough for themselves? The experience of personal bankruptcy is often difficult, if not

impossible, for those with adequate self-esteem to grasp in a meaning-ful way.

Were the rejected *capable of giving* genuine love? Did they have the capacity to love another person with a kind of love that would be requisite for a close personal relationship (such as a happy marriage) or for having a *feeling* of personal love for God? The answers, obviously, depend on what is meant by love.

If love is taken to mean doing only *things* for others, then I think many rejected were capable of such expressions. At the same time, some rejected predictably would have questioned their motives for doing so, convinced as they were that all their actions were ultimately self-seeking.

Love, however, which involves a *personal reaching out* to another with warmth, affection, tenderness, care, respect, and reverence, with pri-mary concern for the other, is a different kind of experience. Then it goes beyond a giving of mere *things* to a donation of *self*. As such, it constitutes a personal affirmation of the real value of that other *as a person*. This kind of love is not motivated by the desire to gain, but rather with the hope of enriching the other. It implies the willingness, even eagerness, to do whatever is needed to accomplish that end. "For-otherness" rather than "for-selfness" constitutes an integral as-pect of this authentic human love. Moreover, the authenticity of any human love utterly devoid of true affection appears to be suspect (52).

Were the severely rejected capable of giving others the genuine, affectionate love characterized by "for-otherness"? Without consider-able psychological help, normally requiring the assistance of profes-sionally trained persons, they usually were not able to love in this way. Because this kind of love requires that the one giving the love be other-centered rather than self-centered, it appeared to have been be-yond most of my rejected clients.

Since this authentic, affectionate, human love postulates a giving of self, it connotes that one's self is possessed of the potential to enrich another (52). The rejected were not able to give this genuine, affection-ate *love* to others, precisely because they regarded their "shoddy selves" as incapable of enriching others. Some rejected were capable of express-ing passionate warmth in certain of their interpersonal relationships, but these expressions were not of the self-giving nature that would be inher-ent in authentic affection. After all, passion and affection are not inter-changeable terms. Presumably, even a rapist might be intensely pas-sionate, but obviously he would be giving nothing of himself. His action would be essentially a *taking* or getting of pleasure—which has nothing whatever to do with the authentic affection of love.

If these rejected were not able to *give* warm, human love, were they able to *receive* it? Were they capable of being personally enriched by being loved by others? The following quotation will help to clarify the answer:

> In the experience of being loved by someone else, a person is being presented with an affirmation of his personal worth by another human being. He must, therefore, be capable of accepting this affirmation in such a way that he becomes a more adequate person. This kind of acceptance is not merely an assent of the intellect. It is much more than that. A person can give solely an intellectual assent to something and still manage to hold it very much at the surface, where it cannot penetrate deeply into his feelings and emotions. An inadequate person can sincerely say, "I do accept the love I receive," and by such a remark mean that he takes and holds it safely outside himself as one might accept and hold an apple merely to look at. The fact is that until and unless he eats and digests the apple it cannot nourish him. In similar fashion, a human being is fulfilled as a person only by accepting love in the sense of permitting it to become an integral part of him.
>
> Real acceptance of an affirmation given by another in love means that a person takes it deeply within himself. As a result, he remains free of the gnawing doubts typical of a person who can accept another's affirmation of love only insofar as he can interpret it as something else. In fact the presence of persisting doubts, demanding more and more proof of love even from those who have been tested and proved true, is the tell-tale sign that love is being "accepted" in the sense of merely being looked at. One who is psychologically empty, and thus feels certain that he is personally worthless, simply cannot believe that anyone who would know what he is could really love him. To admit, even to himself, that he is really loved by one who knows him would be for him to claim that he is somebody of value, which, in his eyes, would be preposterous. Therefore, he must alter any expressions of another person's love until it appears to him as something other than love. (52, pp. 58–60).

Consequently, the rejected were not able to *receive* human love, any more than they were able to *give* it, unless they had obtained psychological help.

Damaged self-esteem was also experienced by some rejected as being *closely linked with guilt feelings*. This association was communicated by such self-reference terms as: "I'm . . . no good," "despicable," "hateful," "loathsome," "rotten," "a louse," "evil," "cowardly," "mean," "depraved," "repulsive," "disgusting," "vicious," and so on. During one counseling session, a man bent very low from the chair in which he was sitting and began repeatedly to tie and untie his shoelaces. Finally, his face only inches from the floor, he turned his head sideways in order to look up at me, and he sobbed: "This is how big I feel . . . I am this low and this small . . . I am a coward . . . I can't. . . . " He continued to sob in utter dejection.

The hurtful *social* consequences of these feelings of low self-esteem that were tied in with guilt feelings were grave. Some rejected, for instance, had characteristically gone looking solely for specific social situations that would enable them to counterbalance or alleviate their feelings of personal worthlessness. One rejected man, a confirmed alcoholic, assured me that he was "a real nobody with a moral record that stinks to prove it." He mentioned that his social life centers around the cheapest bars where, after a few drinks, he begins to talk in a loud voice and others listen. "These guys really look up to me," he said, "and when I buy a round of drinks I am really a big shot."

Other rejected had carefully worked out unhealthy, bizarre patterns of relating closely with others. Their interpersonal relationships had been kept safe only at the price of twisting them into travesties of authentic human relationships. A man who had long recognized that his parents did not love him felt that by his dishonest living he had emptied himself of everything worthwhile. "I strive to fill the resulting empty void within me, which I know can be filled only by God, with possession of other people. My possession of others," he explained, "means getting enough of their acceptance and trust to let me see inside so that I can really understand what makes them tick." To this he added that he could not, of course, let them inside him or let them know him.

The guilt-tortured rejected required no proof of their want of personal worth; it was so self-evident that it stood in need of no proof. Many of them were painfully aware of this. Nevertheless, some repeatedly referred me to the "proofs" that they were no good. As I have previously indicated, I became convinced that they regarded these "proofs" as *manifestations* of their worthlessness, rather than as evidences from which they concluded to such worthlessness. This seemed to be especially so when they had the conviction that their lack of personal worth had an expression in their immoral conduct.

There was something of a vicious circle here. Exceedingly frustrated at feeling worthless, these rejected tended to seek compensations for their frustrations in hostile or sexual behaviors which were morally unacceptable to them. Subsequently, they came to view these moral failures as the clinching "proofs" of their being no good. A man whose constant feelings of inadequacy and insecurity were terribly painful hated himself. His undeniable "proof" that he deserved this self-hate was his long list of personal and moral failures and, most especially, the harm he had done to innocent persons.

Even where there had been no outward revelation of their lack of personal value, some rejected remained wholly convinced that the "proofs," far from being absent, had simply remained well concealed from the eyes of others. One rejected man took a very dim view of himself at all times because of his motives. No matter how fine a thing he had appeared to others to be doing, he knew that because he was selfish he had an angle in doing it.

Reasonableness was not given its day in court as the rejected confined themselves in the dock. Without a fair hearing, they pronounced themselves guilty and sentenced themselves for life among the dregs of humanity. A woman felt she had been undermined by her mother all her life in almost everything she had ever attempted to do. No matter what she tried to accomplish, her mother—in her own subtle way—had let her know that she hadn't done it right. At the same time, she also felt certain that her mother, out of a sense of duty, had sacrificed her entire life for her. Whenever she tried to oppose her mother in anything, her mother cried and so made her feel exceedingly guilty. With the passing of the years, she became convinced that she hated her mother without reason because her mother had not realized she was undermining her. She hated herself for so unjustly hating her mother. "This is why I *know* that I am no good," she concluded. As she went on to explain, it was an undeniable and so a nonnegotiable fact that she was loathsome. That she could hate her mother without reason would be all the proof anyone who came to know her would need. In her eyes, this feeling toward her mother has revealed her for what she is—a despicable person.

The existence of such immoderate and obstinate judgments that the rejected passed on themselves—in order to find themselves seriously wanting in personal worth—raises the question: Where did these judgments originate? Because many rejected felt they had always been that way, there was no occasion to search further. Nonetheless, a few reported looking beyond the way they felt for an adequate explanation. The interesting point is that they almost never reported the source as being situated in their perceived parental evaluation of themselves as unloved, unwanted, and, so, of little worth.

Mainly, those who had searched further failed to find satisfying explanations. Within the context of trying to explain why she had been rejected by others early in her life, a woman wrote:

> . . . I'm considering the question of why I was not accepted by my
> age-mates. The ugly head of myself as a boisterous-loud-bossy-mouthy
> individual is raised. Along with this is raised my feeling of hate of
> myself as this person—of my struggle to keep this unacceptable person
> from view. Why loud, etc? I think the answer lies in the over-
> permissiveness of my mother. I felt I could rule—if I remember cor-
> rectly. I didn't care for the feeling—I felt out of step, different. My
> reaction, as I see it now, was to exert more power—I must have gained
> some satisfaction. Why hate of myself as this person? In grade 5 I re-
> ceived a report card informing my parents that I was a loudmouth—Dad
> informed me that I had to straighten out or else. I think that it was at
> this time that I began to compensate, to cover up.

This woman began her analysis of why she had not been accepted
with what, to her, was the indisputable feeling of her personal unacceptability. She then proceeded to explore the history of her behavior in order to see if she could discover when she had first
become aware of this low self-evaluation. In thus following the characteristic pattern of the rejected (of viewing her behavior, not as
causing her to be undesirable, but as manifesting the unacceptable
person she really was), she unwittingly closed herself off to any
other explanation.

What was the association between badly marred self-esteem and feelings of incompetency? Some rejected experienced a complete lack of
confidence to do even some of the ordinary things they wanted and
needed to do. In them, a damaged self-concept coexisted along with a
deep feeling of childish incompetency. On the other hand, a number of
the rejected felt highly confident in several areas and some demonstrated significant achievements. They had exceedingly high motivation to achieve in a notable fashion. Moreover, the gifted rejected openly acknowledged their possession of unusual talents. But this in no
way offset their low self-evaluations.

I found that a considerable number of those rejected who gravely
lacked confidence did so particularly in their dealings with people. This
was evidenced especially in such interpersonal authority-role positions
as, for example, teaching, nursing, being a den-mother, being a cub-
scout or boy-scout leader, supervising others, and so forth. While they
desperately needed successes in such interpersonal areas, they felt certain that they could not succeed in them. A few were so frightened of
any interpersonal risk that they would become mentally paralyzed at
the prospect.

The presence of intense anxiety at the threat of having to undertake
tasks in which they felt incompetent appeared to mark off clearly the

rejected from the nonrejected persons. The nonrejected seemingly did not experience a comparable *intensity* of anxiety when confronted with tasks in which they were lacking important competencies. Being found wanting in what, in their eyes, were salient abilities did not seem to concern them greatly. This almost cavalier view with regard to the personal lack of important capabilities was almost never experienced by the rejected. In their eyes, such lacks were so many materializations lucidly displaying to others their personal voids.

Were there other areas of personal damage discovered in the rejected? It would be a grave mistake to conclude that damaged self-esteem was the only serious psychological hurt found in the wake of rejection. Other writers have mentioned additional psychological wounds; for example, Newell found that rejected children were much more retarded in school subjects than were nonrejected children (139). I have not attempted to include in this book a complete listing of all such hurts—indeed, a comprehensive listing of them would not seem feasible. They took such myriad forms that it was exceedingly difficult to even identify some of them.

The following lines, written by a rejected woman who had moved to another part of the country and had received further professional help there, exemplify the difficulty in identifying such psychological injuries:

> You probably already know how much a neurotic wants to tell everyone, "My God, how I've suffered!!!" Why, I don't know. You usually feel worse after your lamentations—probably because of several reasons. First, you're not quite sure the person believed you and you feel like an ass for telling him. Sometimes you feel guilty afterwards because, if a loved one does believe you, you're sorry now he's worrying so about you. And last, but not least—and this I've found is the most important of all—a neurotic is afraid to stop lamenting his woes for fear everyone will think he's well again, when he's really not.
>
> Right now I'm not seeing either [X or Y, names of two clinicians]. I've mulled over the idea of going back to [X] but actually my therapy is complete, my problems have been discussed and rehashed over and over, and one thing we all know is a person can't get well unless he wants to; so I don't know whether I should start seeing [X] again or not. You know, it's a very strange thing—a neurotic will tell everyone who'll listen that he'd rather have cancer, be armless, legless, blind, and that he'd crawl on his knees for thirty miles to get well, and yet he says he cannot do the trivial little things that are suggested, such as going to a theatre with friends. . . . There have been countless times when only the thought of death could soothe my mind. But not any more. I don't want to die until I've learned how to love God without neurotic fears.

> Most of my life I've done good, more because I feared punishment from
> God than out of love for Him. . . .

Obviously it would be exceedingly difficult to categorize properly the
personal hurts of even this one woman; but, nonetheless, her emotional impairments, I think, are unmistakable.

Here, very briefly, are some other distressing psychological hurts
experienced by the rejected. There was the terrifying feeling of *aloneness*, of being a stranger among other strangers. This aloneness was far
removed from the warm, comforting pain of loneliness which implies
the existence of another who loves and is loved and whose absence is
only physical. The aloneness of the rejected cried out to them that,
whether present or absent, those who ought to love them did not. It
trumpeted within them, "No one really cares." The closely related
feeling of *not belonging* also was theirs.

Fear in some very distressing form seemed to be an inseparable companion of the rejected. In addition, the awareness some had of their
running in fear from their obligations painfully spelled out their cowardliness. They suffered as well from frustrating feelings that they
were not free to be themselves, to fail, and to be unself-conscious. Add
to these their not being free from tension and of always feeling on
edge. Some of the rejected had the fear that they were moving into
mental illness. There were also fears that they were not complete persons, or that they would take their own lives.

A feeling mentioned by a number of them was that *something inside
them had died*. They had to live with the constant pain of utter frustration. Many, if not all, carried within them incredible intensities of
largely stifled anger, resentment, hostility, guilt, and depression. They
dragged out their days in a gray, depressed world (52). Moreover, the
experience of being whipsawed between needed affectionate acceptance and the fear of once again being rejected was never far from
them. Hatred of themselves and also of others was exceedingly distressing to them.

Findings in the literature on personal damage associated with rejection span many experiences and behaviors of both parents and children. For example, Winder and Rau found unhealthy aggression, dependence, withdrawal, and depression in preadolescent boys to be
associated with parental ambivalence, punitiveness, demands for offspring aggressiveness, restrictiveness, and poor self-concept in the
mothers. This same study found the child's unwholesome dependency
related to both maternal rejection and low-esteem in the father (209).
Many such findings have appeared in the literature, but it is difficult to

ascertain what inferences may be drawn from them with regard to our subject matter.

Intense jealousy appeared to be universally present in the rejected. Basic insecurity and resentment were ingredients of this jealousy. Other hurtful phenomena closely related to damaged self-esteem in the rejected included persevering, unsatisfied, psychological hungers. At least since the time of Freud, psychologists have known that strong, unsatisfied childhood desires continue on at some psychological level. Ungratified desires in the rejected, instead of maturing over the years in terms of the *kinds* of gratifications sought, persisted with the original, immature characteristics.

I vividly recall my first encounter with this phenomenon of the continuation of an unsatisfied psychological hunger. When I was in my late twenties, I was visiting an elderly Catholic priest, whom I knew well, at Christmas time. Beneath his well-decorated Christmas tree, in his home just adjacent to the church, was an impressive array of toys designed for boys about ten to twelve years of age. I asked him: "Father, why did you go to all this trouble and spend this money for these toys? The altar boys probably won't give them more than a passing glance, if they even bother to come in here at all." He answered: "I didn't buy these toys for the altar boys. I bought them for myself. When I was a boy, I longed for toys like these, but we were always too poor to buy them. Now I can afford them and so, at last, I am enjoying them." What surprises me now is not that this same hunger had endured all those years, but that he was psychologically strong and courageous enough to admit his longings, first to himself and then to me.

Unsatisfied psychological hungers in the rejected hung on, as well, beneath the trappings of both envy and jealousy. A successful middle-aged man confided that, deeply mortifying as it was, he wanted to tell me about his envy of persons who were doing and enjoying the things denied him as a teenager. When a high-school-senior boy came to his home to take his daughter to the prom, he wanted to go along so badly that he could scarcely believe it, and he even fantasized having a teenage date of his own. He recognized that he also keenly resented this boy wearing clothes that he could not afford when he was in high school. Though he knew and openly acknowledged to me that it would be wholly ridiculous at his age, he still longed to be one of the cheerleaders at the high-school football games, and afterwards pile into the old car with the gang and head for the local hangout. He had no explanations for these desires aside from the fact that he had longed for them, in vain, during his youth. No one, including his wife, even dreamed he had these cravings. Moreover, even in his wildest daydreams, he remained aware that he could never allow himself to act on any of them. Nonetheless, they persisted.

What did the rejected feel were their most pressing unsatisfied psychological hungers? Most of the rejected reported these to be their ongoing hungers for affection and for warmly accepting parents. Among psychologists, David Levy is known principally for his writings on maternal overprotection. It happened, however, that during his investigations of maternal overprotection he also examined, by way of contrast studies, cases of maternal rejection. Later, maternal rejection—a by-product of his primary interest—captured his attention, and he prepared and delivered a scientific paper on "affect hunger."[3] He referred to "affect hunger" as the love cravings of individuals who suffered lack of maternal love in the early years of life (104). It should be noted that Levy did not treat paternal love or its lack, but was concerned solely with a lack of maternal love. He even raised the question of whether this lack produced a deficiency disease of the emotional life comparable to a vitamin deficiency.

While "affect hunger" was found more frequently in rejected women than in rejected men, it appeared likely that this painful experience was universal in the rejected. Those who, as children, had felt unloved by their mother, father, or both, carried feelings of emptiness where love should have been—often for the remainder of their lives (104). The rejected lived with an emotional hole in the center of their being, from which hungers for affection and love (so badly needed, yet never felt to be there) continuously welled up (73). In a large number of the rejected, affection-hungers were nearly all-consuming (73, 150); they were insatiable. Rejected women, especially, developed into relentless affection-hunters. They became obsessed with affection-hunting.

In contrast to male affection-hunters, however, many of these women maintained that their absorbing hunger was not for sexual relations, although they openly acknowledged that their affection-receiving relationships with men usually became sexual relationships. Their yearnings, they insisted, were for profusely bestowed affection which, at times, even ruled out sexual expression. They were driven by an insatiable longing for affectionate expressions, usually from a specific man, and often at the very time that they did not want sex. Some women found their male companions very frustrating, in that they almost never were able to make this separation between sexual and nonsexual tender affection. As a rejected woman walked past the bed where her husband was sitting, he reached out and grabbed her but-

[3]The paper, "Primary Affect Hunger," was read at the 93rd Annual Meeting of the American Psychiatric Association, Pittsburgh, Pa., May 10–14, 1937.

tock. Although she is a very responsive person sexually, at that moment she desperately wanted him to gently touch or stroke her hair or put his arm around her or hold her very close. She immediately pulled away from him and told him that she did not want sex. She said his uncouth response was: "Stop deluding yourself, girl. To me you're just another piece of tail." She will not forgive him and has never let him touch her since. Now she constantly looks elsewhere for the affection she so badly needs. Some women who were lesbians sought affection from other women, of course; but some women who were not lesbians sought affection, for its own sake, from other women as well as from men.

A large number of the rejected, driven by affection-hungers, found they were unable to separate affection-seeking from personally unacceptable relationships. They were thereby catapulted into ongoing struggles with their consciences. How did they resolve such conflicts? Rationalization was the route some had unknowingly taken. A rejected woman who was torn between her moral standards and her affection-hungers remarked, "I am afraid I will kick over the traces in order to get affection, if not love," and then added, "Everybody is self-seeking, anyway, so you have to pay for affection."

Others employed some form of drugs to blunt ther moral sensitivities as they relentlessly pursued the satisfaction of their cravings. One woman, constantly starved for affection and acceptance, could stand it for only so long. Then she would go out to a bar and drink until she had dulled her moral sensitivity. Later, she would leave the bar in the company of some man she had picked up there, always with the clear understanding that she would engage in sexual relations only if he would be both gentle and affectionate with her.

One snare that female affection-hunters frequently used against the men they stalked was gifts (73). These were personal gifts, either expensive or else made with their own hands. They especially gave gifts that the men would wear touching their skin—bathrobes, socks, gloves, shirts, and so on. They felt these gifts gave them a "presence" by virtue of which they were in physical contact with the men.

They frequently gave gifts with specific instructions that they were to be placed on the recipients' desks or hung in their offices or bedrooms. Through such gifts they desired to gain three goals. First, they hoped they could thus keep the others frequently, if not constantly, mindful of them. Second, they again acquired, in this way, an imagined "presence" with the recipients. Employing such "presence" as a launching pad, they were able to take these relationships, in their fantasies, as far and in whatever directions they wanted to take them.

Then all they needed was to be able to reinforce their fantasies by periodically talking to these other persons, seeing them, receiving mail from them, and so forth. Third, they hoped in this way to keep these men under obligation to them. It was much easier for these women to enjoy vivid imagery if their fantasies could be repeatedly reinforced. With their fantasies adequately reinforced, their imagined romantic and sexual relatings to others proved almost as satisfying as actual physical relations with them.

The kinds of fantasy-energizing employed by some of these women, however, would prove surprising to many men. One young rejected woman almost worshiped her strong, gentle boss—a man of great personal integrity. She had discovered, by accident, that when she stood a few feet distant from him it had quite a stimulating effect on her. Thereafter, often when he was busy at his desk, she would stand near him, pretending to sort out some typing she had done or some such thing. If she could manage to remain within about six feet of him, she would experience unmistakable and, at times, complete sexual arousal. He had not the slightest suspicion that such a thing was happening to her.

Other rejected women had similar kinds of experiences. One who was seeing a professional man regularly for rather lengthy periods of time would sit several feet from him in his office. This proximity, even though she was usually able to carry on a conversation, excited her to sexual arousal, including repeated orgasms. As a religiously inclined woman, she was troubled by this. She said she had talked about it to a woman friend who was also seeing this same professional man. The other woman told her that she also had had such experiences, stimulated by the same physical proximity to him; but she explained that she felt sure God had allowed her these rewarding experiences and, so, she had welcomed them.

A pattern evident in a number of the rejected, particularly in women, was a lengthy testing of others to see whether they could be trusted enough to relate affectionately with them. Almost from the moment they were satisfied that they could risk such relating, the relationships had tended toward excess. Their demands on the time and attention of these individuals soon became exorbitant (104). It was a picture of people endeavoring to make up for lost time, as if their hungers of years could be sated in a matter of hours. In most instances, even while pursuing such affection, they continued their testing procedures. The other individuals were constrained, in terms spelled out by the rejected, to prove again and again their trustworthiness.

These women seemed unaware that such behavior appeared to be highly unreasonable and, at times, almost suffocating to the other persons concerned (73). A number of these affection-hunters, for instance, couldn't resist knowingly badgering others in order to insure that they would be constantly thinking of them while they were physically absent. Their reiterated, unreasonable demands, along with their patterns of clinging adamantly and possessively and their attempts to capture and monopolize attention, inevitably resulted in driving the others away (104). They remained blind to such paradoxical behavior. As early as the late 1930s, Newell had noticed in the rejected a pathetic desire to be liked while at the same time their behavior seems calculated to insure their being disliked (140). Rejected affection-hunters experienced both stark surprise and desolating disappointment when the men they were pursuing sensed they were being roped and branded and so cleared out.

A further characteristic of this affection-hunting behavior was its insatiable, cannibalistic-like character. It was as though they were striving to feed emotionally off other people in order to satisfy their own affectional hungers (73). They could never get enough tenderness, concern, or attention. A number of these women, after losing their friends because they had been so affectionately demanding of them, gave not the slightest indication of changing or even questioning such a behavioral pattern. They appeared to have been trapped in it.

Devastating as were the end results for some of them, perhaps there were some gains from such self-defeating patterns. One woman who had repeatedly acted in such an emotionally demanding way toward her friends that, one after the other, they walked away from her, wrote immediately after she had driven one more away: " . . . I'm splashing in self-acclamation at my egocentricity and enjoying every minute of it. Am receiving my due punishment—self-inflicted." Her statement seemed to indicate some assuaging of her guilt. At any rate, there appeared to be some secondary gains from such painful, self-defeating patterns in her behavior.

Those deprived of parental affection felt a continuing, gnawing void. Lewis found a persisting hunger for accepting and loving parents (106). This hunger was either directly or indirectly felt by a large number of the rejected. Those of both sexes had said, in effect, to a number of men clinicians, myself included: "You are the father I might have had." One woman clinician said that she and other women clinicians had frequently been told, in substance, by the rejected: "You are the mother I should have had." In both of these situations, of course, psychoanalysts would see textbook examples of classical, psychoanalytic "transference," i.e., displaced parental-affection hunger.

The mother and father relationships for which these rejected still yearned were not in terms of healthy adult-to-adult associations. They were, rather, relationships such as a child seeks with "mommy" or "daddy." A rejected man wrote:

> . . . I've always been looking for a father, often consciously, especially in bosses and teachers. Of course, I couldn't find one and didn't, but the tension was always there. [Name of former boss] was paternal in some respects. The only time he took off after me in front of the bunch for something I said to him, I simply broke down and bawled like a baby (in private) for several hours, feeling like a six-year-old who looked for affection and approval and found none. That was after therapy had begun; otherwise, I would have bottled it up as always, and built up a little more hostility.

These childish cravings for parental affection were a continuing source of frustration for the rejected. A middle-aged woman has been obsessed by an intense longing to be held in the lap of some warm, motherly woman whom she would want to have rock, cuddle, and quietly talk baby-talk to her. She would want this woman also to sing her lullabies. She has been searching for such a woman for years. It has been a most thwarting search because of her certainty that this hunger is destined never to be satisfied. Even were she to find such a motherly person, she explained, she could now neither permit nor accept such mothering.

Such affection-hunger disguised itself so well psychologically in some rejected that its presence was not even suspected in the very behaviors that were actually pursuing its satisfaction. A man who was coldly rejected by his father has been baffled for years by a consuming desire which he periodically experiences. This recurring desire, though he is heterosexual, is to search for some teen-age male prostitute to hold and lavish abundant affection on. This has remained the case even though he now knows from experience that his affection usually has not been returned.

To date he has not had even a suspicion that, in this way, he has been attempting (it would appear) to satisfy his own hunger for his father's love by means of two unconscious identifications. As the older man in this relationship, he has unknowingly been an extravagantly affection-giving stand-in for his own father. At the same time, the affection-receiving youngster has been a substitute for himself at an early, affection-deprived age. Through this double substitution of persons, he has unknowingly endeavored to appease his own persisting hunger for his father's affection. He knows only that at times he has the almost irresistible urge to go looking for such a boy. He also is aware that such an experience is never really satisfying.

Occasionally, I encountered rejected persons who recognized that they had been consciously substituting other people for their parents in certain affection-receiving relationships. To a greater or lesser degree, they understood that they had desired affection from these others only to the extent that they had somehow been imagined stand-ins for their parents. For years, an attractive woman has deliberately been searching out a specific type of man. The man must be at least twenty years older than she, unmistakably gentle, kind, and considerate. In addition, he must promise that, once in bed, he will hold her tenderly for lengthy periods, her back to his stomach, with his knees drawn up so as to cradle her. While so doing, he must also talk affectionately and fondly to her as if she were a child. If a man will not fulfill these requirements, she added, she does not even consider having intercourse with him, since she regards sexual relations as his reward for giving her the desired warm, compassionate affection. All the while she is being thus cuddled, she imagines the one holding her to be the father she never had but always wanted.

Extrinsically valued persons also experienced the persistence of a hunger to be accepted just for themselves. While a number had received approval from their parents on one score or another, it had never been *for themselves*. A few of them placed the blame squarely on themselves for the fact that their craving for intrinsic parental acceptance remained unsatisfied. One woman's mother and father never knew the real her because she had never revealed her real self to them, and, therefore, they could never actually accept the real her—so, she blamed herself for her continuing yearning. Her acceptance by her parents exclusively in the role of fulfilling their expectations seems also to have set the pattern for her interpersonal relationships with other people. Since she never found anyone she trusted enough to reveal her real self to, any acceptance she ever had was for something other than her real self.

In the rejected, a frequent experience akin to damaged self-esteem was the feeling of childishness (212). While they were still small children, parental giants had decreed that some rejected were hopelessly helpless, weak, infantile individuals. Now, no matter how much these rejected told themselves differently, in their deepest feelings they really remained such. Their mental representations of their childishness, in fact, were repeatedly reinforced by their feelings of helplessness.

Some rejecting parents had stressed, for instance, the personal bankruptcy of their children in terms of their dearth of abilities. When the parents had also been overdominating, they had clearly conveyed to their children the feeling that the children were to do only what they were told because they were simply incapable of doing any thinking or any other important thing for themselves.

The particular aspects of destructive parental evaluations which had become the focal points of concern for these rejected were those which their parents had most clearly communicated to them. A rejected, middle-aged woman feels deep inside that she is still a little girl. Her rejecting parents had instilled in her, until she left home, the idea that she was a helpless child. Secretly she craves the affection needed by a little girl, although she doubts that she could accept such affection, at least openly, even were it available. Not even her husband knows about this longing. There is no way she can tell him since she is sure he would not understand. She wonders if the continuous resentment she feels against her husband and children is due to the fact that, without their realizing she is a little girl, they have imposed adult burdens on her.

Some rejected experienced these feelings of childishness predominantly within the area of adult accountability. A middle-aged man hates adult responsibility. He can't face it because he feels he is a child. He explained: "If I felt like a man, I could do the tasks of a man and face a man's problems. But I feel I am a child, so I can't do the things of a man. I can't shoulder big responsibilities." He gave no indication of finding this admission in the least embarrassing. He was simply explaining to me the way things were.

A few rejected became aware of their feeling of childishness principally by reflecting on their somewhat puzzling responses to others. A young college woman has come to realize that her roommate has been mothering her, right down to tucking her into bed at night. She both likes this mothering treatment and hates it. In no way does she want to be an adult with adult responsibilities in this hateful world. Because she is not an adult, she said, adult responsibilities are far beyond her powers.

Even those rejected who had succeeded in holding their dependence on others to a minimum and had functioned largely in a self-sufficient way experienced feelings of childishness. Those who did not feel they lacked any really important abilities nonetheless felt deeply within themselves that they were still little children and, as such, quite helpless in regard to certain undertakings.

Some rejected experience great intensities of such feelings *only in certain situations*. Each time one woman returned to the home of her parents something baffling and very painful happened to her. The moment she entered their home, she withdrew almost completely. She didn't really hear any of the conversation, much of which she sensed was pointed in subtle fashion at her, nor was she able to think of anything to say even though she is an intellectually gifted person and an accomplished conversationalist. Her feelings were those of a six-year-old who had nothing worth saying, so she just sat there. After she left the house, it would take her at least a couple of hours to relax, smile, and shake off the childish feelings.

Even when some rejected were prepared to confront a situation which in the past had made them feel childish, this response continued to take place. A middle-aged woman was repeatedly cautioned by her husband never to go near her rejecting mother. He insisted that, regardless of where the meeting took place, in her mother's presence she immediately became a helpless, dependent little girl once again. She agreed that her husband was entirely correct in this. When she was not near her mother, however, she did not feel this inadequacy.

The feeling of childishness was implicit within the difficulties and inabilities experienced by some rejected. Fears of doing almost anything have for years been disabling to one woman. These fears have invaded her teaching, as well as her planning, living by herself, making it on her own. Nor have these fears been lessened by successful doing. This has been particularly true of her teaching, in which she feels certain she has been successful, but to this day she is deeply apprehensive every time she walks into a classroom. "The old adage," she commented, "that 'nothing succeeds like success' is the fallacy of fallacies."

Other rejected found that with successful performances the shattering fears associated with specific undertakings were gradually attenuated, but they experienced no reduction of fear in other untried undertakings. Each time they contemplated the challenge of doing something new (particularly something in the public eye), they once again were inundated with intense feelings of anxiety. One young rejected man had mastered his preoccupying fear of reading aloud before a particular group. Although somewhat fearful each time he did so, he no longer suffered an excruciating fear of failing in it. In addition, the fear of failing in his one special field of studies no longer petrified him, since he had earned high grades in that field. However, he would become terrified at the prospect of having to talk to a different group. He would awaken at night in a cold sweat when he dared to contemplate the prospect of applying for graduate school.

Strong feelings of childishness have kept a few rejected trapped helplessly in unacceptable situations. A divorced woman's mother lives with her and repeatedly criticizes and corrects her in front of her own children. She also independently disciplines the children regardless of their mother's wishes. Her justification for doing so is, "These are my grandchildren, and I'll do what I want with them." Meanwhile, seething with anger and resentment, the daughter would dearly love to really tell her mother off, once and for all. Unfortunately, she desperately needs her mother and could not possibly take care of the children and the house alone. Were she to object too strenuously, she fears her mother might walk off—as did her husband—leaving her once again in the impossible position of having to go it on her own. What frustrates her most is that her mother drops little hints of knowing she is trapped and must put up with the situation whether she likes it or not.

Some rejected endeavored to recall the origin of their feelings of childishness. Invariably, they remembered its being present very early in their lives. A few were able to link it to a specific early experience. One rejected woman finds that any chore, no matter what it is, proves most fatiguing—even exhausting. This even includes such things as brushing her teeth. She thinks it is because she fights these chores. She vividly recalls that as a child she was told they were too difficult for her and adds, "and they are."

Before she was six, she was invited to her first party. Her mother stunned her by insisting that before she could go she would have to do the dishes—a colossal task. She did not know how to do the dishes. Her mother had never shown her how and had repeatedly told her that such chores were too difficult for her. So she had just walked up and down, worrying about the enormity of the undertaking before her. Only much later could she bring herself to try to do something about the dishes. As a result, she was very late for the party.

Ever since that time, she has been late for almost everything. She knows she will be late for every appointment or commitment, and fights herself not to be late, but, nevertheless, she comes late. As soon as she is confronted with almost any task, she automatically begins to stall. Usually she walks up and down, sometimes for hours before doing anything about it. Each time she has asked herself why she finds it so difficult, her answer has been, "Because it has to be done." That, she insists, is why she dislikes and fights it. She feels that, in some way which she doesn't understand, it restricts her liberty. In some vague way, it is still her mother saying, "Do this," when it is too big for her. When she reflects on it, she sometimes literally gets sick to her stomach. Now, any time an authority figure tells her, in effect, "This has to be done," it ties her stomach in knots and leaves her feeling nauseous.

Some rejecting parents, on the other hand, had assumed that their unloved children were capable of taking care of themselves, to the point that they scarcely bothered with them. This situation was strikingly exemplified by the attitude of Mr. Doolittle toward his daughter, Eliza, in the musical, *My Fair Lady*. A number of these rejected became quite self-sufficient.

Rejection, then, was associated with feelings both of helplessness and of high competency on the part of the children. In either case, the children felt not only unloved but unlovable, and they also experienced some aspect of childishness.

In this context, even some loving, warmly accepting parents unfortunately instilled in their children feelings that they were not very capable. Such was the impact, for instance, of loving but notably overprotecting mothers (105). Hurtful evaluations by overprotecting parents, however, appeared to be limited to the *abilities* of their children. By contrast, hurtful evaluations by rejecting parents directly affected the children's feelings of *personal adequacy* as well as their abilities (141). The harmful effects of both kinds of parents remained over the years.

What were the implications for *social* living with regard to personal damages in the rejected? The impact of parental rejection, specifically on the interpersonal relations of offspring, was very damaging. Other writers, as well, have found hurtful social aftermaths resulting from rejection. According to Meerloo, because people are basically oriented toward social relating, the very hurtful experiences of the rejected had wide ramifications in their relationships with other persons (126). Pemberton and Benady found consciously rejected children damaged in their ability to establish close relationships with their peers and teachers (145). Newell concluded that these rejected children have been hurt so frequently that it is almost impossible for them to accept a close therapeutic relationship (140). Roudinesco, a psychoanalytically oriented clinician, making the same point, maintained that the affectionless type of character produced by lengthy maternal separation in early life was irreversible because it rendered the important therapeutic device of transference useless (168). Levy also subscribed to this position (104).

Much of the content of this book pertains at least indirectly to the area of impaired *interpersonal relationships* in the rejected. Nonetheless, because of the manifest importance of the social aspects of human living, it seems well to include here some interpersonal considerations which either have been insufficiently treated or have not yet been mentioned. This presentation is by no means an enumeration of all the harmful experiences and behaviors of a social nature found in the rejected, but rather those I encountered in the wake of rejection. In general, the socially harmful aftermaths fell into two categories: (a) those that related directly to the rejected themselves, but indirectly to others; and (b) those that related directly to others. I will deal with these separately, because they were reported to me separately.

First, there were the painful experiences in the rejected relating directly to themselves that ramified into their interpersonal relationships. The rejected felt inadequate, hostile, anxious, and so forth. They felt inadequate in themselves, and they also felt inferior to others (104). Such feelings had unmistakable social implications. Had a human pecking order been established, they would have felt they were far down the line.

Hurtful experiences of the rejected were not always clearly expressed in behavior. Whether so expressed or not, these experiences necessarily had some effect on their relating to other people. One rejected man has always felt strained and anxious. His parents were also tense and fearful. A couple of the other children in the family who had received no love, but at least were given some attention by their mother, have been troubled and edgy, as well. He believes that his brothers and sisters now share his experience of never feeling at ease with other people.

A number of the rejected, because of the way they felt, were forced to follow some specific behavioral pattern such as being eternally vigilant in their social relationships. They were never able to afford the luxury of being unself-conscious and, as a result, never became wholly engrossed in any discussion. One rejected woman over the years has been forced to be content with acting the role of a good listener in any social gathering. On occasion, she has ventured a hopefully intelligent question, but has never been able to contribute anything more to any discussion. She feels that, as long as she can maintain the appearance of a pleasant, attentive listener, others will not discover how inadequate she is.

Second, there were damaged feelings and behaviors which related directly to others. A key to understanding the unwholesome interpersonal relating of many rejected was the way they viewed other persons. For the rejected, other people had existence solely to the extent that they fitted into their own self-preoccupied framework. They viewed others, not as valued persons in their own right, but only as they related to themselves. Certain people were regarded as need-fulfillers, others as threats, while still others simply had no meaning for them and, therefore, no existence in their eyes. I would think that every clinician—at some time—must have found the rejected unreasonable in their demands on him as one of their need-fulfillers (104). That he had other obligations, needs for privacy, rest, and relaxation, or that he was not able to see them on demand, was not to be tolerated. Didn't he understand? They *needed* him. Nothing else mattered. Karen Horney very astutely summed up their attitude toward others as: "My need is your obligation." Their needs were paramount—they could not afford to be interested in the needs of others.

A number of the rejected tried to describe how they saw others. One woman wrote:

> . . . I know people only as extensions of myself. I feel people much like I used to feel things—strange and distant. Strange because they are distant. Distant because of lack of communication. Lack of communication because I am overbearing—trying to force others, their notions and ideas, into my own idealization. And, finding this unacceptable, I quit—leave—either physically (take my dolls n' dishes) or mentally. Trying to prove to myself that I'm self-sufficient. I like to think that I accept people for what they are, but rather, I accept them for their imposition upon myself through which I can gain emotional satisfaction at being a martyr—or gain satisfaction by applying these impositions as reasons for various behaviors, e.g., tired, cranky, and therefore the imposition should not be repeated because of the latter. Well, I let my mind wander through the process, but I can't understand it.

This experience of "feeling people strange" was a familiar one for the rejected. A man wrote: "I never talked to my mother for even one hour about personal things in my whole life. The one unforgivable thing at home was to complain, so I never complained. Things were always fine—always." Now he feels that he is a stranger even to himself and, as such, is coming into frequent contact with other strangers. He asked, "Aren't all people strangers?" This man still feels that subservience to or dependence of almost every kind on other people is abject. As a norm of his social behavior, he asks himself what is fitting or proper in the behavior of one stranger to another. When, as a Catholic, he receives Christ in Holy Communion, the latter is a stranger in the house of a stranger and so is treated accordingly. Indeed, to act otherwise toward Him or toward any other stranger would be to act out a lie.

He explained, "Christ was a stranger who, in order to do His Father's will, spent time among strangers, and if obedience to the Father's will means the same for me, I, too, will do it." He never prays, because it would have to be forced and "would be as meaningful as spinning a prayer wheel." He is a teacher; and he pointed out: "When one teaches, he doesn't care anything about these strangers before him. He simply wants to get the work done. It is just another job."

This feeling of the rejected that others tend to remain strangers appeared to be closely related to their experience that they did not belong in a group. At least, they sensed they could belong only in a few specified groups. All during his preadolescence and adolescence one man had never really belonged to any group. "Despite this," he said, "I have some fairly close pals. It was most important to me that the kids actually thought I belonged. I acted as if I belonged. That is, I imitated those who really did belong. The kids would inevitably begin to suspect that something was wrong. Fortunately, I was not openly discovered to be a fraud because my family moved frequently, saving me each time they moved. Though I didn't belong to any of these groups, I have always known that I could belong to the wrong kind of group."

Men, particularly, who could not experience a sense of belonging with their social and economic peers felt comfortable with the "wrong kind" of group. Some were strongly motivated to seek out the "wrong kind" of companions in the social outcasts and the dregs of society. Why? Such companions were need-fulfillers. This kind of companionship seemed to provide them with something of a social bomb-shelter, in which they felt safe and relaxed. One rejected man was wholly at ease only with "pick ups" and such, even though he had absolutely no feeling for them as human beings. He could feel very much at ease "in any cheap bar with women and men who are down on their luck." In fact, he even felt elation in the realization that in many aspects he was their superior and they knew it.

Despite their distressing feelings of social uncomfortableness, the rejected, for the most part, did not become social recluses. They continued to relate to others. What kinds of social relationships did they form? In general, they established needed associations which were rewarding but safe. These relationships allayed their feelings of insecurity.

Some rejected experienced strong desires to associate and be identified, in a secure way, with persons who were recognized as successful. By the same token, they had the conviction that they could not afford even to be seen with those who happened to be out of favor. One rejected man summed up this view of relating to others. When a person with whom he had previously been friendly fell into social disrepute, he explained that he had avoided him like the plague, and added, "After all, isn't that what friends are for?"

A number of the rejected, however, readily established relationships with "little" persons who unmistakably had never had and never would have social recognition. Such associations appeared to be mutually parasitic. The rejected who formed such relationships had the rewarding, lifting experiences of playing the role of patrons to these underdogs. Meanwhile, these unfortunate "little" ones—the nobodies of the world—recognized these patrons with gratitude as their benefactors, defenders, supporters, and backers. Most of these rejected, however, appeared to be wholly unaware that defending such social inferiors had offered them gains. They did not notice that it allowed them, by contrast, to feel superior. Neither did they appear to see that, in addition, it frequently furnished them ample justification for attacking others, particularly authority figures.

Some rejected sensed that it was safe to associate closely only with social leftovers in society, who were in no position either to invade their personal privacy or to spurn them. While he was still in grade school, a rejected man had picked up with a social castoff. They needed each other. He felt superior in the relationship, and also had the rewarding experience of a steady companion. At the same time, he hated the feeling of dependence on this other boy. Shortly before he finished high school, he was—with a sense of relief—able to drop him. He still feels that safety dictates that he remain apart from his peers. He is now alone, but feels less insecure.

The patterns of unhealthy interpersonal relationships many rejected formed almost invariably eliminated, as far as possible, every element of having to trust others. Some of them had learned costly lessons early in life as a result of depending on or trusting other people, and they had determined that they would never again allow themselves to be placed in a position where they would need others. That would leave them exposed, and they felt such exposure to be both perilous and unwarranted. They readily recognized that they somehow had to live with other people; they did not, however, need to depend on them in any but absolutely necessary areas. A young woman who is still in college does not trust anyone, nor will she. To do so would leave her, as she put it, "wide open." Much as her boyfriend has proven himself, she cannot and will not trust him, because "he might take me for granted." Despite his strong objections, she continues to go out with other boys—"not," she explained, "because I like them, but solely because the competition *makes* my boyfriend be wonderful to me."

Even as small youngsters, some rejected had given the appearance of being little adults, inasmuch as they had operated with the greatest achievable amount of independence. As far as feasible, they earned their own way and made their own decisions. They did things only because they wanted to and never willingly because others wanted them to. One woman always hated to go to anyone for help of any kind. The need to bring a problem to me was most mortifying for her. "I hated to come; I hate the dependency," she said later. In fact, dependency on another person literally made her sick. When she first came, however, she immediately asked to be told what to do about her problems. Much later, while she was glad she hadn't been told what to do, she was also disappointed. Her disappointment, she explained, lay in failing to get the relief she thought would come from being told what to do. She felt childish and would have been relieved of the responsibility of making a decision, hateful as being told what to do would have been.

Another behavioral pattern which characterized many of the rejected was an insistence on doing only what *they* wanted to do. With a few of them, at least, doing solely what they wanted had become a rule of life. At times, their feeling that they were compelled to do their own will precluded even listening to advice from anyone else, regardless of its source. A few rejected openly declared that other persons were never going to tell them what to do. All during his early life, one man always got whatever he wanted, even though not easily. He would, for instance, dedicate himself to getting from his mother something that he really wanted and that she didn't want him to have. When she finally gave in, he found that he no longer wanted it and so just dropped it. Now, he insists, he simply cannot allow anyone to tell him what to do. He cannot trust God, because that would mean having to surrender completely to Him, which he just could not do. He cannot allow even God to tell him what to do.

In some younger rejected, this need to do their own will was rather abrasively manifested in the area of discipline. They fought against anything parents or other authority figures endeavored to impose on them. A college student, not yet twenty years old, simply cannot tolerate discipline from either of his parents. He is even unable to accept being told what time he is to come in from a date. His summary statement to me was, "No one tells me what to do." His grandmother had lived with them during the early years of his life. In her eyes, he could do no wrong. She gave him almost everything he asked for. Openly she had told his mother, in his presence, "Your disciplining and correcting your son are really saying clearly that you do not love him." Again and again she reminded his mother, "You don't love him or really want him—you never did." He now holds that his grandmother was speaking the truth.

Some rejected recalled having this overwhelming need to do their own will very early in their lives. A rejected woman, though not always successful in getting her own way, has never surrendered. At only two years of age, she got so mad when she couldn't have her own way that she became sick for a couple of days and even ran a temperature. To this day, she has a real temper. It still flares when anyone tries to tell her what she ought to do.

The inability of some rejected to surrender to God posed a problem. While they could not afford to let God tell them what to do, they were tortured with guilt for knowingly disobeying Him. This dilemma was unknowingly worked out for some of them below the level of their awareness. They engaged in types of behavior forbidden them by their consciences or steadfastly refused to do what they felt in conscience bound to do. Thus, they succeeded in resisting God's will. At the same time, for reasons unknown to them, they experienced certain forbidden behaviors as compulsive, or were utterly repelled by what they felt they ought to do. In either case, they did not feel free to do otherwise. In this unconscious way, their dilemma was automatically solved. They did not have to surrender to God's will, and yet did not feel guilty about what they couldn't help. The rejected who experienced such behavior patterns did not have even a suspicion of the presence of any psychological mechanism of a purposeful nature.

In the aftermath of rejection, relating to other persons inevitably remained throughout life a challenging and hazardous matter. In order to deal with it, the rejected developed their own specific coping patterns.

A few handled it by withdrawing and keeping their contacts with other persons to a minimum (126). In justification of such social withdrawal, some focused on the negative feelings involved in dealing with others. One rejected man is particularly resentful of people who ask him to do things for them, and especially of those who want him to correct their mistakes. At the same time, he feels forced to bury such resentment because its expression could have the wholly unacceptable consequence of their disliking him. There is always the danger, as well, that they might ask him to do something he could not do well. Unable to refuse the request, there would then be no way in which he could avoid obvious failure. Faced with the likelihood of becoming thus trapped in failure, his resentment becomes all the greater. Moreover, it has become increasingly difficult for him to keep it from showing.

This feeling of the peril implicit in dealing with other persons ultimately forced some rejected to go through life as "loners." One rejected man can't return the friendship and warmth of others, for were he to do so they would expect much more of him. "You would find them leaning on you, and you would have to live up to their expectations. You would have to do what they want you to do," he explained.

A few rejected worked out a plan of interpersonal operation, according to which they staked out the areas that were safe for socialization while carefully avoiding hazardous areas. The mother of one rejected man had what he regarded as a strange, social-climbing set of values with which he thoroughly disagreed. Even early in his life, he felt that his mother just could not understand, and so he came to the conclusion that he could not communicate with her on any really important matter. Neither could he talk to his father, who felt he had to side with the mother. Now he finds that, though he can communicate with his age-mates, he is simply unable to talk to or even remain comfortably close to older people.

The psychological damage so manifest in the social spheres of the rejected showed myriad facets (104). Universally, the rejected had been psychologically crippled in their relating warmly to other persons, and had experienced considerable personal damage. While such injury appeared to center on low self-esteem, it had by no means been limited to that area.[4] Such personal damage had ramified very deeply into their lives.

---

[4]One study which confirmed lower self-esteem and more egocentricity in the rejected was David Willenson's "Relationship of Adult Personality Characteristics to Perceived Parental Behavior: A Partial Validation of Ausubel's Theory of Ego Development" (Doctoral dissertation, University of Houston, 1959). In addition, the impact of rejection on such areas as anxiety, hostility, and social behavior is well treated in D. Ausubel and D. Kirk, *Ego Psychology and Mental Disorder* (New York: Grune & Stratton, 1977).

3
Concealing the "Real Self" from Others

One thing the rejected shared in common could have been expected—both logically and psychologically—in view of their feelings of personal worthlessness. They felt they had to keep others from seeing their "real selves" (40, 63). Were any other person to see them as they saw themselves, there would simply be no way for them to avoid what would, in effect, be a repetition of their original rejection (67). Once again, they would have been weighed and found wanting.

The responses of the rejected to situations they perceived as dangerous took many expressions. Of these responses, their external actions covered a wide range of activities which they had learned in order to cope with the aforementioned perils. Foremost among these actions were distancing maneuvers specifically designed to keep others from really getting to know them.

Did they recognize these behaviors for what they were? In employing one of these self-concealing behaviors, the rejected usually saw clearly *what* they were doing, such as withdrawing, role-playing, flattering, exaggerating, bragging, and so forth. Often, however, they did not appear to see clearly *why* they were doing it. For instance, those who suddenly felt it necessary, on some pretext or other, to leave those with whom they were talking appeared to have had very little, if any, suspicion of the real reason they needed to leave.

In general, these self-concealing actions—which were psychologically unhealthy—nonetheless provided needed protection, and perhaps other gains as well. They had been repeatedly reinforced over the years, until the rejected knew of no other safe way of coping socially.

Almost invariably to the extent that they let down their guard, they found themselves helpless in trying to deal with others. When they dared to express openly their real feelings and thoughts, others responded to them in highly undesirable ways, such as getting angry or taking advantage of them. When they ventured to show something of themselves to others over lengthy periods of time, they sensed that these others had somehow been able to penetrate their defenses sufficiently to see the lack of worth within them. Such devastating experiences only confirmed their worst convictions of being nobodies.

The more deeply they were hurt, the more they were driven to self-concealing behaviors. The more self-concealing they became the safer they felt, but the more they were tormented by the hunger to be warmly accepted just for themselves. What about the future? Those who dared to seriously contemplate the risk of further self-exposure realized that the carpet was steadily being pulled out from beneath them. There was a progressive erosion of their self-confidence and of their hope to be able to receive for their "real selves" the interest, admiration, and acceptance from others they so badly wanted.

A number of the rejected had tried many ways to safely expose their "real selves." Almost all such attempts failed dismally. This was true for methods they had thought of themselves as well as for those suggested by others in whom they had confided. Almost without exception, such experiences left them frustrated, deeply discouraged, and increasingly convinced of the necessity of keeping their "real selves" concealed.

Much as they resented and even hated their discerned parental evaluation of themselves, the rejected nevertheless subscribed to its correctness. That they really were what they felt their parents thought they were—unacceptable and unlovable—remained an unshakable conviction. At the same time, in what appears to be a logical contradiction, the rejected were preoccupied with and committed to the goal of disproving that parental evaluation.

A few of the rejected, nonetheless, were temporarily held back by fear from actually doing anything to disprove that evaluation. As already indicated, the means generally employed to disprove it were either the path of significant achievement or that of seeking directly to satisfy their hungers for love and affection. Either path, however, placed them in a dilemma—whichever they chose, they were left exposed to inevitable failures that would, in their eyes, constitute naked revelations of their personal worthlessness.

A significant background consideration that seems pertinent here is that each person's overall parent-child relationship seems to constitute something of a psychological mold that forms a characteristic pattern for relating to other people that persists for the rest of his life. The rejected constituted no exception to this generalization. Affection-starved as children, they desperately needed warm relationships with others. Some assigned a priority to satisfying hungers for acceptance and affection. Others concentrated on accomplishments that, hopefully, would be recognized and rewardingly acclaimed by the right people.

However, because the rejected always lived—at some level of awareness—in dread of a repetition of their original rejection, they tended to play it safe. Thus, they found themselves reluctant to approach others warmly. Regardless of the strength of their security-motivated inclinations to avoid people, for the most part the rejected did not become modern hermits; they went on living, as *safely* as they could, with other people.

They continued to sense that the satisfactions of their social hungers were inextricably linked with real dangers. Those to whom the rejected looked for affection, or for commendation, were thereby given the opportunity to hurt them—hence, the ambivalence in regard to relating to other people that was so frequently experienced by the rejected. At one and the same time, they desired and feared personal proximity with others.

Their hungers for love and approval existed, then, side by side with an almost paralyzing anxiety. With every possibility of their being loved or esteemed, there was also an associated anxiety. The hungers continued unabated as their every opportunity of being satisfied was checked by the opposing tendency born of fear. Many felt it was better to continue hungry but safe than to put themselves in a position where they could be crushed by others. This also seemed to explain why many of the rejected endlessly had to test the trustworthiness of others.

The rejected reviewed their own social records. They were forced to search out, often at a high price paid in personal suffering, their own most promising patterns for dealing safely with those who were simultaneously both needed and feared. Their struggles to disprove their deeply hurtful parental evaluation had left them highly vulnerable. The anticipated, unavoidable rejections would be confirmations of their unlovableness and unacceptableness. Nevertheless, many of them continued to strive, despite their feelings that there could be no acceptance for the unacceptable and no love for the unlovable.

The prime consideration in all such endeavors to repair their damaged self-esteem was *safety*. They tried to keep themselves as well barricaded as possible against the prying eyes of others. The specific measures they utilized in order to keep their "real selves" thus concealed were those they had made use of with some success over considerable periods of time until such measures had become characteristic of them.

Were such contradictory behavioral patterns—of being strongly drawn to others at the very time they were strongly inclined to remain safely distant from them—found in all the rejected? My findings do not warrant any sweeping generalizations of this nature. Nevertheless, of the hundreds of rejected who talked professionally with me, I do not recall one who failed to experience such ambivalent inclinations. Regardless of other considerations, most rejected appeared to have worked out their own peculiar patterns of protecting themselves so as to keep their "real selves" well concealed at the very time they were bidding for rewarding responses from others. Following are some of the more frequently reported patterns used to keep their "real selves" hidden.

A few of the rejected retreated, out of fear, from all efforts to disprove their unacceptable parental evaluation, despite their longings for acceptance. They assigned preeminence to their remaining *safe*. For the time being, they withdrew from the risks of relating closely with other people. However, the persistent urge within to disprove their hurtful parental evaluation had not disappeared; it was only being held in check.

Some rejected chose to let others close to them, but only physically. These others would never come to know them as persons (212). A girl who had arrived at puberty in her eleventh year was institutionalized as an incorrigible, sexual delinquent before her fifteenth year. Anyone who really knew her, she felt sure, would have to reject her. However, before being institutionalized, she had achieved singular popularity with a group of older boys in her home neighborhood. In fact, she told me with some pride that she had been known throughout her part of the city as "the queen."

She explained the grounds for this reputation as follows: Regularly, one or two cars carrying just the boys and herself would head for a vacant house which they used. Once there, she would quickly undress and sexually accommodate all the boys present, one at a time. She felt she did not have one serious rival in the entire city: "The other girls did not dare to compete with me and they hated me, since they knew that the boys looked on me as the queen." She was not in the least anxious about this kind of relationship with the boys because, as she put it, "they got to know only my body and my body is O.K." She would not dream of letting any of these boys get close enough to know the real her "because that would disgust them." She had thus worked out a pattern of the most rewarding social responses she felt she could afford. In fact, as she pointed out, this was the only possible way she could relate closely to these boys.

The placing of psychological distance between themselves and others took forms of extreme withdrawal in a few rejected. At least some of these withdrawals would be classified among the serious emotional illnesses. A woman had been deeply hurt many times as a small child by those she loved. Finally, she received a deep hurt from an older sibling. When this happened, she decided that she would not let people hurt her any more. Determined that no one would reach her experientially, she put her doll—which she felt represented herself—inside the closet and closed the door on her. In so doing, she symbolically put herself in there. From that moment on, she determined never again to admit to herself any feelings, especially fears. She became a feelingless thing and no longer a person.

Now, as a young adult, she wonders if she should venture out again from her self-structured, nonfeeling world. A multitude of questions arise within her, all centering about whether it is worth it to come out. If she does, couldn't they get close enough to be able to see her and so hurt her again? Her world is lonely, cold, and dark—but safe—because she allows no one to enter that world. She still hates herself.

"What is outside?" she asked. She had dared to put her hand on the doorknob, because someone approached her walls and invited her out. "If there is just one friend out there," she inquired, "would that be enough to risk going out for?" And how would she act out there? "How could you go up to someone and say, 'Hi!' and feel you were really his equal? How could you be his equal? Aren't you a nobody, a thing?" Later, she answered very slowly: "Perhaps not. You have your hand on the doorknob and feel afraid. If you feel afraid, you are not a thing. You feel, and a thing doesn't feel." Still later she added, "It's wonderful to be able to sit here and think and talk out loud with someone." She asked: "Is there happiness out there? Is it worth it? Or is the pain greater than the happiness?" Meanwhile, she is safely avoiding almost every personal contact. She is still a seriously sick young woman who has found it necessary, out of fear, to retreat psychologically from others.

Some rejected felt it necessary to their safety to remain as far as possible from others, *both* physically and psychologically. When he was still in high school, one man wouldn't dream of going out for the track team, although he knew he could run circles around the school's fastest sprinter, "because," he explained, "if I got out in front, they would all be looking at me." Whenever he was called on in class he went through hell. Before any class in which it was likely that he would be called on to answer, he "sweated blood." Whenever the teacher asked him a question, he would blurt out any answer—even one he knew to be wrong—in the hope of thus "getting off the hook." Before written examinations, he suffered tortures. He picked his present job primarily because he can be alone most of the day. He used to talk nonstop in the presence of his wife's parents "because of the pressure of the situation." As long as he kept talking, he was in control of the topic of conversation and they could not get one threatening remark in.

He said it has taken his wife several years to accept the fact that at home he just does not talk. He doesn't say ten words in a week, and as far as possible avoids being in the same room with his wife. He explained that, since he could not continue to talk nonstop to his wife throughout the years of their marriage, the next best way to keep her from getting close enough to see within him was to strive to hold all communication with her to an absolute minimum. He has pretty well succeeded in doing this, even though, he admitted, she has not been happy about it.

Some of the rejected carefully structured their everyday behavior, for the most part, so as to avoid close physical contacts with others. If that first protective arrangement failed, they retreated to some kind of psychological citadel within which they would be safe. One woman's first line of defense is to stay physically away from people she knows. Usually she is successful in putting some distance between herself and anyone she recognizes approaching her. She has worked out several routines to give the appearance of justifying such actions in the eyes of others. For instance, the moment she identifies someone she knows coming toward her on the street, she stops, looks at her watch, shakes her head in apparent disappointment, and hurries back in the opposite direction. If she happens to be downtown, she may hasten into a store directly across the street where she pretends to be looking for something until the other person has safely passed by. She has found that people usually do not follow her across the street. When such actions fail to keep people physically at a distance, she retreats psychologically. She has built psychological walls so high "that no one can get over them." Even while she withdraws to safety, she remains aware that she longs to be loved.

Some of the psychologically protective situations that the rejected devised were unusual ones. One rejected woman spends as much time as she can in the sanctuary of her own room, reading books, listening to music, and daydreaming. When she is forced to go out, she tries to remain as much as possible in crowds where she is safe from anyone who might try to approach her intimately. If such a person persists, she finds some reason for moving more deeply into the crowd and staying there until he gives up.

Some rejected—particularly those beyond their twenties—settled for deliberate role-playing as their characteristic means of safely coping with other persons. During therapy, a number of these role-players repeatedly expressed their longings to be accepted for themselves. They readily admitted, however, that even if they were to choose— being aware of the dangers involved—to strive for such intrinsic acceptance they would not know how to go about it. Through the years, they had played so many roles in their endeavors to be what people expected them to be that they simply had no idea who or what their "real selves" were. The statement "just be yourself" was meaningless to them. One woman said: "I've thought about just being me, but who is the real me? I've played so many different roles for so many years that I not only don't know who the real me is, I question whether there is a real me." Immediately she added that she has been tortured by the hunger to be accepted and loved just for herself.

To even think of dropping their protective psychological armor on the very thin hope that their "real selves" might be found to be likeable was madness. Their experiences, in the main, had only served to negate any such hope. So they went on playing the same old protective, self-concealing roles, with the consequence of repeatedly experiencing the same frustrations as their hungers to be accepted and loved for themselves continued unabated.

Occasionally, rejected role-players finally worked up enough courage to let go of the roles they had been playing. It was the experience of some of them that it had been a tragic mistake to do so. A man who had been playing roles all his life once risked dropping the roles when he was with "the perfect girl." Then, when he asked her to marry him, she said no. Her reaction taught him never again to drop his protective role-playing. That was the lesson of his life. Better to be lonely, he said, than to allow himself to get hurt that way again.

With time, these role-players learned to employ specific roles which gained for them the safest social responses from others. Some rejected adhered almost exclusively to one particular role, while others varied their roles in accordance with the perceived expectations of others. This latter group engaged in self-glorification through name-dropping, self-laudatory narrations, boasting, demeaning potential competitors, identifying closely with prominent persons, and similar behaviors. A few became so agreeable that others could not possibly dislike them. Others engaged in open flattery, feigned admiration and respect for others, demonstrated the appearance of strength of character by taking strong positions, and so on.

A girl in her late teens feels she has been forced to go around most of the time wearing a phony smile in order to keep people from really knowing her. At other times, she wears a long, sad face in order to get some sympathy. She finds this role easy to enact, since she feels "like a

Sad Sack anyway, because no one really cares." Moreover, she carries the depressing conviction that, no matter which role she plays, people eventually will discover what a "nothing" she is.

The dread that sooner or later people would see through the self-concealing roles and discover that it was all an act was the experience of a number of rejected role-players. According to one man: "By acting a role or playing a part, you keep others from getting to know you for many months. Then they begin to accept you and begin to get so close that they threaten to be able to see through the role and view your real self. That is *very* threatening."

Some of the rejected role-players became obsessed with the fear that others would penetrate their defenses and see them in their stark worthlessness. A man who hates himself simply cannot show people his *real* self. On his first visit, he asked repeatedly, "What do you think is the matter with me?" When he became satisfied that I was not going to answer that question, he remarked: "Whenever I get the feeling that someone is looking at me objectively, I can't stand it. I feel like a bug being pinned down to a table and being dissected." He then quoted, in its entirety, the passage from Shakespeare's *As You Like It* that begins, "All the world's a stage. . . ." He went on to clarify how he always plays a role, especially when the relationship is very important to him and he must strive to impress another. Under such circumstances, he doesn't dare be just himself. At the same time, he acknowledged that because acting a role is phony it inevitably shows up under close and prolonged scrutiny.

This man feels he is quite childish and all mixed up inside. He wants to marry but is deterred mainly by the fear that the girl will see through him and, pretending to accept him, play him for a sucker. "It's so hard to really know someone," he added, "because everybody plays roles." One characteristic I have discovered in my clinical experience with the rejected is that they simply assume that everyone has had the same experiences as they have had.

The feeling that role-playing must inevitably become so transparent that it would lead to a disclosure of their basic unacceptability seemed to be closely related to the emphasis some of the rejected bestowed on the present moment. They assigned a high priority to the here and now.

The rejected played roles designed to conceal their "real selves," even when fully convinced that they were placing their whole psychological future in jeopardy by doing so. A number of the rejected were openly aware that they would inevitably be found out for the nothings they felt they were. Even though such a dreaded eventuality was clearly foreseen by them, they nevertheless continued on a course that sacrificed their entire future to the attainment of momentary gains. In reality, many of them felt that they had no choice in the matter. The only way they could afford to appear before others was under the protective cover of a self-concealing role.

Some rejected openly acknowledged that the roles they played in order to keep their "real selves" hidden from others would necessarily exact a high price from them later on. One rejected man shields himself from others *now*, and largely disregards the future. He is sure his social withdrawal and repeated lying to other people will expose him in the long run. Nevertheless, here and now, they help to shelter him. He insists that he can afford to concern himself at the moment only with keeping his true self concealed.

The conviction of some rejected that they must concentrate on the present, despite their certainty that their exposure would sooner or later be inevitable, exercised a considerable effect on their daily behavior. One man who feels his parents do not love him desperately wants people to like him. At the same time, he quite helplessly acts in ways calculated to make them dislike him. His explanation for this contradiction is that he needs the momentary concealment such behavior affords him and, besides, he knows it is inevitable that sooner or later they will reject him anyway. It is simply a matter of time until they discover that, deep down, he is not likeable. He maintains that he can't win for failing.

Among other protective devices—which were not strictly role-playing but which were employed for self-concealment by some of the rejected—was the aggressive use of their voices to offend others by laughing at, taunting, rebuffing, or in other ways verbally assaulting them. This type of behavior which kept others at a safe distance and hid the "real self," also expressed the hostility of the rejected.

Some rejected felt that a strong behavioral offense was the best protection against people they sensed were trying to get too close to them. Although one young woman longs to be loved and accepted, the need to be safe is so great that she immediately rebuffs every personal approach of another. To anyone who has seriously tried to get close to her she has said something such as, "I'd really appreciate it if you would let me mind my business. Please just leave me alone." The most frustrating result for her has been that most of her acquaintances now give her a wide berth!

The protective stratagems used by the rejected to keep people from seeing their "real selves" were usually not fully recognized as such. A few, for instance, held others at a distance by deliberately instilling fear into them until they became leery of any close relationship. One man has frequently cut people down mercilessly. He feels that if he can really hurt people, and they come to appreciate his abundant ability to hurt them, he will earn their respect—even though he readily grants that they won't like him. He added, "If they think I am low and mean enough to carry tales to those who could make serious trouble for them, why shouldn't I do it?" This carrying of tales gives him satisfaction and, in addition, makes them even more respectful of him. The satisfaction he gains from really hurting someone in such a way—even after he has rationalized it—is not substantial, because he remains conscious of its shameful aspect and feels guilty. What puzzles him is that he keeps right on doing it.

Frequently, the carrying out of these strong tendencies to hide the "real self" also wounded others. One rejected man generally gets along well enough with people. Occasionally, however, he becomes aware that someone is starting to get too close to him psychologically. He is thankful that God endowed him with a sharp tongue with which he has always been able to mount a sudden, devastating, verbal assault against anyone who is crowding him. The victim, invariably stunned by the unexpected, virulent nature of the attack, backs off in hurt bewilderment. Someone thus wounded does not soon again attempt to invade his personal privacy. Here, hostility was the effective instrument he used to shield the "real self" from the eyes of others.

Another fear-inducing maneuver some rejected used to protect themselves took the form of frank and repeated admissions of their ungovernable tempers. These open admissions were calculated to warn anyone who might want to get intimate with them to stay safely distant. Trembling with emotion, a man said:

> At times I really fear for people who try to crowd me in any way. I am always careful to warn them about this problem of mine, on which I have been working, but have by no means conquered. It is my temper. It can start up suddenly without any warning whatever, especially if someone should try to invade my personal privacy. It really scares me because, when—entirely without warning—I break into one of these uncontrollable rages, I know I could easily kill a person with my bare hands. I always try to caution people about it so they don't get hurt, but some nevertheless disregard the warning and keep crowding me. I really fear for them.

It is hardly necessary to remark that he was saying this primarily for my benefit. Others, however, later volunteered the information that he frequently talks about his ungovernable temper. In addition, they testi-fied that most of the people they know keep a safe distance from him.

Some of the rejected discovered that it was impossible to keep their "real selves" concealed from others. They then retreated to their next line of defense. They unknowingly acted in a way which protected them from getting hurt by brainwashing themselves. They convinced themselves that what others thought and felt about them was of little or no importance. For a long time, one woman kept feeling and telling herself that it did not matter what others thought about her, and she had pretty well convinced herself that this was true. Now she knows that it is a lie. It does matter—it matters very much. She wonders how she was ever able to persuade herself otherwise.

The rejected who had, on the whole, successfully kept others safely distant appeared to feel a need to justify such isolating of other people. Frequently, it was because—on one score or another—they were sim-ply unable to let people get close to them. A few of the rejected, for instance, indicated that since they were not able to communicate with others they had to stay away from them. Tension causes one man to forget many things. This forgetting greatly increases the difficulty he has in conversing with other people, so he just does not try to talk to others. This has left him cut off from people and powerless to do anything about it, but he feels less threatened.

Even when they were caught in their own homes by visitors and were unable to avoid being close to others physically, some of the rejected found safe psychological distance by noticeably becoming en-grossed in television or something else during the conversation. They felt that, because these persons had violated their privacy, they de-served such treatment. Besides, it was impossible to really talk to them.

A number of the rejected used their *life professions* in order to keep their "real selves" hidden. Into these they had carefully structured some well-controlled, safe, interpersonal relationships. They had se-lected "avoidance vocations" which provided them with built-in safe-guards against the unwanted invasions of others into close proximity to their "real selves." Following are some examples.

As a librarian, a rejected woman lives in a well-structured world that allows few conversations—and those are strictly confined to whispers. Moreover, she feels professionally justified in limiting almost all dis-cussions to topics centering around books and other publications.

A rejected man working in a laboratory has a vocational shelter into which only a select few are admitted and then only on official business—an arrangement which he insists be strictly observed. He has consistently discouraged all attempts at personal communication in the lab.

A college teacher holds to a minimum her contacts with her academic colleagues. In addition, she declares that academic rank and disciplinary needs warrant her carefully controlling the nature and extent of student contacts, both within and outside the classroom. Outside the class, her students have learned that they may ask to see her about class matters only.

In the military service, a man has discovered a life-structure lived almost entirely according to regulations. This has enabled him to avoid making almost all important decisions in which he might risk personal failure. Thus he has confined almost all of his interpersonal relating to military regulations. In addition, his "real self" has not been exposed in his major policies and practices, even where either or both of these later proved to be blunders. These were not his mistakes, he feels certain, since he was only carrying out the orders of those who had made the decisions.

Behaviors and situations which a few rejected felt to be dangerous because of their potential for self-revelation would not be considered as such by most people. A few rejected were convinced that anything they wrote would inevitably disclose their "real selves." One woman simply cannot accept the assurances of others that she is worthwhile. She sees herself as a "dim bulb," and no amount of evidence to the contrary alters that conviction. As a college student, she could not write her assigned themes and do her other written assignments "because in them I showed myself to others. I could just imagine them going through each of my themes word for word and so discovering what a no-account I am." It got to the point that she simply couldn't do them. She had to lie repeatedly in order to try to explain the absence of her written assignments to her teachers. Another woman said: "I don't want to type, write, etcetera. I'll be found out—I'm hiding behind a self-structured shield."

Finally, the rejected who characteristically employed devices calculated to guard their "real selves" from the eyes of others were not likely to employ them in every contact with other persons. Such devices tended to appear only in those situations which they sensed as dangerous. In addition to those already indicated, these situations included:

—being left alone with someone who made them feel uncomfortable.

—being in the presence of someone who was trying to prove them wrong in a discussion.

—feeling that they were being made to look stupid, ignorant, or naive, in a social setting.

—being informed that they had failed in something or had made a flagrant blunder.

—being ignored.

—being embarrassed.

Among additional psychological techniques which were utilized to maintain safety in such threatening situations were the following:

—alleging the press of business or duties as grounds for having to leave the scene.

—using the habitual pattern of "I have to get going," with no reason assigned for leaving.

—shifting to a monosyllabic pattern of speech or grimaces and shrugs when the conversation became threatening.

—lethally using what appeared to be humor to drive the other person to cover and get others to laugh at him.

—engaging, while smiling and apparently joshing, in injurious sarcasm or vicious remarks to or about another person or his family.

—refusing to take anything seriously; viewing everything as being in jest.

—playing the role of an uninhibited punster.

—turning the conversation, as skillfully as possible, to a safe topic which they had carefully prepared. Having already armed themselves with an impressive array of facts and well-reinforced views on the subject under discussion, they felt fairly safe. This did not need to be a monologue. Others were permitted to speak as long as they confined their remarks to the safe topic.

4
Endeavors of the Rejected to Disprove Their Low Self-Evaluations

In the interest of better understanding the characteristic experiences and behaviors of the rejected, it may be helpful to place them in perspective against a meaningful background. This includes, first of all, the unsatisfied need of the rejected for warm, parental love. Everyone, as the offspring of two people, possesses the innate right to be loved by them. These two, as parents, have the corresponding obligation—whether or not they recognize it—to provide their child with life's necessities, including food, shelter, protection, and, especially, nourishing love. Indeed, warm, personal, parental love is an essential ingredient of the child's personal growth (119).

In the rejected, where this ingredient of authentic parental love was withheld, their hunger for it continued unabated through life. Indeed, the rejected had an abiding experience of emptiness which never ceased crying out to be filled. Maslow implies this in his remark, "The feeling of rejection is itself a motivating state" (119). The lasting, plaguing void that was a consequence of the absence of warm parental affirmation appeared also to be inseparably tied to self-hatred or, at least, to damaged self-esteem. For the rejected, this was a privation in the sense of an emptiness where something badly needed ought to have been.

The distinctive nature of a privation becomes strikingly clear when fleshed out in a concrete way—for instance, if someone were to display an empty shoulder socket from which the arm had been torn away. The first element in this background, then, was an injurious privation of badly needed parental love and affection.

Another element in the backgrounds of some, but not all, of the rejected was that their original privation had been compounded by further privations. These additional privations came from their personal, social failures. Even while they were still youngsters, many of them had engaged fruitlessly in a relentless search for longed-for recognition, particularly from their peers.

Athletic performance was one such avenue open to the boys who represented their schools. These athletically gifted boys had, therein, a source of peer commendation which for a time stopped just short of peer worship. Regardless of personal appearances or other personal characteristics, the athletic heroes of the moment found no difficulty whatever in getting their choice of dates or gaining immediate entrance to any group they wished to join.

Many rejected men, lacking such athletic ability in their school years, concentrated instead on getting high grades, joining a small group of the school intelligentsia, participating in extracurricular activities, or owning a type of automobile that was notably different. Others strove to join "in" groups or to get recognition by drinking, taking drugs, proving they had "guts," or similar behaviors. For none of these achievements, however, had they received the gratifying attention given the school athletes. But whether the rejected excelled in athletics or sought recognition through some other means, their achievements, after a time, proved very disappointing and left them frustratingly empty.

On the other hand, girls who happened to be popular with the right boys appeared to have in that popularity one sought-for manifestation of peer recognition. Distinct advantages in such competition, however, invariably went to girls who were well endowed with physical beauty. In order to compete in this arena, rejected girls who were less physically attractive had to possess or offer something more than physical attractiveness, such as noteworthy peer achievements, successful role-playing, easy sex, and so on. No matter how popular they were, however, the girls had been left somehow dissatisfied.

The rejected felt thwarted over the years because they were never able to get really satisfying recognition from their peers and others. Frustration and anxiety inundated them. They ran the gamut of potentially fulfilling patterns of accomplishment in vain. It's hardly surprising that whenever the rejected asked the advice of a clinician about what to do, they appeared to be waiting to pounce on the clinician as soon as the advice was given. In substance, they were saying: "That's stupid. I tried it and it doesn't work." Most of them had, in fact, tried again and again for "success" through the *same* futile channels. Even if they achieved their goal, they still felt deeply dissatisfied.

With envy, they observed their peers relate and converse easily and interestingly with other people. Some tried to imitate such behavior, but it just didn't come off. Apprehensive and understandably self-conscious, they inevitably began to bore others. The rejected who managed to receive acceptance from others were not always able to handle it. The feeling that they were "in" with others proved very heady stuff for them. Without really understanding why, a number of the rejected spontaneously rebuffed the very responses from others which they sought. After this occurred a number of times, the latter became reluctant to offer any further expressions of acceptance. This was very harrowing, and these rejected experienced great difficulty in handling the resulting, smoldering anger within.

The avenues to recognition that some of the rejected tried but failed at were legion. They observed others repeatedly receiving rewarding social acceptance for the "right" responses, for example, the fast quip or the perfect squelch. Their own experience was that it usually took them hours to figure out such "right" responses. Times without number they encountered people capably handling almost any situation with humor or kidding. Their own such attempts came through as strident, barbed remarks. They studied those who appeared to take disappointments, jolts, and even failures like so much water off the back of a duck. When they tried to model their own responses on such patterns, it was simply pretending. Personal setbacks mattered deeply to them; there was no shrugging them off.

In general, the rejected appeared to be in a rut. Many of them saw only *one* way of endeavoring to accomplish their goals, but they had, without success, run the gamut of other possible paths before choosing their present route. Try as they would, they found they couldn't win. On the other hand, most of the rejected did not give up.

Without exception, the rejected had been damaged by a lack of parental love. Many of them had also been repeatedly stung by their social failures. Add to these the other individual hurtful experiences of the rejected, and the background which produced their low self-evaluation is complete. Since such an evaluation was unacceptable, how did they try to get rid of it?

In general, the rejected focused on either of two areas in their strivings to disprove their low self-evaluations. These were personal achievements and/or the acquiring of love and affection from others. There is no contention here that the rejected who were driven either to achieve or to obtain affection were wholly aware that they were thereby seeking to disprove their low self-evaluations. Nevertheless, this interpretation seems to be well substantiated by my clinical findings and by those of others. It also provides a meaningful key to some of the otherwise baffling behaviors of the rejected.

Whether or not the strings of social failures had been added to the incredibly painful, persisting experiences of emptiness, almost all the rejected continued to press on in their efforts to give the lie to their self-evident, low self-esteem. Although it remained in their eyes unquestionable, their abject self-concept nevertheless was wholly intolerable for them. A primary motive in their lives, even though seemingly involving a contradiction in logic, was their determination to disprove their adamantly retained, low self-evaluation. They were out to refute their unquestionable lack of worth once and for all.

How did they describe these efforts? Some used terms such as wanting to prove themselves, succeed, excel, surpass, achieve, accomplish, create. Others spoke of their reaching out to people and of their longings for acceptance, affection, love, and constant attention from others (150).

The achievement-driven rejected needed to reassure themselves and to impress others with their successes. The others they wished to impress always included specific people. The affection-hunting rejected gave no gift of self in their affectionate relationships. Their need was to get the gratification for which they hungered. Preoccupied with winning affection, they usually targeted on one specific individual at a time from whom they hoped to derive such rewarding responses. However, a lesser number of affection-hunters searched indiscriminately for affection and, especially, sexual gratification.

The previous relationships of a number of the women affection-hunters with men were based on intellectual or other nonphysical grounds. The new experience of being physically sought after by men proved to be heady stuff for some. Through it, a few of these women experienced a new sense of themselves. They felt that they had come alive, as persons, in being warmly sought after by others they found attractive. In addition, a few found themselves awakened sexually toward others for the first time in their lives. With no previous experience in handling such responses, they felt almost as if instant adulthood had been thrust upon them. They came to feel that sexual relating was the key to their worth as women.

Though I have encountered no mention of this in the literature, I have observed in the rejected a sex difference with regard to being oriented toward achieving or affection-hunting. For the most part, rejected men had a compelling need to *achieve*, whereas the majority of rejected women were preoccupied with their longings for love and had an almost insatiable hunger for *affection*. Where affection was not to be had, these women sought the intensive, sustained attention of others. In the past few years, an increasing number of rejected women have experienced a consuming need to achieve, but have maintained their great hunger for affection in a strong secondary position. However, most of the rejected men have not been aware of an increase of comparable strength in their affection-hunger. In any case, the common denominator of these various expressed longings seems to have been the ongoing search by the rejected for grounds to disprove the self-evident fact of their personal nonacceptability.

The sex difference in achieving or affection-hunting orientation appeared to hold true also for the fantasy lives of the rejected. Almost invariably, rejected men pictured themselves in their daydreams in the roles of heroes; famous political, industrial, movie, or stage personalities; or living dangerous, intriguing lives. On the other hand, the fantasies of rejected women centered around their ardently affectionate (including sexual) relationships. Unless these rejected women happened to be lesbians, their fantasized relationships were usually with men they knew well or men who were figments of their imaginations. Occasionally, such fantasies were not with any specific man, real or imagined, but with a nonidentified male body. In these imagined relationships, the satisfactions received by the women were almost exclusively in the area of physical sex. It involved neither giving of self nor feelings of personal attachment on their part. Physical gratification was used in their fantasies to feed themselves emotionally. In their experienced arousals, vivified by their active imaginations, they were able to keep their partners gentle, kind, considerate, tender, or any way they wanted them.

Most rejected men actually used *themselves* as the source for disproving their damaged self-esteem; that is, they sought this disproof in their own accomplishments, for which they hoped to win important social recognition. Rejected women, by contrast, sought the wished-for refutations of their self-devaluation in *others*. They searched for it in the affectionate acceptance or satisfactions granted them by *other* people.

It seems undeniable that endeavors to repudiate the fact of their low self-esteem, whether recognized as such by them or not, held a high priority in the behaviors characteristic of the rejected. What specific kinds of *achievements*, particularly by the men, could be given such an interpretation? Some clung to unreachable levels of attainment. Often I found the rejected demanding a level of perfection of themselves that was increasingly revealed to be a standard which no human being could ever reach. One man is so demanding of himself that he finds it difficult to explain to his wife. He *has* to be most precise in everything he does in order to make up for those things with which he can't cope or at which he fails. If he does not do perfectly in the things he undertakes, he *has* to punish himself.

Some of the rejected recognized that demanding this kind of perfection of themselves was unreasonable. Nevertheless, these demands on themselves remained nonnegotiable. This entire pattern of inexorably insisting on striving for unattainable goals appears to have been psychologically protective. They never really had to put to the test their assumption that the complete attainment of these goals would bring them the promised feeling of self-worth, because the goals would always remain unattainable. As long as the assumption was never adequately tested, it could not rightly be said to have been tried and found wanting. They seemed to sense, at some level of knowledge, that this protected them from the need to prove their self-worth through other unfamiliar, more threatening channels. Untried ventures could have left them still more exposed to disastrous failures.

One noteworthy channel used by some rejected who were demanding perfection of themselves was that of religious piety or external religious observances, either within or outside religious communities. Over the years, I have had in counseling a number of rejected men and women from religious communities who *had* to excel and to be *perfect* in the observance of their community rules and regulations and in their prayers. Any defect on their part in one of these areas would have left them feeling insecure and worthless.

Other rejected persons who were not members of any religious community also strove for perfection in external religious practices. After a rejected Catholic woman has attended Mass each morning, she spends two additional hours praying in the church. Her husband periodically upbraids her, because the children have no one to prepare their breakfast or get them ready for school. She has found it very trying that she is not able to make him understand. She pointed out that, in requesting her to discontinue this practice, he is asking her to renounce her self-respect, for she would then be going against her conscience.

Obedience was another channel used by those demanding perfection of themselves. In contradistinction to reasonable, wholesome patterns of obedience, something quite different appeared in the behavior of these rejected. They committed themselves inflexibly to perfect-to-the-letter obedience to parental, religious, or other authoritative norms. These rigid patterns held the promise of their receiving rewarding recognition for conscientiously implementing the decision of others. Their observance was the measure of their worth. In such unbending patterns of observance, however, they were safe from making wrong major decisions, since they were avoiding, as far as possible, the making of any important personal decisions whatever. Working within such a context, they avoided being responsible for themselves as persons while still proving their worth.

By attempting to eliminate the major risks inherent in living through the use of such a pattern, they sought to develop an immunity to failure—but only at the price of operationally surrendering their dignity as human beings. A rejected married man with children feels that his security lies in doing what he is told. When he is told to do something, he can usually do it well. While he appears to be talented in some areas, he has shown no initiative. Unless he is told what to do, he would never undertake anything, "because it would not be of any value. My security is in doing well what I am told to do." Lately he has come to recognize that, if he acts only when he is told to do something, he does not have to shoulder the responsibility for it. If he should fail, it was not his idea in the first place. The failure would be the other person's for giving him an unsuitable task. While he does not appear to be producing any salient disproofs of his damaged self-esteem, through this channel he is managing to avoid exhibitions of his low self-esteem.

Some rejected appeared to have recourse to their own talents or personal characteristics, real or imagined, as the sources promising ultimately to furnish them grounds for self-acceptance. A few of these rejected explicitly recognized such qualities only when they had somehow been challenged. A rejected man was very upset when he had to face the fact that he was "yellow" in a fearful situation, even though the others present did not recognize that he was cowardly. "That awareness," he said, "pulled the rug out from under me, and my will to keep trying took a nose dive. Until that moment I had never questioned my courage."

For some rejected who had failed to accomplish anything noteworthy in their lives, the mere claims (made by themselves) that they possessed superior abilities became independent sources of feelings of personal importance (10). Such claims were doggedly maintained by some, even in the face of unbroken records of failures and nonachievements. Those who had anything but distinguished records repeatedly mentioned that they possessed incredibly superior abilities. One man announced publicly that he would need only a few days in order to straighten out, once and for all, a number of the most highly complex national and international problems facing our country.

Often the most frequent and severe criticisms of those in positions of top authority came from the rejected who only too obviously were poorly endowed to fulfill such roles themselves. The persons making such assertions seemed to sense that they remained safe, inasmuch as they could never be tested in these matters. Extravagant claims to very unusual abilities which had never, in any way, been demonstrated were made by them in relative safety. Such alleged abilities, for instance, were claimed in executive, artistic, and athletic areas.

The rejected making such claims seemed to sense that at least two psychological cushions protected them from the risk of having to demonstrate the claimed abilities. One cushion was the *hypothetical* or conditional nature of the claimed undertaking. They stated that, *if* they were to undertake any one of these things, they would unquestionably succeed at it. As long as that "if" remained, they knew they could not be forced to substantiate their claim.

The other cushion was the dimension of *time*. There was no commitment to any undertaking as long as it remained in the future. They were in no way irrevocably committed to demonstrate in the present such an event. Behind these two psychological cushions, they were safe. They could continue to make self-enhancing claims without serious fear of refutations.

On the other hand, not all the rejected who claimed outstanding abilities lacked them. Notable personal talents needing only adequate recognition from others appeared to some rejected as their justification for denying their low self-evaluation.

Because the need to find grounds for disavowing their base self-evaluations, whether recognized or not, was so powerful in the rejected, a number who had staked out their research for these grounds within the confines of their personal talents played fast and loose with reality. The fact that an assessment of their abilities would not have warranted realistically considering such lofty goals simply did not enter the picture. These goals of the rejected were selected in terms, not of their actual capacities, but of their personal needs. Hence, certain of their talents had to be expanded in their minds until they equaled the magnitude of those needs. Psychologically, it was a matter of life and death. These rejected *had* to be able to reach the goals they were certain they needed.

One rejected man who envies his successful former classmates persists in his assertions that he has more brains, looks, and all-around ability than any of them. After speaking at length of his superior talents, he remarked with pride that on a number of occasions he has been very favorably compared in appearance with some of Hollywood's leading male movie stars. He then named two leading men, in particular. He said he knows he is their superior in looks, as well as in intelligence. To me, he appears to have a relatively high "normal" I.Q. and to be slightly above average in physical appearance.

Many rejected scored notable successes solely within the realm of their fantasies. One rejected man has never really achieved in the outside world because he hasn't had to do so. Instead, he has always substituted, as his own, exploits from science fiction and western stories, which he has devoured at every available moment since his school days. He is still achieving in this way.

A number of the rejected were wholly preoccupied with a specific urge to achieve in one particular kind of undertaking. At times, this was in an interpersonal area. One rejected man who hates his mother invariably finds himself strongly attracted to any woman he thinks can dominate him. Then he experiences the strongest urge to dominate her. "In fact," he said, "I just have to dominate her."

A great number of rejected committed themselves to living up to the expectations of others. Some were still seeking hoped-for recognition from *parents*, because they seemed to sense that, if they could ever really succeed in pleasing their parents, the tumult within them would cease. A young man, long tortured by emptiness and aloneness, is very conscious of his relationship to his father, a professional man. He feels deeply that his father must never be disgraced by an action of his. Permeating him is the fear that he is going to be a supreme disappointment to others, especially to his dad. During high school, he just *had* to excel and did so in sports and various other school activities; but these did not prove at all satisfying to him.

While he has not said explicitly that his father rejected him, he appears to give strong indications of it. It seems that, in place of openly recognizing his father's rejection, he has been focusing on the less painful, haunting fear that he might disappoint his father. He remains confident that if, just once, he could conspicuously achieve in some really important undertaking he could make his dad proud of him.

Other rejected, after having been rejected by one of their parents, went all-out in their efforts to succeed for the other one. They appeared to hope that, if their nonrejecting parent was highly pleased with their accomplishments, they would no longer be filled with turbulence.

It is wholly understandable that those with loving parents would want to make their parents proud of them. In these rejected, however, I encountered quite a different kind of thing. They were harassed by the need to succeed in the eyes of the nonrejecting parent. This suggested that the acceptance they experienced from that parent was based on extrinsic valuation. Apparently, somewhere within them was concealed the knowledge that the nonrejecting parent wanted them, not for themselves, but for what he could get from or through them. They had not yet sensed that his acceptance was directly proportionate to their ability to fulfill his needs. As previously indicated, such extrinsic valuation shares the common denominator with rejection that one is not loved for oneself. Accordingly, whenever an individual who had been clearly rejected by one parent went all-out for acceptance by the other parent, the relationship usually failed to prove rewarding.

A man who had been rejected by his father identified very closely with his mother. He is now certain that she figures prominently in his constantly striving for status and reputation in everything he does. Even during his school years, he knew that he had to hold offices and get high grades; otherwise, he felt his mother would have been disappointed. He knew she was very desirous that he be a success. Secretly, he knew that she would be very pleased if he chose his present profession. Even his piety, which he had assumed was for God, he now sees was in imitation of his mother and was one more endeavor to excel for her. His mother recently died, but he finds that his pattern of motivation persists. He knows this, finds it most frustrating, but feels unable to change it.

A few unhappy Catholic priests, rejected by their fathers, knew without doubt before they entered the seminary that their mothers would be most pleased if they were to become priests; but most of them were unable to recall explicit remarks of their mothers to that effect. Nonetheless, they had sensed how intensely gratifying such a commitment on their part would be to their mothers. In addition, they somehow knew that this consideration had entered rather strongly into their decision although most of them had tried to look at other motives. After they were ordained as priests, they experienced persisting inner turmoil and anxiety. However, they strove to believe they had taken this big step from a motivation of love and service to God and their fellow man, even though they remained clearly conscious of how tremendously proud their mothers were of their being priests.

In somewhat similar fashion, some Catholic nuns knew they were fulfilling their mothers' dreams by entering the convent, but they tried to tell themselves that this was not their prime motive and wouldn't let themselves think about it. A growing dissatisfaction, however—sometimes experienced very early in their religious life—caused some of them to later re-examine their original motivations for entering.

A few rejected appeared to feel that they really merited the keen disappointment of their parents precisely because of their lack of achievements. Accordingly, they felt obliged to try to rectify the matter by significant attainments. One man, who felt he was not wanted or needed at home, remarked: "I *must* be great so my parents will be able to look up to me, and so that, perhaps, God will bless my family through me."

How did the achievement-driven rejected explain their consuming need to achieve? Most of the rejected saw no need to explain it. They assumed that it was simply part of being human. Every person had to prove himself! What further explanation was necessary?

What were the more commonly undertaken endeavors to score in this fashion? One that was often attempted was striving for the appearance of success so that it could be ostentatiously displayed to others. Everyone is familiar with the often-puzzling spectacle of persons seemingly constrained "to keep up with the Joneses." Such patterns were frequently found in the rejected. Few of those with whom I dealt had notable wealth, and a number of them indicated, at least indirectly, their envy of the affluent and their ambition someday to join their ranks. In their eyes, wealth spelled success. Accordingly, a facade of belonging with the well-to-do had to be maintained, regardless of almost every other consideration. They strongly hoped that in the future it would be more than an appearance of affluence—it would show itself in their residences, automobiles, clubs, and so forth. Some said that it would be paraded especially by their beautiful wives wearing expensive jewelry and clothes.

Name-dropping and the relating of incidents calculated to impress certain people who counted was usually part of this same picture. Even those few who eventually succeeded in reaching the economic level that permitted them to display the image of opulent success failed to find relaxation in it. Such achievements failed to lessen notably their basic yearnings.

Did not some rejected experience failure to achieve in any recognizable way? Yes. How did they account for such a lack of success? What were their justifications for what appeared to be failures for which they were culpable? Some who had accepted without question the position that notable achievements were essential to their existence had been holding back and doing nothing because of fear. Did they openly admit that fear was the explanation? Practically never. They invariably offered some other explanation. Frequently they had justifying reasons for not succeeding in noteworthy undertakings.

Among such justifications was the assertion of a total lack of interest coupled with the claim that they could excel if they chose to do so. This exonerated them from having to make the efforts necessary to achieve certain designated goals. At the same time, to bolster the correctness of their claim, they casually referred to some of their lesser results, which had been effortlessly achieved, as corroborating evidence in support of their seemingly grandiose claims.

One rejected man, who was in graduate school, repeatedly mentioned in the presence of his classmates—as well as to me—that for him graduate studies were "a breeze." He laughingly remarked that anyone who had even a passing acquaintance with him could see that, though he never cracked a book, he was getting straight B's. Several times he dropped the remark that he could very easily surpass the two students who were generally recognized as outstanding in his classes, and immediately added: "It just isn't worth the trouble. It really doesn't mean a thing to me."

Another student happened to volunteer to me the information that more than once she had seen him deep in study when he apparently thought no one was noticing. My impression was that he did possess superior academic ability—together with a very poor self-concept. However, I would seriously doubt that his intellectual gifts were on a par with those of the two superior students.

Other justifications for not achieving took the form of personal problems well known to others. These rejected thus stood justified in their own eyes, as well as in the eyes of their friends, for not being productive. One rejected man has had no notable experiences of success. His chronic illnesses (colitis and ulcers) have been very painful to him. After several months of counseling, he spontaneously raised the question of whether these illnesses might not be giving him an honorable retreat from having to strive for success. He suspected that his ill health, which was rather common knowledge, might have provided him with protection against risking ventures that could have ended in abysmal failure. Meanwhile, he remains deeply angry and resentful at being forced to stand still while his former classmates are going ahead. He accepts no part of the blame for his having been frustratingly stagnant. Instead, depending on how he happens to feel at the moment, he places the blame on his health, God, the Church, his parents, or society.

Another form of justification the rejected used for failing to achieve was a serious personal problem of which others would scarcely be aware. A young rejected man reported that his big problem is compulsive, habitual masturbation. He feels this problem has made it impossible for him to achieve just about anything he has ever tried to do. Later in counseling, he began to wonder if he hasn't needed this problem which, to him, had become so bad that it had kept him, while still in college, from really concentrating and therefore succeeding in his studies and many other important things. Later still, he questioned whether it was true that he simply could not admit to himself the possibility that he might be lacking in the ability to accomplish these things. Nevertheless, he feels it helps that he still can explain to himself his failures to achieve as being due to his problem—though he has no deep peace within.

An intense fear of failure which kept some rejected chained so that they could not achieve anything significant was, at times, unwittingly displaced onto something else. A man is obsessed with the fear that he will lose his Catholic faith. He feels certain that he is unable to realize any of his real potentials because of this fear. Since he is forced to spend the bulk of his waking hours on the all-important undertaking of shoring up that faith, he is left neither the time nor energy to accomplish anything else. Without his faith, he feels sure, he would be able to do absolutely nothing. Instead, he would "then hit the bottle and go to seed completely, probably going from house of prostitution to house of prostitution."

Some of the rejected felt that the real culprit responsible for their not achieving was some aspect of the environment. One rejected man asked me to reread Erich Fromm so that I would better understand the enforced slavery he was experiencing. "As Fromm put it," he explained, "the system itself is evil. I simply cannot accomplish anything in such a corrupt arrangement. The Establishment holds a man in a straitjacket. He's utterly helpless. Believe me, I personally have much to contribute to society but, until they radically change this distorted, unjust system, I'm helpless. I'm forced to remain productively impotent in the chains with which the whole setup has shackled me."

Some of the rejected found less dangerous ways of experiencing achievement, though they did not recognize them as such. The psychological mechanism of *identification*, for instance, was unconsciously employed by some rejected in order to share, what was in their eyes, the unquestionable greatness demonstrated by the notable achievements of others. This sharing was based on their real or imagined relationships to those other persons. A rejected man who experienced failure in just about everything he attempted periodically calls long distance to a man who, in his opinion, has received professional and social recognition and who had befriended him years before. The following are characteristic of his remarks on the telephone: "You're all I've got. You're a big shot, and I know you. I can always fall back on the fact that I know you. I made my mark in life. I can look back on the time when we walked and talked together."

A few rejected women identified closely with such women as "Mother of the Year," or the one chosen on the television program "Queen for a Day," or with some other publicly honored woman. A large number of wives derived their sense of personal value primarily from the occupational status of their husbands. Wives of professional men, for example, felt superior to the wives of nonprofessional men.

Those women whose husbands had specialties in medicine, for instance, regarded themselves as personally and socially superior to women whose husbands were general practitioners.

This type of evident identification with husbands' occupations would seem also to explain, in good part, a reaction encountered more than once—the unexpected, outraged response loosed against an individual who made uncomplimentary remarks about a given profession or occupation. Such a response came most frequently from the wife of a man engaged in that profession or occupation. Such a reaction spoke volumes about an important source of the woman's self-esteem.

Another form of psychological identification frequently found in the rejected was their relating themselves mentally to their own children in such a way that the children became extensions of themselves. The future outstanding attainments of their children would be theirs. Parents who felt they hadn't made the grade themselves would get a second shot at it through their children.

There were those who chose specific goals to be attained by their children. Some rejected men who were now fathers had plans to still make the positions they had always wanted on their universities' teams through their sons. Rejected women who were now mothers felt that this time, through their daughters, they were going to correct the mistake of marrying below themselves. The boys who did not take readily to the desired area of athletics and the girls who dared to date boys whose fathers were social "nobodies" suffered.

Some rejected parents who banked on making it through their children had no specified goals for the latter to attain. A rejected man with a drinking problem has pinned his hopes on achieving vicariously through his son. Although he feels that he has thus far failed to accomplish anything worthwhile in his life, he sees his great chance to succeed in the person of this son. He constantly talks about "my son" and almost never about "my children," though he has more than one child. In fact, he has openly admitted to the family that he can afford to pay attention only to this child. On occasion, he has become enraged when his wife or someone else has corrected or tried to discipline this boy. He protested, "No one must tamper with my investment in the future."

Repeatedly he has asked me, "What will happen to me?" He said that he intended to stoop to almost any depth to get his drinks, then immediately begged for reassurance that he would not become an alcoholic. Having sold everything else in the house that he could to pawnbrokers for liquor money, he is now considering selling the furniture piece by piece. When his wife remonstrated with him about this, he told her openly that he does not care what happens to their home, to her, or to anyone else, just as long as this son is all right. He added, "I am living for that boy."

Identification, however, was not always a safe mechanism; indeed, some forms of it were replete with dangers. Some rejected who used identification found they were exposed to dangers which arose from *comparison*. A woman whose sister married a nationally known man frequently told her friends such things as: "Betsy [not her sister's real name] phoned me again last night from Europe and, as usual, talked on and on. You wouldn't believe the way she and Bill [not her husband's real name] lean on my judgment. Now they want me to pick them out a house to buy here. It's to be a little thing in the neighborhood of $150,000." Her friends were impressed.

Then came the day when her sister and brother-in-law arrived in town. She soon found herself walking around in their shadow. Her friends were using her as a stepping stone to get closer to them. Physical proximity, carrying the threat of comparison, destroyed the personally enhancing effects of her identification. Even more destructive was the experience of threatening psychological proximity, as one visitor asked her: "Did anyone else in your family ever do anything?"

Finally, were there feelings and behaviors characteristic of the rejected who were committed to significant achievements? To begin with, there was their high competitiveness, which implicitly seemed to say that they were searching for their font of personal worth primarily in how they compared with others. The exaggerated competitiveness of the rejected, it would seem, stemmed from the fact that their enduring needs for grounds of self-acceptance tended almost invariably to express themselves in comparisons with other people. Their feelings of personal inadequacy were never absolute; they were relative. "How," each of them repeatedly asked himself, "do I compare with this other person? Better? Worse?" Because they continually measured themselves against others, they remained invariably alert to almost any recognition given to others.

By the same token, they felt vulnerable to comparisons with others. It was enough for them to glimpse even the possibility of such comparisons being made to precipitate negative defensive reactions. A rejected woman, very conscious of her appearance, narrated that when she and her husband had been in a social situation, he had had the unmitigated gall to comment about another woman present: "She wears her clothes very well." Trying not to let her outrage show, she asked him, in cool indignation: "Just what kind of a slob does that make me?" She added: "As yet, I have not been able to forgive him for this insult."

This heightened awareness of the achievements and talents of other people, together with this constant tendency to compare themselves with others, was well described by Alfred Adler (3). To the extent that the rejected perceived any basis whatever for their being compared with others, praise or commendation of those others became threatening. Any remark which could be interpreted by the rejected to imply "Look at what that person has accomplished, and what have you done?" was devastating.

Some rejected habitually belittled the recognitions accorded to others. To the extent that they could reduce the stature of those who were being honored or acclaimed, the possibility of threat from comparisons with them was considerably lessened and their own stature could even be thereby enhanced. The quests of the rejected for grounds of thinking better of themselves appeared to be inseparably linked with their tendencies to lessen substantially the status of anyone capable of being menacingly compared with them. A rejected man who has managed to be self-employed during a good part of his life has, at times, worked under someone else. While in the subordinate position, he characteristically spoke of his business superior in such a way as to imply that he was completely independent of him. Occasionally, he spoke of his superior in patronizing terms. A listener could readily have received the impression that, in reality, he either has no one in a position of authority over him or that such a person was his superior in name only.

Such put-downs also formed the core of what some rejected presented as hilariously funny incidents. One rejected man has narrated humorous experiences in which he invariably presents himself as superior to another who might appear to be occupying a more important position than his own. On one occasion, referring to such a person, he recounted an amusing situation in which he felt sorry for "the poor little guy." He went on to indicate that he has had to rescue or protect this person in a number of situations in which "this born loser" felt helpless or inferior.

The use of belittling remarks offered the rejected the opportunity of lashing back at authority figures. The rejected demeaned persons in positions of authority over them by quoting, in their absence, alleged remarks still more prominent people had made against them. Such remarks attributed to a prominent person could not easily be verified. In fact, it was impossible to verify them in certain situations, such as after the death of the one being quoted. The rejected individual narrating one of these disparaging remarks would even begin with an apology for the other—such as, "He really shouldn't have said this, but . . ."—and then would proceed to quote a devastating remark calculated to undermine the stature of the authority figure being disparaged.

Achievement-hungry rejected endeavored to lower the stature of the parents who had rejected them. Where they had been rejected by both parents, their recall of parental behaviors and characteristics tended to focus on the personal failures of both parents. Those rejected by only one parent worked to diminish the personal standing of that parent. To the extent they were successful in doing this, they appeared to lessen somewhat their own feeling of hurt from parental rejection. There seemed to be further attenuation of this hurt when they were able, by recall, to enhance the accomplishments, wisdom, personality, and so on, of the nonrejecting parent. One man has repeatedly gone out of his way to lavishly praise the achievements of the parent who accepted him and, at the same time, has stressed in subtle ways the pitiful accomplishments of his rejecting parent. His attitude toward the rejecting parent has been patronizing.

What behavioral patterns were characteristic of the rejected (particularly women) who placed the emphasis of their endeavors to be somebody, not on their achievements, but on obtaining warm, amorous responses from others? For the most part, their preferences were primarily for reassuring, affectionate acceptances which usually included (but were not limited to) sexual expressions—but, if these were not forthcoming, then for conspicuous, sustained attention. They clung to their conviction that being loved just for themselves was not feasible; but, nonetheless, they never gave up their search for authentic love. Meanwhile, they settled for the closest approximation to genuine love and affection available to them. A woman whose parents never gave her any love or affection is convinced that she is not lovable nor even likeable; yet, without love and affection, she feels that she is a nobody. She is afraid she "will kick over the traces, morally, in order to get some affection, if not some love," because she is so starved for tenderness. She added: "Everybody is self-seeking anyway, so you have to pay for affection."

Rejected female affection-hunters usually found that their efforts to obtain acceptance and affection sooner or later backfired on them. Almost every such expression toward others ultimately carried with it the seeds of defeat. One woman feels that she has the proof in her moral record that she is not lovable. Nevertheless, she longs to be accepted for herself. Lacking this, she sees herself as having nothing. For some years, now, any clear evidence of affectionate acceptance (including sexual) by another, especially a man, has given a real lift to her self-concept. Her problem has been that, once she has permitted a man sexual liberties, it has been assumed that she would continue to do so. This immediately created, in her own mind, a doubt about the basis of her acceptance by him. Being sought after because she was a satisfying sex-object has ruined the uplifting effect of the relationship and is unacceptable. The result has been that every relationship with a man which began as gratifying for her inevitably has become such that she could no longer tolerate it.

Rejected female affection-hunters quite helplessly functioned in a manner designed to thwart the ultimate attainment of the very goals they hungered after. Their unceasing demands for affection and attention drove away those they were pursuing to feed their affection-hungers. Their affection-hungers, once turned loose, proved insatiable (54). They were never satisfied, no matter how much affection and attention were obtained at any given time. For the most part, they appeared to be on a collision course. By their relentless striving for complete possession and enslavement of the affection-givers, they inescapably invited eventual rejection. In time, they almost inevitably appeared to be so affectionately cannibalistic as to repulse those on whom they preyed. The feeling by the others that someone was attempting to feed emotionally off them was, after a time, experienced by them as personal violation, and so made their continuation in these relationships insufferable.

The rejected who failed to gain affection and so settled for seeking constant attention also appeared to operate in a similar self-defeating manner. Their excessive and unreasonable demands almost inevitably drove the people from whom they were seeking attention to cover. A rejected woman who is very lonely and depressed and afraid of "almost everything" claimed that, without understanding why, she *demands* so much attention from others that she continually loses her friends.

Some of the rejected women who focused on their needs for love and affection assigned a priority to satisfying these hungers in *safe* ways. Rejected single women, including some lesbians, longed to have babies of their own to whom they could give and from whom they could receive love and affection. They sensed that both the giving and the receiving of such love would be very safe.

One or another psychological mechanism was employed to remove from their affection-hunting behavior aspects which some rejected found personally unacceptable to them. In this way, they unwittingly succeeded in keeping these behaviors from becoming morally or otherwise personally intolerable. In order to attain and keep the popularity with men that she needs, one young woman feels she must yield to their requests for sexual intercourse. However, she cannot reconcile with her conscience the picture of herself as a sexually promiscuous woman.

This problem has been unconsciously solved for her. She has come to feel that these things are not actually happening to her but to some other truly unfortunate young woman. At the time she is engaging in sexual intercourse, her experience is that she is sitting off at a safe distance impersonally observing a young woman and a man across the room engaging in sexual relations. In a way, she does know it is she to whom this is happening; but, at the same time, she knows that her more real self is viewing the event from a distance in the role of a totally uninvolved observer. In order to make clear to me the impersonal nature of her spectator role, she mentioned that she has even imagined herself leisurely eating an apple while observing these "other" two people making love. Here, of course, the defense mechanism of dissociation was enabling her to reconcile with herself behavior that was incompatible with her moral standards.

Within this context, Becker maintains that schizoid persons, tending toward dissociation of their emotional and intellectual lives in order to alleviate their anxiety, mentally separate themselves from their bodies during the act of sexual intercourse. He adds that prostitutes, too, are said to actively practice such self-body separation to keep their inner persons intact and pure, no matter how degraded they might feel physically (15).

In close relationship to the priority some rejected assigned to winning affection from others was an intense fear that not everyone would like them. They were obsessed with fear of being disliked by anyone. Under the impact of this dread, they apparently paid little attention to and gained little rewarding experience from those who indicated that they liked them. The fact that even a large number of persons obviously cared for them didn't help. Regardless of how many people clearly were fond of them, if they felt even one person disliked them, it seemed to have the shattering effect of reinforcing their worst convictions about themselves.

For these rejected, being disliked appeared to run closely parallel to failure. Just as a thousand successes could not offset the devastating weight of one of their failures, so a multitude of people who cared for them could not counterbalance the lethal impact of one who disliked them. Their only recourse was to ensure that no one would ever dislike them. One rejected woman said that if she even suspects that someone does not care for her—even if it's a small child—"it just gets me . . . upsets me terribly."

In some of the rejected, this absorbing fear of being disliked dictated their distinctive pattern of relating to other people. One rejected man described his characteristic approach to other people as: "I crawl. I always crawl." With others, he continually apologizes, submits, and excuses himself "so they won't be able to dislike me." On several occasions, he has tried to enter one particular department store, but simply could not force himself to go through the door. His reason for being unable to enter was: "There is a person working in there, and I think he doesn't like me, though I'm not sure of it. But that's all it takes. I can't go in."

In some rejected, another experience that is closely related to the fear of being disliked is that they do not feel free to say no to the requests of others. It would be unthinkable for them to run the risk of having other people not like them if they refused. At the same time, they deeply resent being asked to do things for others. One rejected man finds that it is emotionally exhausting for him to have to take care of or even listen to the troubles of others in the family. Whenever he is asked to do any of these things, he feels resentful and angry; but he explained that he has never really been able to admit these feelings clearly to consciousness because of all the things his parents did for him. He concluded, "So I am just torn up inside." Now he finds he *has* to help, not only those in the family who appeal to him, but even those who have not asked but need him. The resulting bitter feelings that he both voluntarily and automatically pushes below his awareness have left him drained. He never understood this, he added, until very recently.

Some rejected remained painfully aware of their vulnerability resulting from their inability to say no to others. Because one rejected man has never learned to say no, he feels he is imposed upon continually. He summed it up this way: "Once people find out you will do things for them, they pour it on and *never* say 'thanks' or 'nice job'. They show no gratitude whatever. This just kills me."

Associated with the inability of some rejected to say no to others was a need to avoid any relationship that would, in almost any way, obligate them to others. They felt that any such relationship would sooner or later leave them exposed to unacceptable requests from others. One rejected man can't really return friendship and warmth to others, "for then," he explained, "they would expect much of you. You would find them leaning on you and would feel you have to live up to their expectations. You would have to do what they want you to do."

A partial explanation both for this inability to say no and for the resentment against those who asked might be that doing what others wanted was sensed, at some psychological level, as a repetition of the pattern which their rejecting parents had established. In addition, the rejected apparently felt they needed all their energy and time for their own endeavors in their search for grounds of self-acceptance. Having to do what others wanted, then, was resented seemingly as a repetition of hateful experiences, unacceptable interference, delay, and waste of needed energy.

Finally, a few rejected hit upon a combination of both achievement and affectionate acceptance in pursuing their goals. One rejected man now sees that a sexual conquest early in his life was motivated principally by striving to achieve success in a challenge and also to obtain deeply affectionate acceptance. He believed it when told that if he could get this girl to give herself to him he would really be *somebody*. Though his success didn't prove very satisfying, he was aware of seeking both the rewarding affection and the sense of accomplishment. This pattern has also held true, he added, of every sexual conquest he has made since.

Such a combined striving for both a significant achievement and a gratifying affective experience assumed, in a few of the rejected, the stature of being the preoccupying desire of their lives. An attractive woman had ardently desired for more than a year to experience tender expressions of affection, together with sexual intercourse, with the most outstanding man she had ever known. Humiliating as it was for her, she finally had to tell him of her desires. She was utterly frustrated when he kindly, but firmly, declined. At that time, she had no desire for this type of relationship with anyone else. She felt that, if her desire had been fulfilled, she would have experienced both an unbelievable warmth of affection and the achievement of her dream.

A comparison of these strivings of the rejected with those of people who felt warmly accepted and loved by their parents may help to point out the differences between the characteristic behaviors of the two groups. Every reasonably healthy person yearns to achieve some cherished goals and also needs to love and be loved. How, then, did the endeavors of the rejected, both to achieve success and to gain love, differ from those of the nonrejected? Apparently, there were three major differences.

First, there was a difference in terms of the *goal*. Many warmly accepted people spoke openly of their desires to realize themselves, achieve, create, express their uniqueness in some worthwhile way, and give and receive love and affection. This was far removed, however, from the constant endeavors flowing out of the absorbing need of the rejected to prove themselves. This kind of constrained hankering after goals is so difficult for the nonrejected to grasp that very few of them would fully comprehend one rejected man's candid remark that *"everyone* has to prove himself, and therefore *everyone* secretly longs for the highest positions of authority. Anyone who denies this is simply dishonest."

The needs of the warmly accepted, to express themselves and to relate affectionately to others, implicitly expressed their own affirmation of themselves as persons. By contrast, the needs of the rejected to prove themselves implicitly acknowledged the *absence* of their own affirmation of their value as persons. Only rarely did the rejected recognize their persistent urges to "score" through notable achievements or affectionate conquests as attempts to prove their worth *as persons.*

Alfred Adler hypothesized that everyone's foremost drive in life is a striving for superiority in order to compensate for his feelings of inferiority (3). I take issue with his position that *everyone* feels thus inferior. In my judgment, Adler correctly described the major goal of many, but not all, people. I readily agree that those who feel inferior have a compensatory drive to superiority. However, Adler appeared to single out achievement as the sole means to this goal, to the exclusion of the search for affection and/or attention, and I am at odds with this point of view.

Very few of the rejected, of course, recognized their drives for achievement or affection as compensations for their feelings of inferiority. Nonetheless, it did not occur to them to labor assiduously at tasks that did not give promise of notable recognition from others whose acknowledgment they sought. They apparently were not able to afford the luxury of pursuing something for its inherent interest. There was an almost incredible disinterest in what did not promise them enhancement in the eyes of others. Compliments from others appeared to constitute their life-sustenance.

A few rejected indicated their puzzlement at people who appeared to engage in any undertaking purely and simply for its own sake. How an individual could spend hundreds of hours, for instance, studying— solely from intellectual interest—the culture centered around the temple of the moon goddess at "Ur of the Chaldees," near the Tigris and Euphrates rivers, was unintelligible to one rejected man. What could this person possibly gain from such a study? What was in it for him?

Second, the *motives* underlying their behaviors differed. The endeavors of the rejected that were motivated by their search for disproofs of personal inadequacy differed from those of the nonrejected in terms of the intensity of the motivation. Even though the nonrejected were, at times, acutely aware of their needs to achieve and to give and receive affection, these needs were never the obsessive, compelling, driving, "do it or die" kinds of experiences they were for the rejected. In the rejected, even when inherent risks kept them from undertakings to prove their worth, these coercive urges continued to push inexorably for satisfaction at some psychological level.

The vexing needs of the rejected to search for grounds of self-acceptance were unmistakable. Getting the Ph.D. degree is a passion with one rejected man—he is unable to rest until he acquires it. He explained: "Then maybe they will *listen* to me—not necessarily believe me, but *hear* me." He hates degree worship in the United States, and remarked: "I resent everyone who has the damned Ph.D." His description of himself was: "A human whirlwind of energy, to whom laziness is simply impossible." He characterized his life as "drive, drive, drive."

The coercive needs of some rejected to excel produced unwholesome patterns of relating to others. One rejected woman *must* excel and lead. Just to go along with the group would be unthinkable for her. She can never ask a question of anyone unless she already knows the answer. Accordingly, she must either look up the answer to any question she has or forget about it. As a Catholic she has found that supernatural motivation and reassurance haven't seemed to help at all, because, despite these, she has remained painfully conscious of her inadequacy and full of resentment. Meanwhile, she would not dream of slacking in her efforts to lead.

Some rejected were so driven by their needs to achieve that they felt as if they were on a human treadmill, running with a frenzy. As a result, they were not able to stop long enough to produce anything significant. One rejected man is constantly, as he put it, pushing, driving, racing, doing. He has to keep going and going, faster and faster. As long as he can recall, he has longed to create—to produce something beautiful which would bear his personal imprint. He has craved this more than anything in the world. If he could only achieve, he knows it would help; but, thus far, he has not been able to do so.

Most rejected felt that to go on living in disregard of successes would be unthinkable. As one man uncouthly but astutely expressed it: "I have certain goals and ideals to attain. If I do not reach them, I'm a shit." Other rejected were equally determined that, unless they could satisfy their affection-hungers, their lives would be shams. If and when the rejected surrendered to fears and withdrew from seeking such successes, they found little peace. While thus in retreat, some of them felt they were being torn apart and they remained empty.

What did the rejected who were not retreating believe they were endeavoring to accomplish? Many felt committed to *disprove* what they thought of as their being inferior in some way, such as being stupid, shanty Irish, mere laboring class, uneducated, uncultured, or of some other "inferior" classification. Very seldom did their efforts take the naked form of trying to disprove their convictions that they felt they were zeroes.

In almost every sphere of their endeavors to attain success, the rejected repeatedly encountered a psychological conflict. The closer they came to their desired goals, the stronger became their avoidance urges. The nearer they came to psychologically exposing themselves to others in order to "score," the more threatened they felt by the increasing proximity of likely failure; hence, the stronger became their inclinations to withdraw. This helps to explain their frequently experienced reluctance to commit themselves beyond the point of return to many of their ventures. There were numerous occasions when the rejected deserved medals for bravery for undertaking challenges that would not have looked particularly hazardous to the nonrejected.

Third, there was a difference in the *satisfaction* derived. When nonrejected persons succeeded in accomplishing their goals, the satisfactions they usually experienced were both substantial and relatively lasting. This does not necessarily mean that once they achieved something worthwhile or experienced the love of others they no longer wanted anything more. It does mean that either of these experiences, when attained, proved rewarding and tended to endure—they could have rested on their laurels had they wanted to do so.

Alfred Adler very accurately described the inevitable lack of satisfaction which the rejected experience, even though he was referring to all people. He maintained that the need is to excel, to surpass, to get ahead of others, and there is no rest—no let-up (3).

Every satisfaction the rejected drew from their successes proved insufficient. It invariably failed to live up to expectations, and even left them feeling betrayed. Almost unbelievably less rewarding than they had anticipated, it also proved fleeting in nature. As one rejected, achievement-hungry man put it: "You begin by running for office when you are still in school. Later you strive for other prestigious goals and, even when you succeed, each of these in turn leaves you deeply unsatisfied."

Some of the achievement-bent rejected recognized that they were being whipsawed between the need to strive and their inability to interpret any success in terms of personal satisfaction. One rejected man works industriously to get the praise of others for what he has accomplished, and then, when it comes, it means nothing. He explained: "Really, you only did well what you were supposed to do.

There is no carry-away whatever from this." Nevertheless, he *has* to keep on striving each day for whatever recognition he can get from his accomplishments, even though he foresees that such recognitions will not be satisfying.

It was evident, then, that the *goals, motives,* and *satisfactions* associated with the endeavors of the rejected to achieve success and to experience love did differ from those that were characteristic of the nonrejected. My clinical findings provided the following insights with regard to frustrating experiences of the rejected.

Those who attempted to prove their personal adequacy by demonstrating one or more competencies discovered that, psychologically, it didn't work. Even when they had succeeded in impressing other people with such demonstrations, they themselves had remained unimpressed. Why? It would seem that they had not experienced a necessary link between their manifested accomplishments and their own assessment of their personal value. They found that they had continued to hold onto their very low opinions of themselves, even after they proved they were able to get better grades, type faster, sing better, make more money, and so on, than others. That they could do something better than others had proved nothing to them about what they *were*; it proved only what they could *do*.

Moreover, when the rejected tried to tell themselves that their personal worth had been demonstrated by what they had done, they could not accept it. They held all allegedly proving evidences up to the unshakable picture of their personal inadequacy, only to discover that the inadequacy had in no way been altered by all such proofs. At times they explained away all such substantiating evidences by logically emasculating all the proving power of these evidences.

A rejected college student, who had gone all-out for grades in order to prove himself, finally achieved straight A's. To his great disappointment, these superior grades really proved nothing. He explained:

> The A in history doesn't mean a thing. Anyone could get one. All you had to do was read and report on four extra books. In math, I simply lucked out. I know where the A in English came from. The prof taught and liked my dad. In chemistry, I memorized every formula in the book. That doesn't take any brains. That A simply says I've got a photographic memory, which they tell me some mental retards have. Besides, a one-semester performance proves nothing. So I got straight A's. Big deal! But could I do it again and again? I doubt it. Besides, even though I got all A's, and even if I should be able to prove I could do it again, *I* know that I could have done better. I should be perfect and I'm far from perfect in every one of these subjects.

Those who were preoccupied with their search for romantic and passionate responses from others had been faced with their own peculiar problems. The void these affection-hunters longed to fill had turned out to be a bottomless pit. Irrespective of the amount of affection they had received, it was never enough (10). They had remained unsatisfied. Nevertheless, they continued to strain for more and more of it, holding desperately to the hope that if they eventually got enough they would be sufficiently gratified and content.

Their experiences had shown the rejected that there was no way they could win in their endeavors to achieve satisfaction. Those who, on the verge of panic, had given up the struggle remained miserable. Those who had persevered in trying to achieve in notable fashion or to obtain affectionate acceptance from others experienced frustration on top of frustration. This held true even for those who had succeeded in accomplishing their objectives. Knowing no other way of striving, however, they had continued in the very same patterns only to experience disappointment after disappointment in their unhappy lives.

5
Fear in the Rejected

It would be difficult to find an area of psychological research that generates more disagreement than that of the study of feelings and emotions. Treating anything appropriately in this general psychological area is admittedly something of a Herculean task. Sigmund Freud, a leader in both academic and clinical investigations of fear and closely related feelings, put the problem concisely: "Shall we ever succeed, one cannot help asking, in understanding the differences between these various affects of unpleasure?" (61, p. 132).

With full recognition that much of this area is still unsettled, an attempt should be made at the outset of this chapter to clarify the meaning of fear. Defined descriptively, fear is an experience characterized by a *specific* feeling of unpleasantness, accompanied by activity of the sympathetic nervous system and various types of postural and motor reactions (206). It should be kept in mind that fear, viewed as an internal behavior, is an immediate datum of one's experience. Everyone knows from his own living what it is to be afraid.

A fear which was universally experienced by the rejected was anxiety (73, 143). The scientific study of anxiety, ever since Freud's early treatment of it, has been replete with disagreements. What was Freud's conception of the nature of anxiety? Unfortunately, though Freud treated anxiety at length in a number of works and specifically in his book *Inhibitions, Symptoms, and Anxiety* (61), he was never conspicuous for his clear-cut definitions.[1] He characterized anxiety as a response to a perceived danger of object loss, and asserted that it was a distinctive kind of unpleasurableness accompanied by definite physical sensations experienced in specific organs, such as the respiratory organs and the heart. Freud understood anxiety as being a specific state of unpleasure accompanied by motor discharge along definite pathways (61).

His analysis uncovered three attributes within anxiety experiences:

---

[1]While Freud used the German word "angst" in the majority of his writings, he employed the words "angoisse" and "anxiéte" to render this term in French (61). His daughter Anna, who supervised the English edition of her father's complete psychological works, approved the translation of "angst" as "anxiety" (62).

(1) a specified and qualitatively distinct, unpleasurable experience; (2) motor discharge phenomena in the body; and (3) some consciousness of both of the foregoing. Not every unpleasurable experience, then, was viewed by Freud as anxiety. Grief and sorrow—though unpleasurable experiences—were not anxiety, precisely because they were not the qualitatively distinctive experiences of being afraid.

Apparently until the end of his life, Freud was inclined strongly to the position that every experience of anxiety was also a reproduction of one's trauma at birth—the fear he assumed everyone experiences while being born (61). The centrality of the birth trauma in explaining subsequent fear experiences was later emphasized by Freud's early coworker and disciple, Otto Rank. Other authors insist that *anxiety* involves a combination of affective experiences. They see anxiety as fear plus at least two of the following: distress, shame, shyness, guilt, anger, and the positive emotion of interest excitement (188).

Areas of disagreement among psychologists and psychiatrists about anxiety are not limited to its definition, however, but reach out to the causes of anxiety, the exact differences between anxiety, fear, insecurity, and phobia, and the differences between normal and neurotic anxiety. There is, nonetheless, a general consensus among authors that anxiety is one kind of a *fear* experience. A treatment of this fear experience termed *anxiety*, as it was experienced by the rejected, calls for further clarification of its meaning. Helpful light can be thrown on the distinction between anxiety and other fears by examining them in terms of what is perceived as being threatened or endangered.

My position, which is shared by some others (10), is that human fear is a person's spontaneous, emotional response to the stimulus of a perceived danger or threat to one or more of his important values. For example, if one were threatened with a broken limb or other serious damage, he would feel fear. If, on the other hand, someone were to threaten to break his pencil, he would not experience fear since, presumably, he does not place a high, personal value on the pencil. Such a "threat," however, might occasion in him some other unpleasant response such as annoyance.

Accordingly, to the extent an individual values highly his marriage, job, social reputation, and so on, he experiences fear when he becomes aware of a threat or danger to any one of these. I employ the term "insecurity" to denote any fear resulting from a serious *identifiable* threat to any important value of a person, aside from his self-esteem. This would include his existence, integrity, safety, well-being, and so on (10).

What then is anxiety? Anxiety is that fear which a person spontaneously experiences when, at some level of knowing, he is aware that the important value being threatened is his feeling of worth—his adequacy *as a person.* Anxiety, therefore, is one's response to his perception of a threat to his own personal adequacy. He need not be *openly* aware of it, but it seems that the identity of such a threat must be recognized at some level of knowledge by the anxious person.

Anxiety, thus conceived, can coexist with insecurity. For example, suppose a prominent adult in the community, acting on impulse, were to climb the scaffolding of a building under construction in the neighborhood. As he moves cautiously along a plank across the face of the building, he hears the plank begin to give way beneath his weight. There is simply no way he can keep from falling. In the few moments he precariously balances there on the cracking timber, awaiting the inevitable crash to the ground some twenty feet below, he is petrified with fear. What is he afraid of? He fears at least some broken bones and, most likely, serious facial or other disfigurements. These fears are termed "insecurity" fears or simply experiences of "insecurity."[2] At the same time, he is anticipating the reactions of astonishment from his family and friends, and their inevitable loss of esteem for him once they learn what a childish stunt he has pulled in climbing the scaffolding. He leans heavily on the good opinion of these people who are so important in his life. To the extent he foresees that they will think less of him, he experiences the fear of loss of self-esteem. This fear is termed "anxiety."

In other words, "anxiety" is the fear that individuals experience when faced with the prospect of really "looking bad" to those whose opinions they value, or of doing something which would make them lose respect for themselves. This explanation of anxiety need not imply their *conscious* identification of such a threat, but only that they somehow sensed it. For the most part, the rejected suffering from anxiety were not clearly aware of any threat that could account for this experience. Later, when some of them did become satisfied that what was being threatened was their self-esteem, they found that their anxiety remained largely unabated.

Much of the lack of agreement about anxiety has centered on the term "neurotic anxiety" (107). Is there any recognized distinction between normal and neurotic anxiety? Freud's original distinction still receives considerable respect. For Freud, while normal anxiety ("real-angst") is a response to a danger we know, neurotic anxiety ("angst") is a response to a danger we do not know (61). One man occasionally—

[2]Freud used the German term "furcht" rather than "angst" if a fear experience had found an object (62).

without warning and with no knowledge of any danger or threat—undergoes a most frightening experience of which he lives in dread. He feels a sudden wave of fear during which he has what he describes as "hot flashes," after which he literally shakes for days. This gradually passes into tension which, in its turn, usually lasts for weeks.

A high negative correlation has been found between anxiety and self-esteem. Of all the rejected who talked to me over a lengthy period of time, I do not recall one who failed to manifest a fear experience which permeated his life. With the exception of the fear of failure (which will be treated later in this chapter), that experience seemed to possess the tell-tale characteristics of anxiety. Other studies seem to bear this out. Koch's study of children from broken homes is one example. She found that, among these children, those who were rejected by their mothers had significantly high anxiety test scores (96).

What were the earmarks of the anxiety experienced by a large number of the rejected? For the most part, they were the characteristics of "neurotic" anxiety, which Freud described as "objectless," "free-floating," and "disproportionate" (62). In the experiences of the rejected, their anxiety frequently moved from one of these three characteristics to another or the characteristics often dovetailed. Accordingly, more than one of these characteristics will be found in some of the following reported experiences.

The "objectless" aspect which characterized much of their anxiety should not be understood as a contradiction of the current psychological position, mine included, that every emotional experience is assumed to be a response to a definite stimulus. The "objectless" experience was in no sense understood to be a denial of the existence of any specific threat or danger to the persons who reported these fear experiences. It was, rather, that they failed to perceive clearly what was threatening them. They were unable to make sense out of their fear. One rejected man's anxiety is so bad that he fears he will "throw in the towel" and move into insanity. He described his life as "fears, fears, fears." He feels it is like fighting a shadow, since he doesn't know what he fears.

The contents of "objectless" anxiety experiences were described in remarkable detail by some of the rejected. In giving these descriptions, they often stressed the element of instability. An "objectless" fear had, without warning, suddenly attached itself to some object. It had just as suddenly shifted to another object and then to still another. A highly intelligent professional man lives in continual fear, which often takes the form of "naked fear," which he describes as "the fear of fear." He feels it is much like the fear he imagines he would experience were he to walk perilously close to the edge of the abyss of nothingness. It is like the fear of ceasing to exist—the fear of being utterly annihilated. He has also feared greatly a large number of things, one at a time, with what his mind tells him is a ridiculous fear. Among the fears that have tortured him are failing in his present profession, various illnesses, insanity, and death.

During the periods between these specific fears, he has returned to the fear of fear. In the face of this horrible fear, he feels completely helpless because he can think of absolutely nothing he can do to protect himself from it. While in it, his whole being is threatened. Frequently he has asked himself if it really isn't the fear of insanity. He cannot be sure. Readily admitting that he is highly suggestible, he suspects that suggestion may be a factor in his torturing himself about one thing after another. For instance, his eyes begin to blur and bother him, then it is his stomach that worries him, and so forth. Always his anguish is about only one thing at a time. When fear is so specified, he pointed out, only a part and not the whole of his being is threatened.

Recently he is beginning to see that each of these worries is, to him, a definite, limited specification of, and substitute for, his fear of fear. When specified as an identifiable threat to a part of him, he can take some measure to protect himself against it. He has also found that, if he can get all wrapped up and enthusiastically involved in some project, he can for a time escape both the fear of fear and every specification of it. This, however, won't last longer than a week or so, and in his relatively unafraid state he then begins to fear the return of the fear of fear.

Moreover, feelings of guilt without sufficient foundation have tortured him for years. He now sees these guilt feelings as other substituted specifications for his fear of fear. In addition, he has come to understand more about the psychological role these groundless feelings of guilt have unconsciously been playing. In them, he recognizes not only additional specifications of his fear of fear, but also a means of withdrawing from the reality of self-determination with its obligations and uncertainties. He recognizes it particularly as a withdrawal from the calculated risks that are rooted in human freedom.

It is characteristic of him to be tremendously concerned about foreseeing and safeguarding himself against all future dangers. He is constantly on guard against every possible future calamity, including his own eternal salvation. All his worries and fears, he has concluded, are ultimately reducible to his insecurity—a basic insecurity, he said, in which the gloom descends on him like a large tarp and enfolds his very being and especially his mind, which he sees as his principal manifestation of living.

The "free-floating" aspect of anxiety in many of the rejected was presumed to be a displacement of their "objectless" fear experiences. They described their tendency to be dreadfully afraid of one specific thing at a time. When they moved away from that one fear, they often moved into a between-specific-fears period during which they were just afraid without being aware of what they feared. Shortly thereafter, they would begin to worry about and become fearful of some specific danger. One man was working dangerously high off the ground in bridge repair. This felt good, precisely because he was high enough to be at a safe distance from other people. Safe in the conviction that he was able to do the job better than most men, he had only one thing to fear and that was that he might fall. Because he was dreadfully afraid of falling, he was utterly puzzled to find himself repeatedly taking unwise chances. Each time he did so, he would experience intense fear. Because he was inclined to loaf on the job, he feared others might observe his poor performance. This made him feel unhappy, insecure, and anxious. There have been other times when he has driven a car so dangerously fast through the city that it has really scared him. What baffles him is that, when he became aware of doing so, instead of slowing the car he invariably increased the speed to the point where he became still more fearful. Also, periodically, he has been almost obsessed with the fear of being beaten up physically by some men.

The anxieties of some rejected presumably were so completely displaced to another person that there was no experience whatever of feeling afraid for themselves. One rejected woman continually agonizes about the harm that can come to her teenage son. When he leaves the house, she literally runs after him to make sure that he is wearing his rubbers if it looks like rain, or a scarf if it is getting cold. All the while he is out of the house she is beside herself with additional distress that other kids or some adult will corrupt him morally. She is apprehensive as well that he could be physically hurt and she would not hear about it until it was too late for her to help him. Even when he is safely at home in bed, she frequently can't sleep with presentiments about what could happen to him the following day. Before her son was born, she had been worried sick for months on end that we would go to war, and before that she had fretted that there would be another great depression in the United States.

There was an unrecognized impatience in some rejected to latch on to some particular thing they could worry over. During the course of several weeks, one rejected man was terribly upset, sleeping very poorly, and trying with all his strength to accept what God was letting happen to him. He felt certain that he was going blind with glaucoma.

Afraid to go to the doctor because a medical examination would only confirm this fact, he lived in agony until he could no longer stand not knowing. The eye specialist gave him a clean bill of health. Despite his great relief, he found that he could not really relax. During the following days, he had a vague sense of uneasiness and was waking up at night in cold sweats. Later, the cold, night sweats ceased, but again he was not sleeping well. Recently, he has been reading everything he can find about the SALT talks. He has gradually become convinced that the Russians are just biding their time to drop H-bombs on us. He has become convinced of the absolute necessity of digging and equipping, without further delay, an H-bomb shelter in his back yard. He is apprehensive, however, that people will laugh at him for doing so.

This behavioral impatience to latch on to one particular thing at a time to worry about and then, inevitably, to go on to something else did not go unrecognized in all the rejected. One man reminds himself of a terrier because of the way he relentlessly persists in worrying about one thing at a time until he has "wrung it dry." Then he finds no rest until he happens upon something else to fuss about. Over the years he has anguished, one at a time, over such things as not graduating from college, losing his job, cancer, the loss of his credit rating, and so on.

The "free-floating" aspect of anxiety manifested in the foregoing examples has been interpreted to involve the unrecognized conversion of unspecified fears, through *displacement*, into specific fears of some identifiable dangers or threats. Faced with specific dangers, the rejected were able to take steps to protect themselves.

Some rejected displaced not just the dangers but also the important values being threatened. Such a twofold displacement defines "phobia," which is regarded as that displaced anxiety in which one perceives some other danger to some other personal value. For example, germs could be greatly feared as threats to one's health. Such specific, substituted dangers, in order to be maintained at the focal point of fear and worry by the rejected, had to remain serious threats. However, if the teeth of these threats were pulled, they could no longer serve as substitute dangers for the actual threats producing the anxiety. Accordingly, they could no longer produce adequate substitute fears for the fear of anxiety.

One woman was terribly worried that she had breast cancer because she was terrified at the thought of a mastectomy. Months later, she submitted to a medical examination—much as she feared it—in order to test the grounds of her worry. The medical examination produced negative findings. From that moment, the considerably diminished fear of breast cancer could no longer function as an adequate substitute for her basic, strong fear of anxiety, and so her naked fear of anxiety returned.

An "objectless" fear of the magnitude of her anxiety could no longer be packaged in her greatly diminished fear of breast cancer. However, during the time that it did serve her as a substitute, without her being aware of it, she was by no means helpless against it. She could and did have a medical examination, which lessened the substituted threat and therefore momentarily succeeded in reducing the corresponding fear resulting from it. Some rejected recognized that whenever one thing they feared had been proven to be no longer seriously threatening, they had shortly afterwards fastened onto something else to fear and worry about.

The "disproportionate" aspect of anxiety in a number of the rejected referred to their tendency to respond to perceived dangers or threats with what appeared to others to be overreactions. Their fears appeared unreasonable and exaggerated. For instance, obsessive fears centered about their having to adjust to changes of job, neighborhood, school, and living arrangement, and were specified, as well, in their fears of illness, death, business reversal, failure, breakup of marriage, and so on.

The underlying assumption in each of these "disproportionate" affective reactions was that the person unconsciously substituted a specific, concrete danger, through displacement, for the threat to his self-esteem. His resulting insecurity unknowingly then became a stand-in for his fear of anxiety. The motivation for unconsciously arranging such a substitute was self-protection. Since he could do something effective about lessening the proximity of the danger, he thereby automatically diminished the resulting, painful fear experience which had taken the place of his anxiety. By contrast, as long as he experienced "objectless" anxiety, the danger he was confronted with remained hidden from him, thus leaving him powerless to cope in any effective way with it.

The "disproportionality" so evident in some of these fearful reactions was recognized by some rejected in an *intellectual* way. At their *feeling* level, however, these seemingly overreactive fears were experienced as responses well proportioned to the magnitude of the threats. For instance, one man's *head* told him that his fear of heights was disproportionate. The fact that merely standing on a chair left him petrified with fear was a disproportionate response to the danger involved. His intense fear was, nevertheless, well proportioned emotionally to such an action, since he *felt* it to be endangering his very life.

The anxiety of the rejected, especially when not displaced, carried with it an awareness of some bodily processes (62). The motor responses experienced in conjunction with feelings of anxiety—especially when these feelings were unconsciously maintained below the level of awareness—were particularly manifested as pressure or tension. Such tension was dreaded by some of the rejected principally because it inevitably interfered with their effective performances.

This pressure had been felt in various parts of the body, often in those directly related to the performances of the rejected. It had, for instance, been experienced in the hands and arms of a pianist and a basketball player, the throat of a singer, the legs of a runner, and so on. In general, a whole range of such pressures, situated even in parts of the body not related to performance, had been experienced. The rejected had been aware of such tension-associated motor responses as: irregular heart rhythm, irregular breathing, visual disturbances, chronic fatigue, feelings of suffocating, fainting, tingling of hands, fingers, and toes, chest constriction, bowel problems, ringing or buzzing in the ears, gastric discomforts, and irritability (47).

The rejected had also been conscious of tension-associated loss of appetite, insomnia, the heart beating as if it would burst through the rib cage, palms perspiring profusely, coldness in the extremities, headaches, trembling, and so forth. One rejected man's head had felt as if a steel band were being steadily tightened around it until he was sure something in his head would burst.

Some psychological situations appeared to be peculiarly linked with the prominence of tension in the experience of the rejected. One was the conflict experienced by the rejected who *consciously* persisted in refusing to face their rejection. These rejected continually denied or turned their attention away from both the evidence of their rejection and the feeling that they had been rejected. One man reported that he has been tormented with tension. At times, along with the tension, he experiences a deluge of delusions in which he is almost certain that he is being persecuted. He has to fight these delusions with every last ounce of his strength, lest he succumb to them. He also spoke of his fears that he is going insane. Repeatedly, he has characterized his parents as wonderful, religious people who have lived by the highest standards.

More recently, he has begun to experience doubts about how his parents feel toward him but, when these thoughts come, he immediately pushes them to the back of his mind. Nevertheless, additional thoughts, along with accompanying doubts, continue to surface in his awareness. His reaction to these thoughts is to become more convinced than ever that he must be great so his parents can look up to him. He remarked that tension has a paralyzing effect on him, since his memory, as well as his thinking, are adversely affected by it. At times undisguised fear will break through into his consciousness and last for days. When it finally goes, he is left with chronic tension.

Other rejected persons spoke of the persisting physiological tensions associated with their failures. Several of the rejected of both sexes reported unbearable tensions related to their commitments to strive for important objectives. These tensions often proved to be utterly baffling. In fact, most of these people did not have a clue as to their meaning. A few of them, however, identified the tensions as the physiological companion-states of their fears of failure, which are present within the framework of all of their significant commitments.

Peculiarly linked to a salient experience of tension in the rejected was the feeling of being compelled to bottle up their resentments. One rejected person who has kept going faster and faster in his work fears he is heading towards psychological exhaustion. He explained that the air pressure on his ear drums is not equal in the middle and outer ears, and so he must constantly readjust it by swallowing and yawning. This condition, he pointed out, is caused by tension-induced spasms of the musculature which normally regulates the equalization of pressure on his eardrums.

For some years he has been aware of mounting tension. His father and mother fought during all the time he lived at home. He felt that he was miles away from his dad in every important way, but nonetheless took his side in the arguments because his mother nagged his father constantly and never helped him to carry the burdens. All his life, he has known that he could never really talk to either of them so he kept everything locked up inside him. He still can't really talk to anyone without the greatest difficulty and reluctance.

Over the years he has stifled every resentment of others and every criticism of others. This is especially so since the time he spoke out to his mother for the way she was being unfair to his father. He will never forget how she clobbered him with the statement: "After all I've done for you and slaved for you, I never dreamed that you could be so ungrateful as to turn on me in my weakness, now when I really need you. . . ." Just recalling it causes tension.

He is convinced that tension makes a man still more terribly lonely. It isolates him, cuts him off, so that even though he can ask intelligent questions he can't communicate. He can't give or contribute anything. Tension keeps him a slave. It will not let him go to other people, but forces him to be introspective and keeps him from making decisions. Just as he did with his parents, he now suppresses his resentment for the way he is treated by anyone in authority. When he does so, he inevitably experiences tension, and the tension leads to fear. For him, tension means unhappiness and terrible insecurity.

It is a vicious circle. Tension causes him to forget many things, and such forgetting increases his difficulty in conversing with others. As a result, he just doesn't try to speak with other people. This absence of communication with other people causes more tension. Once, to his complete surprise, the tension left him for about twenty minutes and it was a different world—one that was "unbelievably wonderful."

The pain of clearly recognized anxiety was so excruciating that a number of the rejected *consciously* used some means to attempt to lessen that pain. Some took the pleasure route, because pleasure seemed to compensate for suffering. One man had abandoned himself completely to sexual pleasures in order to get away from the anxiety. After a time he found that it did not help. His experience of incessant sexual indulgence proved increasingly cloying. As he summarized it, "it's ashes in your mouth."

Some rejected strove to deal with their experienced anxiety by trying to conceal it from the eyes of others. A woman remembers that when she was only five years old she was terrified of dogs because she had been bitten. In spite of her terror, she deliberately teased her own dog until he bit her in order to master her fear of being bitten by a dog. She succeeded in this endeavor to the extent that, afterwards, neither people nor dogs knew how afraid she was of being bitten. She feels this same pattern is being repeated as she sits in counseling, for she is talking about her fears and problems to me so that she won't be afraid of "being bitten," i.e., hurt by other persons, later.

As already pointed out in the discussion on means of concealing the "real self" from others, some rejected attempted to lessen their feelings of anxiety by locking themselves, as far as possible, into the present time. They attempted to close out of their thoughts both the future and the past. An anxiety-ridden man found that it helps to live solely in the present. He strives to disregard both the past and, especially, the future. He knows that certain of his actions and omissions, such as withdrawing socially from others, will be harmful to him in the long run; but he doesn't care as long as it gives him present relief. Regardless of every other consideration, he explained, it is only with the present time, that he can afford to concern himself.

Some rejected consciously sought to reduce the pain of anxiety by removing themselves from painful aspects of reality. They also conjured up antidotes to the pain of anxiety where they had not found such antidotes in reality. When things get really bad for one man, he invariably gets some relief by persuading himself that all reality, especially hurtful reality, is a mirage. When another man is lonely, empty, and hurting, he deliberately separates himself by selective attention from all such feelings until he no longer feels any pain. Still another man is determined that he simply is not going to be without sensible consolation. Hence, he sees to it that he always feels good. He accomplishes this by disregarding everything hurtful, particularly in interpersonal relations, and by selectively letting in only those aspects of life that are pleasant. Then he creatively uses his imagination to invent whatever is still wanting to sustain uninterrupted, pleasant experiences.

In view of the described anxiety in the rejected, it seems well to examine here what some well-known authors see as the source of such anxiety. Do they agree that rejection can be the source of such anxiety?

No concept was more central to Freud's psychoanalytic theory than that of anxiety, but he was sorely pressed to explain the causation of the anxiety he found in so many of his patients. He repeatedly altered his explanation of its source. In 1894 and 1895, he regarded sexual abstinence as a cause of anxiety. By 1909 he felt that infantile masturbation between the ages of three and five was a cause. More specifically, he saw anxiety as the product of a conflict between the child's sexual urges involved in masturbation and his other ego inclinations. In 1912 he said anxiety was the result of a person's masturbatory activity (62).

By 1926 Freud openly acknowledged how little was known about anxiety. At that time he explained it as a person's reaction to the danger of the loss of an important object—that is, one's reaction to the loss of an important object is pain; his reaction to the *danger* of that loss is anxiety. After that, he considered repression as the cause of anxiety; but in 1933 he did an about-face, declaring that repression was not the cause, but rather the effect, of anxiety (62). Finally, he held that the feared instinctual situation implicit in all anxiety ultimately goes back to some external situation of danger. He analyzed the unknown dangers triggering anxiety as unrecognized instinctual dangers (61). It may be helpful to recall that throughout his life Freud suffered from fears, especially the fear of death, and increasingly came to view his world with a feeling of terror (15).

It was late in his life when Freud gave attention to the fear of death as a source of anxiety. In *Inhibitions, Symptoms, and Anxiety* he says: " . . . nothing similar to death has ever been experienced. I therefore maintain that the fear of death is to be regarded as an analogue of the fear of castration, and that the situation to which the ego reacts is the state of being forsaken by the protecting super-ego—by the powers of destiny—which puts an end to security against every danger" (61, p. 130).

Freud's final conception that anxiety's origin was situated in the fear of death has been masterfully developed by Becker, who endeavors to show that death is man's peculiar and greatest anxiety. He finds much of the source of anxiety in the universal terror of death, which in many persons is repressed. He upholds the psychoanalytic position that the child is filled with terror precisely in that he is different from the animal. The child's fears, including anxiety, are fashioned out of the way he perceives the world (15). It would be about as difficult to disprove Becker's position as it would be to prove it; and Freud's position, because it changed so frequently, makes evaluation most difficult.

Otto Rank emphasized the idea he shared with Freud—that the birth process is the font of anxiety. According to this position, the experience of being born causes anxiety in the child. The child is born with a fear of life itself, which is changed forthwith into fear or anxiety of certain people or things (153). It is impossible to establish scientifically that the infant actually experiences fear in the birth process, and I believe that Rank's position is based on a debatable assumption.

For some existentialists, the fundamental source of people's anxiety is not to be found in any specific thing that has happened to them, such as rejection, but instead flows from the human condition itself. Heidegger's conception is that it is in the face of the world itself that one has constant anxiety (80). If this were true, most people—if not all—would be expected to experience some form of chronic, painful anxiety. I have not found this to be the case.

May and DeForest both differ with the position that rejection alone could produce the kind of anxiety which has been described in these pages. While they find the source to be external rather than innate, both differ with the view of rejection as a cause of anxiety for almost identical reasons. May maintains that the source of such anxiety is not parental rejection, but the child's inability to evaluate parental attitudes realistically (122). DeForest locates the source of this anxiety in the child's reaction to the simultaneous parental presentation of affectionate words and hostile behaviors (43). Both positions, in my judgment, do not preclude their data being interpreted as evidences of parental rejection.

Mowrer sees such anxiety as having a source in experiences other than rejection. A person's anxiety originates, according to his thinking, in the denial of his guilt and in his fear of retribution for both his personal repudiation of moral urgings and his past transgressions against society. These two experiences—guilt and fear of social reprisal—are then repressed and become transformed into conscious anxiety (131). In the rejected, guilt and fear of retribution were frequently experienced (as indicated in the chapter on guilt). Nevertheless, these two experiences, rather than appearing to be causes of basic anxiety, seemed to be its by-products. I see no problem in granting that both guilt and fear of retribution could add to the intensity of the basic anxiety already present from the recognition of the parental rejection.

For Goldstein, the source of such anxiety is the experience of a child's being placed in catastrophic, adjustive situations in which he cannot cope, and in which he therefore finds his existence threatened (70). Goldstein would at least seem to allow that rejection could be regarded as one of the adjustive situations which could cause this anxiety.

Horney would probably disagree that this kind of anxiety comes from rejection because of her stress on conflict as the salient source of such anxiety. According to her position, the conflict in question is that which wells up from a person's "neurotic trends" (84). Nevertheless, Horney seems to agree that the "neurotic trends" themselves originated in those persons' experiences in childhood who were not warmly loved by their parents.

White would also take issue with the position that such anxiety arises from rejection. He chooses to analyze this anxiety in terms of a person's perceived incompetency. For White, anxiety and personal incompetency are positively correlated. Accordingly, he sees this type of anxiety as being caused by the feeling of a person that he is incompetent to deal with what is present (208). My difficulty with accepting this position is that the apprehension people sense in undertaking tasks they feel they cannot successfully accomplish seems to be a different kind of experience from the chronic anxiety being discussed here. In addition, perceived incompetency was not experienced by nonrejected persons as being inevitably associated with basic anxiety.

Allport's position appears to be that the source of anxiety is not wholly innate. He seems to concede that a "rejective home" can contribute to this anxiety, but nevertheless maintains that the basic source of one's anxiety lies in his innate inadequacy and dread of life. He maintains that most people are buffeted by the anxieties of existence and the normal fears of death and disaster, and that these, *augmented* by economic insecurity, affectional deprivation, and feelings of guilt, are the fonts of anxiety (9). However, in one of his books, he comes close to the position that parental rejection can be a main source of such anxiety when he asserts that "pathological anxiety" may be nothing more than the manifestations of unresolved infant distress (8).

My position is that a person's knowledge, at whatever level, that he has received parental rejection is alone sufficient to produce this personally destructive anxiety. In all the years of my professional experience, I do not recall even one rejected person who failed to report during the course of counseling at least the basic elements of such anxiety. Each of the rejected, even if he was conscious of no fear experience at the time, revealed at least physiological processes attesting to underlying anxiety. Those rejected who were aware of only physiological concomitants of anxiety early in counseling invariably experienced anxiety later on.

In view of these findings, I suggest the following hypothesis: A person's knowledge, at some psychological level, that he has received parental rejection results in the feeling that he is worthless, unwanted, and unlovable. The anxiety which he sooner or later experiences is the painful aftermath and evidence of his having experienced such a feeling.

The damage to his self-concept that results from such a feeling is devastating. From that point on, irrespective of how competent he might otherwise have been, he feels inadequate as a person. This feeling of inadequacy appears to be the source of his constant anxiety; hence, he spontaneously reacts with fear in the presence of anything that threatens to show this inadequacy to others. This appears to explain also why he experienced anxiety when faced with the prospect of failure. In his eyes, his inadequacy as a person is evident to himself, even if not to others, in his every failure. Meanwhile, his painful anxiety is often attenuated by his spontaneous and unknowing recourse to one of the defense mechanisms. Regardless of the nature of the specific defense mechanism employed, its ultimate function is to reduce the intensity of the anxiety in some way.

Was not the fear of *failure* an affective reaction to the perception of a threat to something other than one's self-esteem? Not really. The fear of failure, as I viewed it in the rejected, was a response to the threat of a manifestation of their personal inadequacy. From this viewpoint, then, the fear of failure was a specific exhibition of their damaged self-esteem, which left the rejected feeling not only that their personal worthlessness had once again been displayed, but also that they had been psychologically stripped naked before others.

The rejected lived in fear. Its intensity varied with changes in situations and other factors. However, there were times when even those rejected whose fears were normally very intense became almost oblivious of them. As already indicated, many of their fears were responses to nonidentified dangers. A number of the rejected awakened each morning, afraid. Afraid of what? Frequently, they didn't know. Some characterized it as not being afraid of anything but, nonetheless, afraid.

However, irrespective of the specificity of both the dangers and objects of their fears, all of the rejected eventually had experienced the fear of failure. Some testified that this fear was unquestionably stimulated by a recognized specific danger—for example, the danger of failing as a teacher or as a parent. But, whether the rejected had been tortured with fears from specific dangers or had been preoccupied with unspecified fears, they had all dreaded failure. Failure for them, even in contemplation, was most disruptive. Because the rejected were drawn so strongly toward people in their bids for either affection or recognition, they felt their failures had usually been witnessed by others. Thus, the truth of their lack of personal worth—so manifest to them—had been seen by others.

In what common areas was failure dreaded? It often was the fear of failing in some kind of performance in the public eye. Frequently, it was an area associated with their life's work, where the threat was readily identified. One man, who is in an administrative position, fears the insubordination of those under his authority. Never far from him is the fear that they might challenge him. One of his dreads is that they will gang up on him in some difference of opinion or decision and, by reason of sheer numbers, overwhelm him or shout him down.

Many rejected had a constant preoccupation with "success." While everyone enjoys success, the rejected—whether it was in the area of achievement or that of interpersonal relationships—felt they needed it as they needed air, food, and water to sustain their lives. There could never be enough success. By contrast, falling short of any goal had inevitably spelled out failure in their eyes. Many of the rejected saw themselves as perfectionists. They tended to view, for instance, a grade of 98 percent, not as excellent, but as falling 2 percent below what it could and should have been. Hence, it was but one more failure, even if a lesser one.

The rejected were ceaselessly whipsawed between their consuming need to succeed and their almost paralyzing fear of failure. This seemed to be the reason why a number of them were so concerned about erecting safeguards in anything they attempted. This experience of being harassed between an all-important need to succeed and a devastating fear of failing produced in them a state of physiological tension. There was no way they could shake it. Their inability to accept their successes as proofs of their personal worth left them helplessly mired in the grip of fear-induced tension.

Everyone experiences failures and dislikes doing so. What then was different about the impact on the rejected of their personal failures? It was havoc. In their eyes, their failures placed the verifying seal of their actual experiences on the low evaluations they held of themselves *as persons*. One rejected woman must punish herself for all her failures "because," she explained, "they show up my lack of true worth."

Did the rejected who were deeply religious find the brunt of their failures notably cushioned by religious considerations? They did not. One young woman cannot understand why she gets and stays depressed and discouraged after her failures, especially in her studies, when she knows of Christ's personal love for her. This, she says, only leads her to feel still more guilty because of the evident weaknesses in her hope and trust in God.

The rejected repeatedly stated their convictions that their failures, especially their moral failures, had clinched once and for all the matter of their worthlessness. Failures constituted, for them, incontrovertible disclosures that they were no good. One rejected woman received no rest until she put herself through the torture of showing me "the most unlovely part" of herself. It was her personal record of moral failures. She could scarcely believe, let alone understand, how I could continue to accept her as a person in view of what I now knew about her. She added that, even though she did not question my acceptance, it still made no sense to her.

The rejected especially dreaded the anticipated reactions of certain people who might become aware of their failures. During the course of one counseling session, a woman agonized in complete silence for almost an hour before she was able to accomplish what she felt she had to do, namely, to show me her *real* self. She then narrated a grave, personal, moral failure. Later she confided that she couldn't fully believe I would still accept her. "No one else," she remarked, "who has ever had even an inkling of what a despicable coward and heel I am, has ever accepted me."

Their moral failures, particularly, furnished incontestable evidence of personal bankruptcy for the rejected. One rejected woman could never hope to respect herself for the obvious reason that she saw nothing in herself to respect. She felt she could make this statement without any qualification, solely on the grounds of her undeniable cowardice, inasmuch as all her life she had cravenly run away whenever she encountered a serious threatening situation. Her life, she concluded, had been one prolonged moral failure.

What were the long-range aftermaths of the rejected taking such a view of their failures? Some felt they were destined to an endless succession of failures in everything they attempted, since there was no way for them to avoid failures. It is the conviction of one rejected man that failures, particularly social and moral failures, are inevitable for him. This is why he *knows* that he is going to hell—the ultimate failure. He pointed out that, in this light, all of God's gifts to him, which should elicit his gratitude, are just more wasted talents to be added to his huge list of failures.

A number of the rejected felt frozen in a position of inactivity. Their personal bankruptcy would show in anything they might undertake. Even what others would regard as lesser undertakings possessed for them the kind of lethal risk one faces in playing Russian roulette. Accordingly, the main thrust of their activities had been to eliminate, as far as possible, the risk in almost any and every venture. One man is constantly preoccupied with endeavoring to anticipate and defend himself against every future risk and contingency. He must have almost the equivalent of a guarantee against failure before he can commit himself to any undertaking. He is resentful that, since this is the case, he has been forced to avoid practically all endeavors when he so badly needs to succeed. It is not, he added, just that he can't afford to gamble; he can't even afford the luxury of what others would consider a calculated risk.

Another man is drifting because he has no goal. He has been looking for years, but can't find anything which interests him. The biggest single thing in his life is *fear of failure*. Failure, he asserted, *crushes* him. With further insight, he has discovered that, as long as he can't decide anything, he does not have to commit himself to strive. He keeps telling himself that he could do many things if he decided to, but he does nothing when he reflects how devastating failures are to him.

Some of the rejected reacted to their failures by descending further and further into discouragement. Most of the early social failures of one young man have been associated with being deeply hurt by girls. He characterized his discouragement as being so pervasive that he has gradually lost all interest in his studies and in almost everything else. In addition, after each failure he has noticed that his sex drive is heightened and, consequently, he has engaged more frequently in masturbation. This behavior has led to deeper discouragement and a still lower evaluation of himself. As a result, he wonders why he should resist further and so falls still more often into this habit. He feels he is caught in a vicious circle leading to ever deeper discouragement and depression.

The fear of failure seemed to be a prominent factor in the *indecisiveness* that was characteristic of so many of the rejected. They often gave the picture of almost endless worrying and stalling. It was as though they were hoping against hope that some miracle would take things out of their hands so that decisions by them would no longer be necessary.

This indecisiveness appeared to be closely tied to an inability in a few of the rejected to do almost anything they felt would involve them in responsibilities. One woman cannot bring herself to answer the phone. Her explanation is that it might be one of her friends or former classmates who would want to meet her for lunch during the week or make some other arrangement. Whenever she agrees to such an appointment, she gets very little sleep the night before and is a nervous wreck by the time she gets there. Knowing only too well that each of these commitments could end in failure, she seeks to avoid them.

The fear of failure held some rejected in a kind of slavery. It ramified to block their freedom in the ordinary living of their daily lives. Several months after Christmas, one man had not yet been able to open his Christmas mail, though he was sure it contained at least one check. He remarked: "I simply can't make decisions."

Some rejected who were almost consumed with their efforts to erect psychological buffers against all future failures were baffled by their behavior patterns. They had structured their lives, as far as possible, so as to be forewarned and forearmed against all anticipated risks. In addition, they had set into operation, wherever possible, measures designed to lessen the likelihood of failures. At the same time, however, they had acted in ways designed to make failure inevitable.

One rejected man longs to go back to school and would like to be a perennial student. In order to do this, however, he would have to insist on assurances from the faculty and administration, and even a guarantee beforehand, that he could not fail in his studies. He is preoccupied much of the time with building psychological and situational dams against future risks and contingencies. Yet, despite his great fear of failure, he is mystified to find that he is repeatedly acting in ways calculated to unavoidably end in failure. This fact only intensifies his fear of failure. He has never held a job more than a few months. Though he does not understand why he does it, he acknowledged that "I invariably begin to drag my feet on every new job." While he knows he has considerable intellectual ability, he has noticed that he is exceedingly slow to learn anything pertaining to a new job. His repeated learning pattern on each job is that he becomes increasingly dependent, making absolutely no decisions for himself, asking others constantly what to do about this and that, until they are finally forced to let him go.

Patterns of self-sabotage (such as that just exemplified), in which the rejected who greatly feared failures simultaneously courted the very failures they feared, were frequently experienced. The explanation for such behaviors would seem to lie in their need to punish themselves, a need that lay concealed below their conscious level but which was stronger than their conscious need to avoid failures. To punish themselves for what? It would ostensibly depend on the personal histories of those involved. One source of the urge to self-punishment was the feeling of guilt. Guilt in the rejected is treated in greater detail in the next chapter, but for the present it should suffice simply to mention that much of this guilt existed below the level of conciousness.

Another font of self-punishing inclinations in the rejected emerged as the unshakable feeling that they were not only wanting in personal worth but were also evil. Inevitably, their personal experiences reinforced such feelings. Their parents or parent surrogates instilled in them the belief that they were bad; and, subsequently, this belief had been "proven" in their own eyes by their evil behaviors. The rejected who felt strongly inclined to self-punishment tended to emphasize their unacceptable moral records as "proof" of their being no good. At some psychological level within them, there seemed to be a conviction that punishment was not only fitting, but even demanded, by their being evil. Thus, their every failure was regarded by these rejected as revealing their underlying evil nature, and this had become a major element in the structure of their self-concept of worthlessness.

In summary, fear in the rejected assumed myriad forms, but inevitably it included that of anxiety. To this exceedingly painful experience was added the dread of failure, which increased the level of fear. While such experiences receded to the threshold of consciousness at times, the rejected were never free from fear.

6
Guilt and Depression
in the Rejected

During the process of evaluating my findings, it was determined that the feeling of guilt was one of the major psychological consequences of parental rejection and that it held a prominent place in the experiences of almost all of the rejected. My findings also seemed to indicate a close link between guilt and depression; therefore, both are discussed in this chapter, although they are treated in separate sections. No implication should be drawn that every experience of rejection was somehow linked to depression, but only that a great number of the rejected who had feelings of guilt also experienced depression.

Guilt in the Rejected

It seems apparent, after reviewing the matter, that the term "guilt" stands in need of clarification. What is meant by guilt? To begin with, it is something immediately experienced. By way of a parallel, if a color-blind individual had never experienced color, it would be impossible to communicate to him a proper concept of red. Any person, on the other hand, who has experienced the color red has no need of a definition of it. He knows what it is. Here the presumption is that everyone, at some time or other, has had the experience of feeling guilty. In fact, anyone claiming a clear exception to this generalization would be regarded by clinicians as a victim of self-deception or as otherwise emotionally unhealthy.

What are the components ascribed to the experience of guilt? Ever since Freud found it exceedingly difficult to distinguish between the sense of inferiority and the sense of guilt, there has been little agreement regarding the make-up of guilt. Sappenfield (171) has pinpointed it as an "anxiety-like" process. Ausubel (10) ascribed to it the elements of shame, anxiety, remorse, and self-disgust, as well as such physiological reactions as sweating, visceral giddiness, and the inhibition of the normal vegetative functions of nutrition and growth. Whatever the differences among the authors, the rejected found every intensity of guilt an exceedingly painful experience—one which they would readily have gotten rid of if they had only known how.

Guilt feelings in the rejected admitted of degrees, in the sense that these feelings were not experienced with the same intensity by all of the rejected, nor in the same degree at all times by the same rejected. Accompanying their feeling of guilt was a tendency toward behavior that would restore their sense of moral worth—an urge to be *cleansed* from that which made them feel guilty. Those with chronic guilt feelings frequently were aware of an urge to self-punishment. In such persons, two characteristics were prominent.

First, although some were not clearly aware of it, this inclination for self-punishment at times took the concealed form of their being accident-prone or self-defeating or self-sabotaging. In the latter case, they operated in a way designed to guarantee their failures in such things as marriage, receiving promotions in rank, increases in salary, and so forth, while at the same time they consciously desired successes in these areas.

A few of these rejected even recognized that they were helplessly operating in a self-defeating manner. This only bewildered them, because they didn't know why. Very few of them suspected any connection with guilt. In fact, some were not even aware of guilt feelings. Certain rejected who had a complete lack of guilt feeling together with self-sabotaging behavioral patterns later experienced a surprising development. In the course of counseling, strong guilt feelings surfaced suddenly in their awareness. Such occurrences invariably took them by surprise, since they had not had a clue of the existence within themselves of such deep, intense guilt.

A second characteristic of the guilt-ridden rejected was a feeling of compulsion. They felt *obliged* either to undertake or refrain from ventures (including important, long-range ones) on the score that they were not morally free to do differently. This was true even of the rejected who recognized that these were things in which they should have felt free. One young man, studying for the Catholic priesthood, said that he *had* to study for the priesthood. "Otherwise," he stated, "I would have no security." He explained that there was something of a parallel in his earlier life when he was in mortal sin: then he *had* to go to confession right away or he would have no peace. The two were very much the same experience of being morally bound.

In such guilt-ridden behaviors, the rejected really *wanted* to do the things under consideration, but they wanted to do them because they *had* to. At the conscious level, they gave their consent; but they also felt they were unable to say no. Below their conscious level was a rebellion at these unacceptable burdens that constituted a kind of moral slavery. Their feelings of guilt were such that they could not do otherwise.

Such experiences were invariably unhealthy in the sense that the rejected felt obliged to do or refrain from doing things about which they should have felt morally free. A form of slavery was the price they were paying to maintain their guilt feelings at a low level—they lived in bondage. In addition, some rejected experienced deep resentment at the injustice implicit in such slavery. A few mentioned that this kind of living "tears a person up inside."

Psychologists assume that every response of an organism has a specific stimulus. What is the stimulus that triggers the response of guilt? There seems to be no generally accepted answer. Brown sees all guilt as flowing out of infantile fantasy (29). Basically, the psychoanalytic position has been that guilt is triggered by self-frustration of superego motives, or self-frustration of conscience (62). Masserman views impulses or deeds forbidden in earlier experiences as stimulating guilt (121). Ausubel reminds us that guilt can be the product of hostile impulses (10). Some rejected experienced intense guilt feelings even when they were not aware that they were doing anything wrong.

The stimulus of guilt is not in the future; it's either in the past or the present or both. Accordingly, guilt is in no sense a kind of fear. Fear is referred to the future—to something bad that can, but has not yet, happened. Guilt, however, is a response to something the person has already done or is presently doing. What is the nature of this guilt-producing stimulus which exists either in the past or present or both? Again, there is no consensus. My position is that it is a person's *knowledge that he is responsible for some act or omission which is in violation of his personal moral code.* That is, he has *done* or is doing something which he thinks he should not have done or be doing, or he has *omitted* or is omitting something which he thinks he should have done or should be doing.

What stimulated guilt in the rejected? Many of them simply did not know, though they remained aware that guilt had ramified in their lives, affecting them deeply. One rejected woman, who had been in therapy for a long time, wrote—in something of a stream-of-consciousness style:

> This brings to mind guilt feelings I had toward a reaction I felt in myself as I perceived a strangeness in the feelings of my parents—guilt toward my mother, anxiety toward my father. This was before the age of five. Until I can recognize and accept my own limitations and faults, I will be unable to see and accept the perfection of Christ in any but an abstract

way. I would like to think that this is the big push that keeps me coming back.

Acceptance is deeper than I would like to think. This I know by observing the areas that used to be unquestionable but which are now under question—these whitewashed structures within my self-esteem, I think. For example, the Church and my religion: this has passed from an uncomfortable feeling to an act of questioning, an active search for answers.

The rejected who thought they knew why they felt guilty had pinned it down to something they had done or failed to do. Without exception, they felt responsible and accountable for this act, omission, or desire, even if and when such a position seemed unreasonable to others or even to themselves.

The stimulus situation which triggered their response of guilt had at times been an *act*. For some rejected, it was external and therefore observable, such as having stolen something substantial or having seriously damaged someone's reputation. For others, it was internal and therefore not observable, such as having secretly indulged in hatred or having deliberately planned to arrange evidences to make an innocent person appear guilty. In each of these instances, the person doing such a thing considered it wrong.

Where the stimulus situation was an *omission*, it referred to something the rejected felt they culpably had failed to do or were failing to do. The omission also was either external, such as a breadwinner's publicly recognized failure to support his family, or internal, such as having deliberately neglected a friend or neighbor who was in dire need.

Where the stimulus situation was a *desire*, it was usually internal but at times had also been expressed externally. Here the rejected usually made a distinction. The term "desire" referred either to their *merely liking* and feeling attracted to something that was morally unacceptable to them or to their determining to have that thing. Some of them, for instance, said it would be very pleasurable to abscond with a million dollars or to sleep with some other man's wife. They normally did not experience guilt, however, unless they made the additional determination to have or do it—for example, looking for a *way* of stealing the money or sleeping with the man's wife. Such a finding appears to be at odds with Sappenfield's position that guilt arises whenever a person has an impulse to behave in a manner contrary to his introjected moral standards (171).

A seeming exception to this finding was experienced as something pathological termed a "scruple," where persons felt guilty at the mere liking or even thought of something which they believed was forbidden them, without any determination on their part to obtain it. A "scruple" is ordinarily presumed to be a displaced guilt. Accordingly, the guilt experienced by such persons was presumed to have been displaced from something else which they really felt to be wrong and for which they felt morally responsible. Their immoral behavior, however, presumably remained unconscious since they were not at the time psychologically ready to face it and deal with it.

Implicit in the element of holding themselves morally responsible—which appeared to be an integral element in the guilt-producing stimulus situation of the rejected—was the experience of psychological freedom. They felt they were at the controls and *could*—and, moreover, *should*—have done differently. They saw the action or omission in question as morally imputable to them. It was the knowledge that they could and should have done differently to which they responded with guilt feelings.

Were there any universally experienced acts or omissions giving rise to guilt? In most, if not all, of the rejected, one of the main sources of guilt feelings seemed to lie in their *counterrejections*. They counterrejected those who had rejected them. One woman wrote:

> Acceptance. Ultimately, it is a choice between the old defenses which would assure some miserable measure of consistency and that which would necessitate the removal of those defenses. It seems to be an all-or-nothing type of decision. Intellectually, I know that until I can accept myself I won't be able to take my place as a productive person, to love, to give.
>
> It seems that I've rejected everything the folks have given me except their evaluation. Have I rejected them? To a certain depth, I think so. But basically I think I hinge on their judgments. At this point my mind wanders to the counseling situation and how I feel about it, the main thought being that I hate to portray my ignorance of myself and of people in general, of information and insights. My thoughts are my worth and you are my judge.

The counterrejections by the rejected inevitably contained resentments, hostilities, and hates against the rejecting person or persons. Such strong negative feelings, particularly against parents, were personally unacceptable in the eyes of the rejected themselves. Many of the rejected viewed such feelings, not only as personally unacceptable, but as seriously wrong for them.

One man who suffered constantly from guilt harbored intense resentment and hostility toward his parents. His mother had made him so completely dependent on her that he felt like a zombie. Repeatedly, when she had been discussing him with others within his hearing, she had remarked: "If I should go down, then he goes down." Speaking of her, he told me several times: "She is a vampire sucking out my life blood." The only solution he was able to see was her death so that he could be free from her.

As long as he could remember, he had hated his father. He had even tried twice, unsuccessfully, to kill him. He thinks that someday he may get another chance, and this time he won't "flub it." Anything he has ever done to his father has never made him feel guilty; but at the same time, he has lived in guilt. He ascribed this guilt to his wishing his mother dead, his cowardly pattern of living, and his deep hatred of people.

In the next chapter, it will be seen that some of the rejected found, to their great surprise, that murderous hatred had surfaced in their consciousness. They had become aware that they were killers. This called for their constant vigilance lest these murderous urges be translated into action. They knew they were fully capable and strongly inclined to hurt or even kill certain people. The unexplained chronic guilt they had experienced before these feelings rose to consciousness remained, but a few had come to recognize these urges as sources of their guilt.

Why had the rejected counterrejected their rejectors? There appeared to be several reasons. To begin with, they sensed the extreme injustice in their rejection and they resented it deeply. In addition, the feeling that their missing parental acceptance was not really wanted seemed to lessen their pain, and this was implicit in their counterrejection. The absence of parental acceptance, affection, and love, didn't hurt as much if they were seen as being unwanted, and counterrejection accomplished this purpose. To the extent that their rejectors were resented or even despised by them, there was a corresponding attenuation of their pain of rejection. They were also hitting back at their parents in this way.

There were other effects of their counterrejections. It is necessary to recall that one emotional experience, if sufficiently intense, can fairly well drown out another emotional experience. The dread of personal inadequacy can, in large part, be replaced by an intense, unspecified anger. In the rejected, the anger had a masking effect on the anxiety resulting from the knowledge of their rejection. Such an emotional substitution seemed less painful to the rejected than the anxiety which it replaced in them. At the same time, because this anger flowed out of a personally unacceptable hatred, it seemed to be the stimulus of guilt, even where that guilt had not yet surfaced.

This unconsciously arranged substitution of the less painful feeling of anger for the anxiety caused by their knowledge of rejection appeared to provide some explanation, as well, for the apparent unreasonableness which characterized the conscious guilt feelings of some of the rejected. To the extent that intense anger remained unspecified, it was less likely to produce guilt. Besides, the anger of the rejected was felt to be justified, in some unexplained way, even when they had no conscious awareness of either its source or its function. Nonetheless, some guilt was present. Self-protectively, some other explanation had to be found, without their realizing what was happening, for this experiencing of guilt. For instance, some felt guilty about the wrong things—things which they knew should not reasonably have been imputed to them.

A few even went looking for personal misdeeds in order to give a reasonable foundation to their feelings of guilt. One woman deliberately did things which she knew were seriously wrong in order to provide herself with some justification for her constant guilt feelings. She knew she was no good anyway, for how else could she explain her ever-present guilt? It made good sense to her to furnish herself with concrete evidences for the guilt with which she lived and with which she was sure she deserved to live.

The rejected who appeared to have unwittingly made substitutions of unspecified anger for some of their guilt normally failed to perceive their remaining chronic guilt as the result of harboring personally unacceptable elements in their counterrejections. At the same time, they were aware of an urge to self-punishment. One woman with no religious affiliation feels so guilty that she must continuously punish herself. She is certain she owes expiation. For one thing, she feels that she should have tried much harder in so many ways. In no way can she convince herself otherwise, even though she really does not know how she could have tried harder.

It is still her deep conviction that she "must pay in suffering for everything." She feels that perhaps this doesn't make sense, but, nevertheless, it is the way she experiences it. She suffers deep guilt both for what she has done and for what she has failed to do, and especially for the hurt that she has brought to others. Besides, she believes she will bring more hurt to people, simply because that is the kind of person she is. It is impossible for her to feel she is right in anything she does. In fact, because she feels so guilty, she can never believe she is right in doing what her judgment tells her is right. She has mentioned repeatedly that she hates her father for what he did to her mother over the years. She can't stand to be left alone with him. She thinks this is foolish because now he is good to her.

Besides that which came from the personally unacceptable elements in their counterrejections, guilt in the rejected appeared to have additional sources. Some reported that their parents, in one way or another, had either reinforced their guilt feelings or had given them additional grounds for feeling guilty. One man wrote:

> . . . I was probably guilty about feeling that I had to take my father's place in the family, but Mom did give me that feeling. . . . Mom had directed all of us from the start with a very subtle, interior direction, badly confused with the moral order (hence, more guilt). She has a martyr complex as wide as a barn, and has used a number of real and severe physical ailments which I know fit right into the neurotic picture caused physically by the overworking of the sympathetic nervous system and other mechanisms.
>
> From this came—and this is extremely important—the following picture: We [children] are better than other people; we must be perfect because we are all our poor mother has in life; to be perfect we must live up to her every desire, whim, idea, and ideal; we must work hard to take the load off her, since she is suffering so much from poor health, overwork, nervous strain, and a paranoiac husband, who, as we all know, is a beast; she is watching us constantly, and we must measure up—this is the most important thing in life. Further, all of her directives are moral; any failure is a moral failure, and we must face the wrath of God; sin is an offense against our mother—God and Mom are the same kinds of people; we must love her. At the same time, it was impossible to love her, impossible to help her (since basically she didn't want help, only sympathy for her crucified self), and impossible to live up to her desires (since success brought no approval because her desires had changed and the old ones forgotten by the time you complied), impossible to live up to her ideals (since they changed from day to day, but were always absolute at the moment).
>
> Results (for me, especially, but also for some other of the kids, as I now realize): an obsession for constant activity; constant guilt and the feeling that it was impossible to be "good"—the only important thing in life—impossible to satisfy God; the feeling that I was constantly being watched, no matter what I was doing; the paradoxical feeling that I had to be better than anyone, but wasn't actually as good as anyone else; the feeling that I was abnormal, that everyone hated me, that no one understood me; a very feeble capacity to love; strong hedonistic and sexual desires (probably looking for some joy in life), and the concomitant feeling that I was morally obligated to a life of severe asceticism; the feeling that I dare not love or like any person, book, thought, opinion,

without first consulting Mom's standards (changeable, as I've said); the feeling that it was morally wrong to express fear, hate, love, or any emotion or inclination; and the severe inability to think or act independently in any way. . . .

I could list a long line of other effects of the situation as well. . . . For one thing, there's my reaction to any situation in which I feel I'm being watched—I normally tend to fall apart and get an enormous hostility headache, a rather frequent phenomenon in [his former profession] for me. And I always felt that I was being watched; I frequently remarked that I never prayed without watching myself pray, never studied without watching myself study—and so of other activities. Now I know who was really watching, even when she was absent. . . .

All of the above has been borne out by a clear look at myself, my reactions, my background, and the "chance" recollections of the past—those things that just seem to pop into mind when your mind is on the subject because of the pressure of the therapeutic situation. I'm working to correct the situation as much as possible, and I think I'm being successful. Now, for the first time in my life, I feel like an independent agent, responsible only to God. I guess it will take some time to cut the umbilical cord completely, but I'm well under way. It's interesting to note that my brothers and sisters have come to many of the same conclusions (about themselves) and were more affected by the "same" environment than any of us realized. They go even further when I lead them into conversation and then ask leading questions about Mom, especially. . . .

Guilt had become the main behavioral determinant in the lives of some rejected, in terms of their reactions to it. Often these reactions were escapist in nature, designed to get them out from under the guilt. A rejected young woman who is still in college needs the presence and strength of her (older) boyfriend. She knows she is possessive toward him. He makes her feel she *is* somebody—a real person in her own right, and not a "kept" child to whom is given a dollar for this and fifty cents for that and who is, as she worded it, "constantly beaten across the head with, 'look at all we have done for you—how ungrateful can you be?' " She is convinced that she has to get away from home to break the psychological dam which has built up inside her.

Some rejected uncovered further sources for guilt feelings. These feelings did not always come, as far as they knew, from things their parents had said or done to them. Some felt that they had somehow either inherited moral obligations as members of the family or they had been imposed on them—in either case, they were deeply resented.

These resentments extended to specific persons, and the harboring of such personal resentments made them feel all the more guilty. A rejected woman, hungry for affection, had allowed herself to be seduced by "a smooth-talking married man," who had abandoned her the minute he discovered she was pregnant. In addition, he informed her that he would deny, even under oath, that he was the father of her baby. She hates the baby and deeply resents having to carry it. She is seriously considering having an abortion. Her guilt for hating and wanting to kill her baby is constant.

A few of the rejected realized that they had gradually become inextricably trapped in guilt. Little by little, they had lost certain of their most important areas of freedom. One woman's mother had been ill-treated by her husband and largely ignored by her other children. Gradually, this woman had to take her mother under her care, because she was all her mother had left in the world. Her mother, while appreciative of her solicitude, became more and more possessive until she pretty well took over her life. By degrees, her mother began to make all her decisions, even going as far as to select a husband for her—one whom, to her later regret, she obediently married. While she remains painfully aware of her mother's grip on her, she deeply resents it and feels powerless to do anything about it.

She constantly reminds herself that her mother has been hurt all her life, and now she is the only one her mother has left. Besides, she feels sure her mother does not realize she is so possessive. There is no way she could neglect or disappoint her mother while she is "down." She feels she can't kick the last prop out from under her. In fact, she can't disobey her mother or go against her will in anything, for that would crush her mother. While deeply resentful of being caught in this position, she feels very guilty that she is so resentful. She is also depressed, since her mother is so pitifully in need of her.

Depression in the Rejected

What is depression? Freud (62) compares depression (melancholia) with mourning, and describes it as characterized by painful dejection, loss of interest in the outside world, inability to love, inhibition of activities, and the lowering of self-esteem to the point of loss of self-respect. Rado (150) agrees with these observations and adds another—the intensely strong craving for "narcissistic" or "self" gratification. Abraham (1) also agrees with Freud's observations and emphasizes an incapacity for love in the depressed. Maslow and Mittelmann (120) hold that if the depression is severe enough the patient manifests, in addition, a delusion of sin and guilt. Fenichel (54) adds that the depressed complain that they are worthless and act as if they had lost their egos, but at the same time they have a continuous need for sexual satisfaction and heightened self-esteem. Rado (151) finds the depressed person's self-esteem abased and shattered. Bibring (19) agrees that depression implies an extraordinary fall in self-esteem. Becker (15) and Adler (3) acknowledge secondary gains for the depressed person, since depression coerces the people around the depressed person by stimulating in them guilt and self-accusation.

Depression clearly is a datum of one's experience. At the same time, it is not clear that everyone has experienced the kind of depression some rejected have known. Whether depression is actually inseparable from rejection, and therefore universally found in the rejected, is a moot question.

As the rejected described their depression, it was a state of dejection, lowness of spirits, discouragement, and helplessness. In this state, absorbed in self-pity, they were self-preoccupied, frustrated, and angry. Their world became overshadowed with a dull gray, their activities tedious and boring. With no impelling motivation for any undertaking, at times they saw no reason for living. Depression was erosive; it increasingly left them physically, mentally, and emotionally exhausted. Lacking energy, they could at best drag themselves through making an appearance of living. Meanwhile, their whole being was slowed down; even the muscles of their faces sagged.

What stimulus produces psychologically caused depression? There is no agreement among recognized writers in this matter. Fenichel (54) believes it is precipitated by a loss of self-esteem, or a loss of hope for a source of self-esteem. Moreover, he views every depression as a repetition of a decision reaction to childhood difficulties. He further believes the primary depression is always triggered by an injury to childhood "narcissism." Jacobson (86) tends to agree, and adds that the child's primary depression is precipitated by his disappointment in the parental omnipotence. Bibring (19) sees the experience of an inescapable situation and a state of helplessness as producing depression, and Horney (85) and Seligman (179) emphasize the depressive's hopelessness.

What stimulus had triggered depression in the rejected? Their depression invariably appeared to involve the knowledge that they were caught helplessly in a situation which was more than unpleasant—it was unacceptable to them. My hypothesis is: *The experience of being helplessly trapped in a personally unacceptable situation produced in the rejected the response of depression.* This by no means implies that these depressed people were, of necessity, clearly aware of being trapped in an intolerable plight.

Usually, they knew only that they were depressed. A number of the rejected awakened each morning depressed, with no idea of why. The cause of their depression seemed to be safely guarded below the level of their awareness. Thus they were protected from coming face to face with an intolerable situation about which they felt powerless to do anything.

In the course of counseling, most rejected came to a recognition that they were trapped. This occurred, however, only when they appeared to have grown psychologically strong enough to cope with the intolerable position in which they happened to be. Before that time, if someone had suggested to them that they were trapped in an unbearable predicament, they would most likely have reacted indignantly with an intensely emotional denial. This response, of course, could have been an indication that they felt threatened by the remark because it hit home.

What constituted this kind of trap for the rejected? It was not the objective situation itself in which they were involved, but rather their *perception* of the situation, that established their feeling of being trapped. Let me use an example to clarify this distinction between an objective situation and one's view of that situation. Some time ago, a newspaper described the final test given to students in a winter-survival course. Two men were required to parachute into an area of snow-covered mountains and make their way, in three days, back to a base camp. They had been supplied with extra, warm clothing, food rations, a knife, matches, a compass, and a few other items. A blizzard which began minutes after they both had been dropped from the plane, some ten minutes apart, and which lasted the better part of three days, had not been forecast—and, of course, not planned for. As a result, the two men were not equipped to travel through the several feet of soft, new snow.

When they had failed to appear at the base camp five days later, search teams were sent out. They eventually found the first man pacing up and down in a narrow, twelve-foot-long clearing. He was cold, hungry, and depressed. Later, he told his rescuers that they had arrived in the nick of time, because he felt he was on the verge of going out of his mind. After they had returned him to the base camp, they resumed their search for the other man. The following day they found him in a thirty-foot-long cleared area, with a deer strung up at the end of it. He was relaxing in an improvised rocking chair, calmly smoking his pipe, in front of a well-banked fire. When he saw them, he said: "Go away. The peace, quiet, and beauty of this place are beyond anything I had ever imagined. Would you mind terribly just leaving me here in peace for another few days?"

In this example, the objective situation itself appears to have been substantially the same for both men. However, one experienced it as intolerable, while the other experienced it as the very opposite. Accordingly, situations themselves were not sufficient to trigger depression in the rejected. Rather, the depression stimulus was contained in their perception of being helplessly caught in a situation which they felt was beyond their endurance.

What were the elements that held the rejected pinned down as captives in such situations? The *fear of failure* kept some of them trapped in intolerable situations which were productive of depression. Such situations were, for instance, their present business or professional positions. Some of them had worked for these positions. They needed them for their rewarding prestige. They also realized that they were less well prepared for any other prestigious occupation. They had discovered that these positions also left them highly vulnerable. Even though prepared, they were frightened. While they could not leave, neither could they free themselves from the haunting fear of failure to which they were thus exposed.

One teacher wakes up depressed every morning. He has just begun to see that his depression comes from feeling that he is trapped. For years, he studied to qualify for the teaching field. Now that he is functioning in the classroom, he feels that it is too late to change. He anticipated that he would be safe hiding behind the teacher's role. Now he does not feel really safe in that role. "What if one of them were ever to openly challenge me or confront me in anger?" he asks, "What if I were to discover that I am boring them?"

Some rejected remained in a depression when forced to stay in an unbearable situation by the *fear of losing* their sole source of *acceptance from their parents*. One man had understood very early that the only possible way he could get acceptance from his parents was by studying for the Catholic priesthood. All the while he was studying, his parents regarded him with pride and undisguised admiration. When he finally became a priest, their acceptance was heightened. Such acceptance was rewarding, but he was miserable as a priest. He feared that if he were to cease functioning as a priest he would not only lose their acceptance, but moreover would be branded by them as a "disappointment" and a "failure." For him, the priesthood was an experienced slavery. He has lived as a priest in continuing depression.

Guilt proved to be the factor closing the trap on a number of the rejected. Even the prospect of leaving the unendurable situation would have flooded them with overpowering guilt. They stood out in clear contrast to other people who, because they felt obliged in conscience to remain in a very frustrating situation, chose to "tough it out." By contrast, the rejected who felt themselves fastened in a situation by chains of guilt were able to make no such choice. They *had* to remain in it. Otherwise, the guilt would have been insupportable.

Many of the rejected who had at least periodically experienced depression earlier did not have even a suspicion that they were thus trapped. Such lack of awareness is understandable, inasmuch as the human psyche functions spontaneously to retain securely beneath the level of awareness anything that would prove overpowering. It remains thus buried until such time as one develops the psychological strength needed to cope with that particular thing.

Some rejected men and women felt they had made a bad marriage choice. Their marriage partner had not proved to be the admirable person they had originally thought they were getting. At any rate, the continuation of the relationship was perceived by them as having become intolerable. But even the thought of divorce and of seeking another mate caused such an insupportable experience of guilt to well up in them that they felt hopelessly trapped in their relationship. Remaining with their mates was not really their choice—they were enslaved. It was something they *had* to do, not because it was right, but because they knew they were not able to even consider any other course. It was not, therefore, a matter of virtue which would presuppose the freedom to do otherwise. Whether or not people who experience freedom feel they *may* do otherwise, they know they *can*, if they so choose. For these rejected, on the other hand, remaining with their mate was being inescapably shackled to their marriage partner by guilt.

Other rejected were held, bound by guilt, in other intolerable situations. A student for the priesthood repeatedly had the same terrifying dream. He dreamed that a thick, sticky, plastic-like substance was growing out of the ground, completely surrounding him. It was rising up in a tent-like fashion, directly over him, to a point just above his head. In his dream, he was forced to tilt his head far back with his mouth open in order to get as much air as possible through the hole at the top, which was gradually closing in to the point of shutting off all his air. Each night he awoke, terrified, just as the hole was about to close and suffocate him. As he discussed the dream, he said,

> I want to be a priest and a good priest, but why did God pick me? Why did it have to be me? I really don't want to be a priest and to live a single life. I want to marry and have my own children. But I'll be a priest. I'll do God's will if it kills me. What choice do I have? I have to. But why did He pick on—I mean, why did He choose me? Some of my friends are much better people. Why didn't He take them?

These examples of guilt enslaving people in their life situations involved "psychological" as well as "moral" freedom. There was no question of these married people or this student for the priesthood *freely* opting to remain in or leave the situation—that would have been a choice. Those able to make such a choice would in no sense have been morally enslaved. These rejected, by contrast, had no such option. It would have been simply unthinkable for them to seriously contemplate an action that would have released within them a crushing burden of guilt. Hence they remained utterly powerless—trapped in what they felt to be an intolerable situation—and continued to exist in inescapable depression. A woman expressed this experience very succinctly when she wrote: " . . . It's a funny thing, but how I envy those people who are completely capable of sin without fear of reprisal."

A number of the rejected whose depression came from their being entrapped by guilt experienced various behavioral happenings that baffled them. Though they had been unable to consciously find acceptable escapes from their entanglements, their psyches had taken over below the conscious level to furnish them with releases. These happenings, in fact, appeared to be various channels unknowingly manufactured by them to permit some escape from their impossible situations. Such channels provided them with badly needed, excusing "reasons" for getting out of their undesirable involvements.

Among such "reasons" were a whole spectrum of incapacitating health problems. One young woman, studying to be a Catholic nun, was convinced that God was demanding convent life of her, although she confided that she herself would have wanted something else. Early in the course of her studies, during which, for some reason unknown to her, she was continuously depressed, she developed a severe vision problem. It became impossible for her to do the required study because the print on the pages blurred so much she could not make out the words. A series of medical examinations failed to show any organic pathology.

The doctors finally told her superiors that the problem was "functional" and that there was nothing physically wrong with her eyes. She was taken away from her studies and placed as an assistant teacher in one of the primary grades. She loved the children and was doing very well until her eyes began to blur to the point that she could not see what she was writing on the blackboard or even recognize her students. This problem increased until she had to terminate her teaching assistantship. Eventually, she was informed by her superiors that this was not her vocation, since God was clearly indicating that He did not want her to be a nun.

The news left her experiencing intense regret but also a surprising feeling of relief. About a year later, she came to tell me that she was thinking of going back to finish her college education. She could now read without difficulty, but had no idea why her vision had gotten better. Neither had she any suspicion why the original problem had occurred while she was still in the convent. She only hoped the problem would not reappear in her future work.

One rejected young man felt he had to be a doctor because, over the years, his parents had repeatedly told him that was the only way he could begin to repay them for all they had sacrificed for him. When his parents were first married, his father was a premedical student, but never made it to medical school. The young man hated the idea. He wanted to be a musician but couldn't face the guilt that would be his were he to let his parents down.

He possessed the intellectual ability to do medical studies, but was failing in the pre-med program because his depression drained him of energy and his almost continuous, blinding headaches would not permit him to study. When he explained to his parents the reason for his poor grades, they took him to a doctor. After a series of medical examinations, the doctors told him they could discover no explanation for his condition.

Two years later, when the director of the pre-med program informed him that he could not recommend him for medical school, he had no choice but to drop out of pre-med. His parents, though terribly disappointed, had to admit it was not his fault. He switched to the music department. Now he wonders if the reason his depression and headaches have disappeared is because music has such a soothing effect on him.

Another unrecognized escape hatch employed by some rejected who were trapped in an unacceptable position by guilt was a compelling, conflictual, moral problem. A man who was studying for the Catholic priesthood had developed a problem of compulsive masturbation. Because he deeply believed that God had marked him to be a priest, he was determined to become one. At the same time, he felt like a "gold-plated hypocrite," because—despite appearances—he wasn't honestly living the chaste life of a celibate. Yet, he could not prevent the repeated moral failures. He was living in dread that his confessor would finally have to tell him that he obviously was unworthy to study for the priesthood.

He felt, in order to be sincere, that he also had to keep his superiors continually informed of how he was doing with his problem, even at the frightening risk that they might feel obliged to dismiss him because of it.

Discouraging as it was for him, he was determined to be what God wanted him to be, unless his superiors or confessor found him unworthy. Finally, he was advised by his superiors to leave, and he did so. More than a year later, he informed me that his problem had practically disappeared. At that time he wasn't sure but supposed that the confining life of the seminary probably had accounted for his problem.

The bail-outs provided for some of the rejected in unacceptable situations gave them a release, not from the situation itself, but from some crucial aspect of it. This had the overall result of reducing the personal violation involved in the situation. One woman, living in a terribly unhappy marriage, is unable to have intercourse with her husband because of her constant frigidity. Hence, they occupy separate bedrooms. She has gone to specialists but has received no help. Surprised that she feels guilty about the separate bedrooms, she also feels sorry for her husband. However, she is very relieved that she is thus freed from having to give herself physically to a man she somewhat admires, but does not love at all, and her depression is not as great as it was when she was still sleeping with her husband.

Where the escape (selected below the conscious level) was successfully carried out, the depression had at least lessened, even if it had not disappeared. However, where the escape had been blocked, the depression had not only failed to diminish but had become reinforced and the hopelessness accentuated. This was experienced a number of times by those trapped in an intolerable situation by fear. One woman, almost devoid of any confidence in her personal adequacy as well as in many areas of her competency, was unable to make any significant decisions for herself. She had married a very dominating man who, in his turn, had the psychologically unwholesome need to make not only his own decisions but also decisions for others. He alone had decided on the choice of the household furniture and appliances and had also selected both her clothes and those of the children.

As she grew psychologically stronger in the course of therapy, this kind of absolute dependence on her husband became less and less tolerable for her. She began to have feelings of being smothered. Finally, she worked up the courage to ask her husband if she could at least go along and give an opinion the next time he went shopping for the children's clothing. Her husband, threatened by her request, turned on her in anger and shouted: "OK! Do the whole damned thing yourself. I wash my hands of it." She panicked. He had confronted her with the impossible. Frightened, she dropped the matter then and there and moved back into persisting depression.

Since that day she has had an increasing feeling that she is suffocating. Because she couldn't dream of trying to make it on her own, there is no possibility of her taking the children and leaving. Neither can she any longer accept a dependency that does not allow her to be, to some extent, responsible for her own person; hence, the deepened, continuing depression.

In a number of situations, the rejected living in depression appeared to be saying "yes" at the conscious level to the enslaving position, while simultaneously saying "no" to it at a deeper, below-conscious level. Such conflict was experienced as one part of them struggling against another part. They lived divided within themselves. A few had found that the depression left them only when they were able to say a definite "yes" or "no" to a given situation and feel it down to their toes. This required them to bring what was below consciousness into harmony with what was conscious. Some had succeeded in bringing about this transition. In order to achieve it, a number had used recourse to professional help.

Just as the injured body tends to move constantly toward physical health as fractured bones knit and wounds heal, so the injured human psyche strives continuously to move toward psychological health. There was an application of this principle in the ongoing drive of the rejected to escape their depression. Even though their thrust toward psychological health had, for a time, been blocked by various obstacles, it continued unconsciously or consciously to try to free them from the psychological traps which had caused their depression.

What *conscious* escape hatches were employed? One psychological maneuver the rejected *consciously* used to escape from their depression was fantasy. One woman feels trapped in marriage to the wrong man. When her husband is making love to her, the lights must always be out to make it easier for her to fantasize that he is really another man who, in her imagination, is her lover. In these situations, her husband is merely a stand-in for the other man. She feels sure that her husband does not suspect that she has never actually had sexual relations with him. She has always imagined that they were with the man of her daydreams.

If, in the course of the night, she feels the need to touch her lover, she is very careful not to touch any identifying part of her husband's body. For instance, she will avoid touching his chin because that would be unmistakably his. Instead, she will touch his cheek, which, inasmuch as it is not identifying, fits readily into her fantasy of touching her lover. This kind of fantasy makes her life less unbearable and leaves her less depressed, although it also leaves her feeling somewhat guilty. She copes with the guilt by repeatedly reassuring herself that she is not really an adulteress because this affair with her "lover," a man she knows, is entirely unknown to him and exists only in her fantasy.

Other ways used by the rejected to *consciously* alleviate their depression covered quite an array, which included refusing to look at the situation or denying its existence entirely. Some had recourse to preoccupying themselves with their blessings, dwelling exclusively on consoling thoughts and memories, and conjuring up in their imaginations whatever was needed to make them feel good. Still others lost themselves completely in work or some cause or escaped into some form of pleasure so that they didn't have time to think.

By way of summary: guilt need not be pathological. The guilt which appeared to be a companion of the rejected, however, was unwholesome. It was crippling, even where the rejected could explain its presence, in that it prevented their living as free people. Depression, on the other hand, does appear to be pathological. At any rate, the depression experienced by the rejected was manifestly unhealthy and locked them into a state of suffering.

7
Anger, Hostility, and Aggression in the Rejected

What do the terms "anger," "hostility," and "aggression" mean? There has been a notable lack of agreement in this matter. Irrespective of the different positions taken regarding their meanings, there has been general agreement that all three are closely associated. In general, the differences in definition stem from two opposing views of the underlying scientific data. For some contemporary psychologists, including myself, these data refer to *experiential phenomena*, which are identifiable as qualitatively distinct *experiences* and so, to some extent, can be described by the persons experiencing them.

A number of psychologists, however, currently view "anger," "hostility," and "aggression" in terms of nonexperiences. Considered precisely as *subjective experiences*, they are not the externally *observable data* to which these psychologists have chosen to limit their investigations. While these people *operationally define* externally observable behaviors, they frequently prefer to define human "anger" and "hostility"—but not "aggression"—as inferences from behavioral or psychological *constructs*. The term construct has been employed by contemporary psychologists as a substitute for "concept" or for a "synthesis of impressions," and thus something *inferred* from observed data.

Their concern with anger and hostility, then, is with their validity as psychological constructs. In reporting carefully derived findings in support of the validity of such constructs, a number of psychologists appear to give minimal attention to defining them. When they attend to definition, they frequently show what appears to be a lack of clarity in their definitions of "anger" and "hostility" and even of "aggression." These definitions appear to be anything but clear.

One contemporary author, who favors a behavioristic approach, clarifies what he means by *aggression* in these words:

> . . . when a person is punished, either by another organism or some accidental aspect of his environment, he frequently gets downright an-

gry. Unless we have been conditioned otherwise, we are not likely just
to sit or take our punishment lying down. This aggression, which punishment generates . . . (112, p. 279).

In view of this clarification, what is "aggression"? He says it is what is
generated by one's being punished (i.e., one "gets downright angry").
But what does he mean by "gets downright angry"? Presumably, in
view of his behavioristic orientation, he refers to some kind of observable behavior. If so, how would such aggression ("which punishment
generates") also be observable behavior in the person who, in fact,
does just sit and take his punishment lying down? Is this author defining aggression as a kind of behavior and, at the same time, saying that
aggression would also be present in one who was *not* engaging in that
behavior? To me, at least, his operational definition is not clear.

I find that a number of contemporary psychologists evidence a similar lack of clarity of definition. In fact, it is exceedingly difficult to find
clear-cut definitions of "anger," "hostility," and "aggression" in the
writings of psychologists who operationally define things in terms of
distinctive patterns of observable behavior. I find such definitions, on
the whole, clear enough in the context of animal studies. With human
subjects, however, these operational definitions seem, at best, to be
inadequate.

For some psychologists, "anger" and "hostility" are practically inter-
changeable terms when they are defined operationally. Though a few
authors endeavor to draw a clean distinction between "aggression"
and the other two, they seldom attempt to distinguish between
"anger" and "hostility." For some of them, "hostility" and "anger"
both refer to *attitudes* and covert *aggressive tendencies*, which they feel
obliged to acknowledge at the human level because of the presence
there of thought and symbolic processes.

Anger in the Rejected

Can "anger" be adequately defined by an operational definition? The
anger which is expressed in manifest attacks or other observable behaviors can readily be so defined, insofar as it is externalized by the behavioral patterns. Yet, as such, it seems to be inseparable from aggression.
Is there an operational definition for that anger which a person deter-
mines *not* to express externally in aggression? To my knowledge, nothing of this nature has yet been agreed upon by those recognized in the
field. Nonetheless, there have been some beginnings made along these
lines in the area of physiological differentiation.

Funkenstein's original research appears to be empirically verified. He found that "anger," even when not expressed in aggression, is associated with the presence of noradrenaline, which is secreted by the adrenal glands. He recorded, as well, seven different physiological measures which differentiate between "anger" and "fear." Nevertheless, when noradrenaline was experimentally injected into human subjects—though they testified that they experienced a state of emotional arousal—they were unable to agree on *identifying* that state *as anger* rather than as some other emotional state (65, 12, 174).

For me, it is at least conceivable that the *presence* of behaviorally unexpressed "anger" will some day be adequately established by distinctive, measurable physiological reactions which accompany it. Among these changes would be such things as pupil dilation, change of skin color, trembling, and recordable physiological changes mediated by the autonomic nervous system, such as diastolic blood pressure, heart rate, galvanic skin response, and muscle tension.

If and when anger is thus identified, will such identification tell us only that anger is *present* but not *what* it is? In this context, there are other interesting phenomena. Even where "anger" has psychologically gone "underground," in the sense that people are not aware of their anger, it still can be detected in some of the identifiable and measurable physiological happenings (such as trembling, sweating, and so forth) normally associated with conscious, intense "anger." For example, some rejected reported early in counseling that they were baffled by the presence of some of these physiological phenomena since they were not at the time aware of any emotion which could account for them.

When such phenomena have been approached from an experiential point of view, some psychologists (including myself) have been well aware of the problems inherent in speaking of the existence of nonexperienced feelings. How can one seriously speak of a feeling such as anger that is not experienced? I do not wish to appear to take such a problem lightly—in fact, it is a highly controversial matter—but since, in my judgment, its discussion does not belong here, I simply choose to acknowledge the existence of what is manifest even though I do not yet understand it. That is, I recognize what appears to be a fact, even though I cannot yet adequately explain it. Clinical evidences support the position that negative feelings such as anger frequently go below consciousness and accumulate there.

One clue, already mentioned, to the existence of such a reservoir of angry feelings was the often surprising and sometimes highly explosive anger periodically experienced by the rejected. Some of them—

later in the counseling relationship—came to recognize that these had been present in them for years, though they had not recognized their existence.

Were the experiences of "anger" in the rejected always different from "hostility" and "aggression" rather than just different labels for similar experiences? If they were different affective experiences, were they mutually exclusive? In endeavoring to answer these questions, let me first attempt to spell out the experiential meanings I ascribe to each of them.

According to Webster's dictionary, "anger" is "a feeling that may result from injury, mistreatment, opposition, etc.; it usually shows itself in a desire to hit out at something or someone else." Were my findings in agreement with this definition? Anger in the rejected was a qualitatively distinct, feeling-response of heightened displeasure. When it was very intense, it was frequently termed "rage" and was usually stimulated by the experience of perceived injustice, mistreatment, humiliation, or some other personal hurt or frustration. It was found to carry with it an inclination to lash out damagingly against someone or something.

Some rejected labeled what appeared to be anger as *resentment*. Throughout his childhood, one man could never express, and so continually pushed down, the resentment he felt toward his father and mother. He now resents and still buries his resentment of anyone in a position of authority over him. At the same time, he cannot allow himself to express his resentment through a hurtful act of any kind. He cannot admit, even to himself, any hurtful inclinations whatever.

What were the characteristics of anger in the rejected? One prominent characteristic was *imputability*. The urge to hurt or injure appeared to carry a specification of its target only when it was sensed to have been stimulated by a *blameworthy* hurtful act or omission on the part of one or more *persons*. There was no urge, for instance, to hurt a blind person who accidentally knocked over and broke a priceless art object.

Anger in the rejected was experienced in its "chemically pure state" when present in notable strength. Even very intense anger or "rage" was triggered at times by things, such as being unable to find something or being frustratingly delayed by circumstances. Such was the factual side of it. However, in terms of explanation, something else appeared. When real rage was occasioned in the rejected by nonhuman elements, the frustrating situations or things invariably appeared to have been reductively personal. These enraged rejected at least inferred that some person was at fault.

Accordingly, the rejected got *intensely* angry *only at people*. They appeared to be incapable of becoming truly enraged at *things, as such.* Even their childhood temper-tantrums appeared to them much later to have been caused by ostensibly frustrating parents or other people. When the cause of the tantrums happened to be some frustrating thing, they felt that parents or others should have removed or remedied the situation and had failed to do so.

I submit this hypothetical statement with due caution, since I have yet to encounter it in the literature. Nonetheless, the reports did appear to warrant the interpretation that the chronologically adult rejected invariably inferred that one or more persons were somehow responsible for all their rage-producing frustrations. It is more accurate to say that their frustrations were seen as person-caused rather than people-caused, inasmuch as some rejected felt that God or the devil was responsible.

Intense anger also seemed to carry at least the connotation of injustice—the feeling that something unfair had been perpetrated on them. At least implicitly, the rejected felt that the persons who caused their anger ought not to have acted that way. At times, the rejected felt personally violated by those things which had enraged them. Again, I have not found this point of implied or connotative injustice in the literature.

Another characteristic of the intense person-caused anger—anger felt to have been culpably caused by one or more other persons—was that it was more *lasting* than that caused by nonhuman situations (47). Those who were angry, for instance, because their balky cars wouldn't start when they were in a hurry, found that their anger subsided much quicker than would have been the case had they suspected certain persons of deliberately tampering with their cars.

Anger resulting from perceived person-caused actions or omissions also appeared to carry a strong retaliatory inclination toward *specific* persons. Verification of this specificity of a human target in person-caused anger, however, proved exceedingly difficult. The very common phenomenon of *displacement*—of taking it out on the wrong person or even on a thing—contributed considerably to this difficulty. When taken out on a thing, this thing at times was felt to be a stand-in for a person. In displacing their anger, the rejected had spontaneously found a suitable victim, but often remained unaware that they were hurting the wrong person.

Further difficulty in verifying the specificity of a human target in perceived person-caused anger was due to either of two factors: the *automatic,* unconscious concealment below the level of their awareness of what was painful; and the *voluntary,* conscious disregard of what was painful. Through either of these devices, the rage itself or the associated inclination to hurt back or both at times remained safely below the level of their awareness. Two reasons why both the feeling of anger and the inclination to retaliate had been kept out of consciousness were that: (1) both would have been productive of unpleasant guilt feelings if conscious; and (2) if such experiences had been maintained for lengthy periods in awareness, they would have become psychologically erosive as they gradually wore these persons down.

An almost incredible *intensity* of the accompanying retaliatory inclinations was experienced by some of the rejected, particularly those who had been harshly rejected. To their utter astonishment, brutal urges surfaced in their consciousness in the course of counseling. In one way or another they became aware that they were potential slayers. Many of the rejected whom I counseled for a considerable time had become aware of a murderous rage which had been deeply buried within. All they would have needed, they knew, was the appropriate situation—for example, participation in a war, mob violence, some kind of authoritative order giving "justification," or sufficient taunting by someone—in order to utterly destroy other persons. Some even described themselves as human bombs, fearful that they would some day be detonated.

They realized that they were fully capable of physically destroying other people or, in some instances, themselves. One rejected man who frequently was aware of such anger was only waiting for the right time to take his life, but he insisted that he was not going alone. He was determined to take several people with him, including at least one priest, because an early confessional experience with a priest had caused him great suffering. He explained that, though he greatly admired me, he didn't really know any other priests and, because I was handy, he had decided definitely to take me with him. The reason he was waiting, he added, was that he had not yet determined the best way to kill all of us together. It is hardly necessary to remark that my weekly sessions with him for over a year were anything but comfortable. Before he had determined the means to be used, he was killed in an automobile collision.

A number of these rejected felt sure that, even if they were to kill someone, they still would not be satisfied. They were certain that they would not get the need to hurt others out of their systems in this way. Somehow they still would not have felt they had gotten even.

The rejected who were aware of such extremely violent urges did not have them as constant experiences, for the most part. Rather, such inclinations periodically and suddenly surfaced in their consciousness

with frightening strength when triggered by certain stimuli. One rejected man wrote:

> I can readily understand how people commit murder, because I always
> felt that I was capable of it. Because of a tiny wrong, real or fancied, I've
> often fallen into a state of fear-hatred for days or weeks which is abso-
> lutely indescribable. At the time, I often thought of it in terms of hell:
> something caught crossways in the middle of my soul which I can't get
> out—a ceaseless fight against something in the center of me which I
> can't stand, won't recognize as mine, and can't get rid of; the desire not
> merely to hit or kill someone, but to annihilate him absolutely. Of
> course, I had it under control (especially since I've always been incap-
> able of expressing anger at all—the consequence would be too disas-
> trous), but I knew that if the object of hatred had really pressed me
> while I was in that state, anything could have happened. This also
> explained why I always turned so bitterly and effectively sarcastic if
> anyone seemed to be getting the better of me in conversational kidding.
> Also, why I found it was impossible for me to pretend to be mad—as
> soon as I pretended, I *was* mad; there was just so much pent-up force
> that the slightest opening brought an overrelease of feeling.

The retaliatory urges of some rejected were directed at rejecting parents, but almost never on the grounds of getting even for the hurt of
rejection. Those who targeted their vindictive urges on parents usually
gave themselves some other explanation for doing so. One young man
hates his father because the latter abused his mother. Several times, he
wanted to kill his father. Once, when his father made a slurring remark
about his mother in the presence of another person, he corrected his
father right there. When his father started for him menacingly, he
stepped back, looking for some weapon with which to kill his father.
His dad saw the look in his eyes and retreated. He said: "My old man
knew that I would kill him. I will, too, if he lays a hand on me or says
anything against my mom or anyone close to me." After a bit of reflection, he added: "I might not kill him, but I would beat him to a pulp."
    A number of the rejected who recognized murderous urges in them-
selves realized that these could readily be displaced onto innocent
people. They felt they needed to keep up their guard to prevent such
tragedies. When one man had been in high school, he did not dare
enter one of the amateur boxing matches because he might have gotten
mad and wanted to kill the other kid.
    The tendency to displace retaliatory urges onto innocent bystanders
was, in a few instances, carried out as recognized displacement.
Though still in his teens, one young man said he could kick his "old

man" to death with no feeling because of what he had done to the little kids in the family. He said that he would kill him but, if he did, he "would have to take off, and there would be no one left to take care of the little kids at home except the old lady, and she's nuts." Meanwhile, he savagely beats up some tramp occasionally, but only if he reminds him of the "old man." "Moreover," he added, "I will take no guff at any time from anyone in a position of authority." He explained this attitude toward authority figures at length. The burden of his explanation was that he will not tolerate anyone trying to be a stand-in for his father.

Was such seemingly unappeasable, violent anger limited to only a few of the rejected? I do not know, and I have not encountered anything on this point in the literature. However, a relevant consideration is that depression seemed to be characteristic of the rejected, and Rado maintains that *every* depressed person is characterized by rage (150). I could not seriously maintain that I received sufficient information to conclude that such apparently unquenchable rage lay deeply buried in *all* the rejected. At the same time, my findings would seem to support such a position. Such intensity of anger did not need to await recognition by the rejected that they had been rejected. It was mentioned by some rejected long before they became aware of their rejection. The seemingly insatiable nature of the anger in those who felt they were powerless to hurt back with equally devastating effects seemed to offer an explanation for one experience of the rejected: even those who had found a way of venting their retaliation directly at the rejecting parents reported that they often expressed their destructive urges toward other persons also.

A social parallel regarding the strength of these anger-derived destructive urges could be found in the intensity of lethal anger reported by some members of minority groups who felt rejected by white society. A friendly, mild-mannered, black man was terrified to go to sleep at night because of a recurring bad dream. In the dream, a faceless white woman, knife in hand, relentlessly pursued him, determined to cut off his male sex organ. Each night in his dream, when she approached him with the knife, he awoke in a cold sweat. In the course of talking to me about it, he came up with this interpretation of the dream, which he felt certain was the correct one: The woman represented "whitey," and the dream expressed his deeply buried fear that "whitey" was determined to deprive him of his manhood—his personhood.

Later on, he was astonished to recognize within him an anger so violent that, as he put it, he could kill a white person—any white person—preferably with his bare hands. He added: "I know that if I did manage to kill whitey I still wouldn't be even, because I'd only be taking his life, not his manhood. However, no need to be alarmed, because I think I have the urge well under control."

This intense anger has been experienced by some members of minority groups and could be one explanation for the sudden eruptions of racial violence in areas such as Watts, Newark, and regions of Central and South Africa (154). As American newspaper accounts have frequently maintained, a few members of minority groups who participated in violent deeds during such racial riots later indicated that they were surprised at the intensity of their own destructive urges.

In this country, members of minority groups have repeatedly claimed that they have not as yet received full status as human beings, since they perceive white society's continuing rejection of them as fully equal persons, but caution is called for in evaluating the causes of their destructive behaviors. Because displacement of aggression is so common, it would be difficult to ascertain to what extent these aggressions are caused by white society's rejection and to what extent minority-group aggressions were being displaced onto "whitey" as a scapegoat.

Such considerations might suggest a similar explanation in still another area of contemporary life, namely, that of the feminist movement. Because some women feel they have been the victims of injustice, they are angry. Constantly frustrated by what they see as ongoing, undeniable discrimination on the basis of their sex, they regard men as trying to deny them full personhood. This explanation might, in part, account for the occasional intense anger of some of them.

There is one further aspect regarding such experiences of some minorities and of some women. Experimental psychologists have demonstrated that the tendency to approach a desired goal grows stronger the closer the organism gets to that goal. As some minorities and some women get increasingly closer to their desired goal of full acceptance as equals, their efforts to reach that goal increase. To the extent that their strengthened drives toward their goals are blocked, their resulting frustrations and angers become more intense.

Finally, in both of these situations—as, apparently, in all experienced rejections—these people feel that injustice has been perpetrated on their persons. This should be expected to heighten their frustrations and, consequently, to further increase their angers and retaliatory urges.

Hostility in the Rejected

What is meant by hostility? Webster's dictionary defines "hostility" as "a feeling of enmity, ill will or unfriendliness. . . . " In substantial agreement with this definition, I regard "hostility" in humans as an *emotionally derived desire or intention to hurt or damage.* That is, there must be present in experience an inclination to damage or hurt, which wells up from some emotion, and this inclination must be consented to. Accordingly, hostility is always internal behavior, which may or may not be externalized in overt behavior. The specific emotion out of which this desire to hurt flows may be anger or another negative emotion, such as fear, jealousy, envy, hate, spite, or malice. In the rejected, it was almost inevitably experienced as the emotionally-toned desire to damage not a thing but a person or persons.

How common is hostility among people? Are humans innately non-aggressive toward one another as has been maintained by Leakey and Lewin (100)? Human history clearly seems to me to refute such a position. On the other hand, is hostility innate in people? I cannot subscribe to this position either. On the basis of my clinical findings, I take issue with the assumption that the socialization process is so exceedingly painful that every child forms hostile death wishes toward his socializers but that these hostile wishes are repressed and maintained below the conscious level (205). Close observance of many young children fails to show all socialization as dreadfully painful.

Again, I have found no support in my clinical experience for the psychoanalytic position that every love relationship has an ambivalent quality, so that it always includes some hostility or rejection (15). I have not found evidence for the assumption that a mother's hostile feelings for her child are unavoidable (15). Neither have I found clinical grounds for Zilboorg's insistence that murderous drives are the only ones capable of maintaining the universal fear of death in a state of low tension (217). Marcuse has allied himself with Freud in postulating a destructive instinct in humans—a death instinct which leads to the release of increasingly destructive forces (116). My clinical experience has indicated no evidence of such an instinct. Moreover, it is well to recall that early in his life Freud had structured his theory around the conflict between sex (the libidinous) and ego (the self-preservative) instincts; only considerably later did he see an antagonism between the life instinct (eros) and the death instinct (thanatos).

Have others found a relationship between hostility and rejection? Symonds maintains that the child who is rejected by either parent is destined, on the average, to be hostile (196). Bowlby, from a different approach, seems to be saying something similar when he states that an excess of separation anxiety and an excess of hostility are very commonly provided by the same experience (25).

Would there be present in all rejected a strong, destructive urge? My findings would seem to support such a conclusion. To begin with, they were all conscious of a strong negative feeling that some of them had labeled *anger*. When one rejected man said, "I am mad, mad, mad, all the time," he was referring mainly to his tendencies to hurt.

Whatever the specific nature of the negative feeling that was the source of their inclination to hurt, one conclusion appeared to be warranted. It was that *hostility appeared to have been present in some form in every rejected person* with whom I dealt professionally. One study has found that, where the child's renunciation of his rejection-produced hostility was the condition laid down by the parents for any acceptance whatever, his hostility was turned inward and resulted in various kinds of self-punishment (73). The Alcoholics Anonymous organization, whose members are believed to include quite a number of the rejected, simply assumes the presence of deep hostility in every alcoholic.

The rejected who were my clients described their hostility in terms of their consented-to desire to humiliate, injure, damage, cause loss to, get even with, inflict pain on, attack—and so on—one or more other persons. Some talked, at times with pride, of controlling their hostility. They felt proud of themselves for refraining from carrying out powerful urges to hurt people. On the other hand, some who had given vent to their destructive urges reported subsequent guilt feelings.

A number of the rejected, aware of such emotionally-toned urges against another, had decided to forgive the other person for the wrong done. In this way they had determined not to carry out those urges. Others had either carried out aggressive behaviors, or they had chosen to bide their time until they could more disastrously hurt the other person. The difference between these two kinds of responses was clear. In the one, they "would have liked to" hurt the other person but determined not to do so. In the other, they "chose to" hurt the other person. This difference between merely "liking to" and "determining to" is of considerable psychological importance. As will be seen presently, the *external* (behavioral) *expression* of such hostility is what is meant by "aggression."

Hostility has long been regarded as being composed of two basic elements: the negatively-toned feeling and the destructive inclination. The rejected have not been able to psychologically cope with these two elements easily. Some of the rejected devised various methods to help them control their destructive inclinations. Others, who expressed their negative feelings and the inclination to hurt back, feared retaliation or had painful feelings of guilt.

One woman's rejecting mother had been dedicated to having her daughter master the piano. Her mother would sit alongside her at the piano by the hour, driving her crazy with her tapping noises. Though this got on her nerves terribly, she kept herself from screaming at or slapping her mother by concentrating on the pressure feeling at the base of her neck and between her shoulder blades. When she was not playing the piano, she "held herself" by keeping her thumb inside her fist and her arm stiff. She knew that if she let go she would scream at her mother. She could not afford to do this because the interest and attention her mother showed her depended on her living up to all her mother's expectations.

Now, she finds that she just can't get mad at anybody. In fact, she doesn't have to do so, because she almost never lets herself see a situation as maddening. Even when she does, she takes it out on things by throwing, kicking, or knocking them about.

Many rejected reported that they experienced hostility only periodically. One young man experiences hostility only when he becomes depressed, although he has no idea why he becomes depressed. He describes himself as a real menace if he happens to be at the wheel of a car when he is in a depression, because he will push the throttle to the floor. While doing so, he thinks he might kill someone—"But," he remarked, "I just don't give a damn."

For a few rejected, hostility became so integrated into their everyday life that, regardless of what happened, it was present. One man is invariably filled with hostility early in the day, when he will explode about almost anything. Usually, he bursts out verbally in such a way as to hurt someone present or damage someone's reputation. For the most part, he is not aware of such inclinations during the afternoons and evenings.

A number of rejected accounted for their hostility as being simply hatred or as flowing out of hatred. An unusually insightful man, rejected by both parents, wrote about his former boss: "I think I hated him all the more because he was the kind of person I wanted to love and wanted to love me—but he wouldn't, so I hated him thoroughly."

Such hatreds were always directed at persons, and a variety of personal targets were specified. The hatreds were focused by a few rejected directly on the rejecting parents. The following letter from a young girl, in which she writes about her hatred for her mother, is reproduced almost in its entirety because of its highly revealing content:

> Right now I just had another fight with Mom. Or rather just continued one we've had for years. We don't throw words or yell at each other— it's just the hatred in our eyes. I called her on the phone. She told me not to wait up for her, but I could tell she wanted me to, so I did—until

twelve o'clock, then I had to go to bed. The next morning she was real crabby. I didn't know how to act and it made me mad because I didn't do anything. All she did was yell, yell, yell. But we're so used to it, it just goes in one ear and out the other, and we let her know it. I hate myself for it, but I hate her more. I don't really, but that's the way I felt yesterday and today. So today I thought I would just try to hurt her. . . . All she did was yell some more, and every time we'd sit down she'd give us one of her looks which goes right through us, but we couldn't let her know so we'd just look back. . . .

I wanted the car to go riding around. I don't have a license or a permit cuz I'm only fifteen, but she usually lets me. That's another thing. I'm spoiled silly. I can usually talk her into letting me do anything but today she said no. She told me to turn off the roast at 4:00, but I told her to tell dad to do it and that I wouldn't. I hope you aren't shocked. I know it's terrible, but I've always gotten away with it. When she came home, we just didn't talk. After supper—I didn't eat when she told me, but when we (my sister and I) were doing the dishes (I hope I don't sound proud of the way I act; I'm not at all, but I want you to know just how it is)— all of a sudden I heard her (mom) yelling and crying and swearing all at the same time. She was saying how dad never did anything but read, why did she ever get married and have us, how she hated herself, and that she was a fool to work so hard for us when we didn't even love her, and that she wished she was dead. I had heard this all dozens of times before, but I felt so guilty I ran upstairs and collided with my sister who was running down to get me and we both ran to her crying and hugged her and my brother came in, too. We said we were sorry but she kept going on and on. This is all what she said. Well, she kept saying that we didn't love her, that she tried so hard and didn't get anything out of it. That she had to do everything alone, that she knew she was crabby but couldn't help it because she had so much to worry about and every little thing we did bothered her. How different she is when she is at work.

The urge to hurt parents was frequently associated with hatred of the parents, at times linked to considerable fear of those parents. One woman's father, who didn't like her, forced her to do the kinds of hard work that should be done by men. He disliked her mother and was hard on her, as well. To neither of them had he ever given affection or consideration. As a girl, she had feared her father and used to run away and hide from him. Now, she vehemently hates her father, especially for what he has done to her mother over the years, and looks for ways to hurt him back. Recently she stood up to him in an argument and won it, and so is no longer as afraid of him. However, she still can't stand to be alone with him anywhere.

The fact that a parent had made himself greatly feared was, at times, the reason for hating him. One woman remembers her father as a wild man, constantly throwing and breaking things and keeping everyone petrified with fear. For this she can never forgive him, and she tries at every opportunity to get even with him. She likes her mother "real well" but does not love her—she hates her dad.

Hatred unknowingly became generalized to situations closely associated with the experiences of some rejected. One woman can't force herself to enter any Catholic church. Frequently, she has gotten as far as the door but is unable to get beyond it. The revulsion she feels makes entering impossible, though she really has no idea why. Later, she mentioned that she hated the woman who had raised her and regrets that she can no longer even the score with her. This woman, long since dead, was a Catholic and insisted on raising her as a Catholic, though her own family background had been non-Catholic. The woman had been unbelievably cruel to her, though she was so pious as to seem in her young eyes to be almost a woman-priest. She had no doubt that the woman hated her; she could see it in her eyes.

Now, whenever she approaches a Catholic church, the woman is so vividly there that she can't stand it. In fact, she feels that this same woman is inside the church, still looking her intense dislike at a little girl—whom she knows to be herself—standing there at the church door. In addition, whenever she tries to think and act as a Catholic, she feels like a hypocrite, because, in some very real way, she is then being the woman whose eyes she could scratch out.

The presence of hostility, whether flowing from hatred or another negative feeling, manifested itself in a few rejected solely through their fears. One woman, whose mother had punished her exceedingly all her young life, lives in constant fear that her children will die. If they are only a few minutes late in returning from school, she is sure they are dead. In vivid, horrifying detail, she fantasizes each of their deaths. The turmoil within her is so great she is fearful that some day she will "flip." Were she ever to do so, her greatest fear is that she would then kill her children and her husband.

At times, the rejected did not have to struggle consciously with the two elements of negative feeling and the inclination to hurt: either or both of them were psychologically taken care of for them in a spontaneous, but unrecognized, protective manner, by being unknowingly repressed and maintained beneath the level of their awareness. Where both the feeling and the inclination were thus repressed, grounds for their existence appeared solely in the unexplained aggressions of these persons.

On the other hand, sometimes a feeling such as anger remained below the level of awareness in some of the rejected, while the inclination to hurt remained conscious though displaced (142). One man gets all wrapped up in espousing or defending almost anything, which he now recognizes as giving him a basis for severely criticizing or verbally attacking anyone in authority. He explained to himself the source of these urges to lash out against authority figures on the grounds that "it's the principle of the thing." Then he looked at me and added, "I really don't know what I mean by that, here." Significantly, Symonds reported a pronounced tendency in rejected children to resent authority (196).

Very few rejected recognized their hostility toward rejecting parents. One man, who had gone to another part of the country and been in therapy there, wrote that he had admitted to the psychiatrist that he had held on to feelings of hostility toward one person he cared for, but only for this person. His letter continued: "O.K.., says the psychiatrist, you'll admit it about him, but you still don't dare admit it about your parents. Gradually I came to realize that he was completely correct. The hostility was very widespread and very complicated. For example, I hated the world but projected it; hence the feeling that everyone hated me. . . ."

The feeling such as anger that underlay the hostility remained a conscious experience of some rejected, while the inclination to hurt was unknowingly maintained safely beneath the level of their awareness. One young woman, who is still in college, is deeply hurt and resentful that her parents have rejected her. Recently, she has been bewildered by what has been happening to her in school. Her parents are very proud and highly pleased when she receives good grades. While she seriously tells herself she wants to get good grades for them, she invariably finds herself so loaded with anxiety whenever she is preparing for any examination that she just can't study. As a consequence, she has been getting poor grades. She doesn't know of any solution to this problem, nor why it is happening to her.

Other rejected unconsciously buried both the feeling and the inclination to hurt back. Nonetheless, they were in some inexplicable way getting back at the person or persons who gave the original hurt or frustration.

Counterrejection of the parents appeared to be universally present at some psychological level in the rejected. This implied a hostility flowing out of anger and/or a hatred for the parents. With very few exceptions, nevertheless, the rejected were not endeavoring to hurt back for having been rejected by those parents. Instead, either they gave themselves no reasons whatever for these negative feelings against the parents or they offered some reason other than their own rejection as their justification for hurting back. Regardless of whether or not a reason was given, they were committing *aggression* against rejecting parents.

Aggression in the Rejected

Can "aggression" be given an operational definition? In my judgment, it cannot be given an adequate one. Some psychologists have presented such a definition by concentrating on the *behavioral* aspect while disregarding the integral element of hostile *intentionality*. Bandura, for instance, has behavioristically defined aggression as behavior that results in personal injury and in destruction of property (14). While this kind of exclusively behavioral approach does indeed seem to be justified when dealing with animals, it has created problems when dealing with humans.

The behavioral approach necessitates lumping together deliberately intended actions and omissions, nonintentional and accidental ones, and those that are intentional but are not intended to hurt or damage another person, even though they are hurtful and frustrating. The unfortunate result of such a mixing together of human behaviors has been something of a psychological hodgepodge. I think it is this kind of approach, which focuses solely on the behavioral aspects of aggression, that has been the source of much of the confusion evident in viewing all competitive sports and events such as debates as "aggression"—and, therefore, psychologically unhealthy.

The element of intention, in fact, has been controversial ever since Dollard and his associates (in 1939) characterized aggression as "any sequence of behavior the goal response to which is the injury of the person to whom it is directed" (46, p. 9). Intention would seem to be at least connoted by them. At any rate, *injurious intent* was adopted as an essential element of aggression in much subsequent research, such as that of Maccoby (113), Berkowitz (18), and Feshbach (56). I subscribe to the position that injurious intent is an essential element of human aggression. In agreeing with this position, many psychologists view aggression in terms of responses *designed* to hurt others (18, 32, 75, 124, 172).

Aggression, then, is any form of *overt, hostile* attack on a person or thing. This external expression can be either a hurtful, blameworthy *act* or a harmful, externally observable *omission* to act where one ought to act. Hence, "aggression" presupposes intentionality; it is presumed to include the element of culpability.

Accordingly, as considered here, no matter how injurious to another a given behavior might be, if it was not an expression of hostility, of an urge to hurt, it is not regarded as aggression. A true accident, for instance, regardless of the damage resulting to one or more persons, does not qualify as aggression, precisely because it lacks evil intent. Therefore, the psychological position I take here is that a parent who spanks his child with the motive of love is not committing aggression; nor is a teacher or supervisor who punishes a child in school necessarily expressing aggression. A football player who blocks or tackles an opponent very hard is not necessarily expressing aggression, even though it might appear to others to be an act of violence. In fact, even in professional football one occasionally sees the perpetrator of such "violence," after he has effectively flattened out an opponent, help that opponent up with a little pat that says, in effect: "Sorry I had to hit you so hard, old fella, but there was no other way of taking you out of the play."

However, much contemporary aggression, because it remains verbal, is not readily recognized. According to the position taken here, a person who *designedly* "just happens" to mention in public a damaging rumor about another is committing aggression against that person. One who, with premeditation, succeeds in publicly humiliating another person is doing the same. This category of aggression would also include the individual who says nothing when his testimony could clear the name of an innocent, accused person, and the individual who does nothing as he watches another person bleed to death.

Several studies were found in the literature that, in some way, relate aggression to parental rejection. Knight (95), Newell (138), and Wolberg (212) report that, the more overt the rejection by the parent, the more frequently the child displayed aggressive behavior. Bowlby et al. (26) mention that mother-rejecting patterns were often found in women who, as children, had been rejected. Pemberton and Benady (145) disclose that children who had consciously rejecting parents had rejecting attitudes to those parents. Bowlby (25) also found that where a young child's hostile impulses were directed to a parent, especially if unconsciously, there was an inevitable increase in the child's anxiety.

Maternal and paternal authoritarian-control attitudes were found by Chorost (37) to be positively related to their children's overt hostility, while parental warmth attitudes were negatively related to overt hostility in their children. Kagan's study (89) of six- to ten-year-old aggressive boys revealed that there was anger between parents and child. Three times as many children from disrupted homes (divorced or separated parents) were rated aggressive by Loeb and Price (109) as were those from nonbroken homes.

Aggressive, uncontrollable children were found by Becker et al. (17)

to have maladjusted parents who tended to vent unbridled emotions and to be arbitrary with their children. Winder and Rau (209) report aggression in preadolescent boys to be associated with parental am-bivalence, punitiveness, demands for aggression, restrictiveness, and low self-esteem in their mothers. According to Becker and his asso-ciates (17), there is strong support for the hypothesis that the degrees of hostility of both parents and the use of physical punishment are related to aggressive behaviors in children. Schulman et al. (175) found that conduct-problem (aggressive) children's parents were significantly more rejecting and hostile toward their children than were the parents of non-conduct-problem children.

Finally, in Sears' study (176) of normal twelve-year-old children, a sex difference appeared that could throw light on some aggressions reported by the rejected. The girls were significantly higher in express-ing their aggression in socially approved ways, e.g., punishment for rule breaking, while the boys were higher in antisocial aggression. It seemed that, in the rejected, aggression had been in keeping with Dollard and Miller's (47) hypothesis that aggression is a consequence of frustration. Certainly in their rejection they had experienced deeply painful, ongoing frustration.

An important factor in understanding the aggressive behavior of the rejected was the underlying motive of their counterrejection. Their counterrejection was not only of the rejecting parents themselves but also of their values, standards, ideals, and everything for which they stood and to which they subscribed. It was against the religious values of the parents that the rejected frequently felt an aversion and through which they often struck back at their parents. One man, whose parents are both church-going Catholics, remarked: "If there is a God, as you believe, Father, how could He have permitted what happened to me? How could He have allowed my father to reject me and my mother to accept me only insofar as I would play the role of the girl she had wanted? I just got a bad deal in my parents. I don't see that a good God could hand out that kind of deal. I don't buy that."

The counterrejections of the rejected zeroed in on those values the parents had most stressed. One rejected woman, whose parents are openly pious and have endeavored to instill into her the importance of religion, could not accept either their religion or their church. Moreover, the sanctity of marriage—about which they had preached incessantly to her during her teens—has been completely rejected by her. She feels that honest love and affection—something they had never known—is what really gives a union its sanctity. Just the thought of the marriage contract makes her nauseous.

A few rejected openly recognized that their rejection of certain values and truths embraced by their parents was a counterrejection of their parents. One woman cannot accept the Catholic religion, or even the existence of God, because of her hatred for her first theology teacher, her mother.

Dollard and Miller made the point that the strongest instigation aroused by a frustration is to acts of aggression against the agent perceived to be the source of the frustration (47). While this position has not been hard to verify in dealing with animals, Wolberg agrees that it has been exceedingly difficult to corroborate with humans (212). In the rejected, powerful factors—particularly guilt—had prevented them from directing aggressions against their parents or from recognizing that they were so directing them. Pemberton and Benady report that a few rejected recognized their aggression against the rejecting parents (145). As already indicated, the rejected who recognized that they were hurting their parents felt it was for some other reason than because they had been rejected by those parents. They were hurting back at the right persons for the wrong reasons.

One rejecting father wanted his son to be the best in athletics and also to be the toughest kid in the neighborhood. The son, however, wore glasses, was anything but tough, and actually hated athletics. Once when his father insisted that the two of them play catch with a baseball, his father began to throw the ball harder and harder at him. He couldn't even see some of the balls but caught every throw, which he knew infuriated his father. Then he wound up and threw the ball his hardest back at his father's bare hands. It stung his dad. He added: "It hurt him. Boy, that really felt good." It was because of what his father had done to others in the family, he explained, that he hated him and welcomed any chance to get back at him.

Some of the rejected remained at least peripherally aware of their indirect aggressions against rejecting parents. One woman was accepted only by her father. Early in life she found that she could not get recognition for anything she accomplished unless her mother benefited from it. In grade school, her teacher advised her parents that she should skip a grade. Her mother said no. From that time on, she lost all interest in school and studies. She has known from childhood that her mother uses her. Now, from the moment that her mother tells her how important it is for her to do well in something, she notices that her performance in that area deteriorates. At the same time, she feels guilty about it.

Frequently, rejected who earlier in life had carried out direct aggressions against their rejecting parents failed to see clearly that this was what they had been doing. Some had been aware of their aggressive behaviors but made no connection of them with hostile feelings. Others had been aware neither of hostile inclinations nor aggressions while they were actually carrying out the aggressions.

One rejected woman is now aware, for the first time, that she was fighting against her parents in many ways though, at the time, she did not realize that this was what she was doing. She deliberately walked pigeon-toed after her parents spent a great deal of money correcting her badly turned-in feet. When her parents insisted that it was important for her to have healthy gums and teeth, she would not tell them about the cavities she could feel with the tip of her tongue. She also managed consistently to get poor grades, whereas her parents put a heavy stress on the importance of her obtaining good grades. She added that the one thing that should have made her suspect what was going on was that she always felt guilty in doing these things.

Rationalization frequently concealed from some of the rejected these aggressions against parents. One woman whose rejecting father is now wholly dependent on her has frustrated him at almost every turn. No matter what he has wanted, she almost invariably has denied it to him with the explanation that "it is for your own good." She has also repeatedly insisted that he do things in which he has no interest whatever so that he "will remain vital and current." As a result, his later years have been miserable ones of utter frustration. A person to whom the father had revealed it relayed this last bit of information to me, along with the fact that their friends have nothing but admiration for the daughter, a very religious person, because she so heroically dedicated her life to her father's care. When they have commended her for this, the daughter has replied that she is glad to sacrifice her life in order to care for her father.

Some rejected continued for years to express aggression toward parents without any recognition that they were doing so. One man simply cannot speak to his mother nor answer her when she asks him anything. Even if she just remarks, "It's a nice day, isn't it?" he is silent. It puzzles him that he can't talk to her; he has no idea why. His father never gave him any affection, and he always felt certain that his dad didn't love him. Much later, he mentioned that he couldn't think of separating his father and mother since, as he put it, "they stood or fell together." While he has given what appeared to be indications of his mother's rejection, he has not openly recognized that his mother, too, rejected him.

It was necessary to exercise caution to avoid interpreting every observed hurtful behavior of the rejected as aggression. What at first sight appeared to be clear-cut aggression against others, at times was not that at all. Hurtful behavior had, for instance, been a device calculated, not to damage another, but to be protective, since it could furnish less loathsome grounds than unlovableness for the anticipated rejection by others that some rejected felt sure was coming. This had resulted in the "protective" hurting of self and/or others. One woman wrote: "I am so used to being hurt I hurt myself rather than let others do it. I know from experience that I will be hurt anyway so I come out against people principally to hurt myself—I would rather hurt me than have another hurt me. This hatred is born of fear." Here, what first appeared to be the desire to displace hurt onto the wrong persons was explained as a means of protecting herself by furnishing grounds other than her own unlovableness for being rejected by people.

A number of rejected men and women, especially at their first counseling session, arrived very late without having phoned that they would be delayed. Others showed up noticeably under the influence of alcohol. Still others initially used very crude language. Later, almost without exception, these persons admitted that they had deliberately acted toward me in such an offensive manner in order to beat me to the punch. They had been sure that I would reject them as soon as I got to know them. They were laying down grounds of their own choosing for my anticipated rejection. This would have enabled them later to be able to reassure themselves that I had rejected them because they had been rude, disrespectful, uncouth, and so on, and not because I found them unacceptable as persons.

By far, the greatest amount of aggression in the rejected was *displaced*—carried out against the wrong persons or even against things. Dollard and Miller (47) and Ostow (142) had similar findings. The aggression which welled up out of the hostility of the rejected was displaced, not only onto other persons and things, but also onto themselves. This is in agreement with Sears' report (176). One woman hates the whole world because it is so hurtful, hates God for making it thus filled with hurtful people, hates herself for everything, and punishes herself for all her failures, which show up her lack of true worth.

Displacement was something spontaneous, rather than something that the rejected had logically figured out. It did, indeed, appear to possess its own kind of logic, but not one that had been consciously worked out. In fact, it had been manifested very early in life before there was much evidence of reasoning. A mother was holding her three-year-old son, who was crying bitterly because his daddy was leaving to board a plane. The child suddenly turned on her and struck her viciously in the face. The destructive inclination of hostility and its externalization in aggression were obviously being *displaced* against the wrong person. At the same time, it required no conscious reasoning process, even though the logically apt selection of the victim as a suitable substitute was evident. It was the other parent's parental similarity to the offending parent which made the substitution suitable.

In the rejected, *displacement* of aggression was a spontaneous, unrecognized function which seemingly gave them the satisfaction derived from getting back at the rejected parent or parents through substitutes. At the same time, it protected them from the undesirable consequences which could have resulted from a recognized, direct attack on the parents.

What were these undesirable consequences which were avoided? They appeared to be the guilt which would have been involved in any recognized attack on their parents, as well as the extremely painful acknowledgment of the rejection-produced psychological hurt. This would have been implicit in the realization that the real reason for wanting to hurt back at the parents was the original, excruciating parental rejection. In addition, the retaliation that might have come from their parents or other persons for their undisguised attack on parents was avoided. In our culture, this kind of behavior is certainly unacceptable.

The rejected who had been displacing their aggressions were well aware of their feelings of hostility and aggression, but nevertheless *failed to relate* them to their own parental rejection. One man who was rejected by both parents knows he is really loaded with resentment and hostility, because they come out whenever he can safely release them. He is, for example, inevitably defiant and abusive to strangers in a situation where he is not known and where there is little likelihood of retaliation. While driving, he has at times slowed his car in a strange place and shouted abusive insults or made outrageous gestures at people on the sidewalk. He has even rolled down his car window and spat contemptuously into another car alongside while waiting for a traffic light to change. On two such occasions, the other driver gave chase. Each time this happened, he pulled over to the side of the road, locked the car doors, put up the windows, buried his face in his hands, and waited for the other individual to go away. Much as he recognizes in himself these strong hostile inclinations, he has no idea what causes them.

In a few instances, the rejected consciously arranged ingenious situations which would furnish them the opportunity of expressing their aggression against others. One woman frequently pretends that she is stupid so that she can secretly laugh at the people she has thus fooled. At the same time, she insists she knows of no reason why she should want to do this.

The majority of the rejected seemed to have unknowingly generalized their counterrejection of their parents to all persons holding positions of authority over them. Seldom have I encountered rejected persons who were cognizant that they were thus generalizing. Nonetheless, they experienced an apparent inability to admit subservience or submission of any kind to persons placed in authority over them. This reluctance to capitulate to such persons reached down as far as the patrolman who stopped them for a traffic violation and stood in judgment on them.

Every relationship of the rejected to those in authority over them appeared to re-present, at some level of their knowing, their original relationship to the parents who they felt rejected them. They did not see that they resisted those in authority positions over them because they were in such positions. Neither did they think that they had any particular problem with those in authority, as such. Rather, they knew only that they disliked and bristled with resentment when they had to deal with specific persons who happened to be authority figures.

Displacement of aggression by the rejected almost invariably tended to be taken out on a substitute that was *safe*. Indeed, the element of safety became a touchstone in the displacement of aggression. The aggressor at least implicitly sensed that the one selected as the stand-in for the real culprit would "take it" rather than threaten to seriously hurt back. A grade-school teacher, for example, might sense that she could safely take out on the children in her class the frustration from the "dressing down" she received from the principal without having to fear that the children would reject her. In turn, they might sense that they could safely take out on each other at recess their frustration for the unexpected and unjust attack by their teacher.

In displaced aggression, there almost always seemed to be an alleged *justification* for carrying out the aggression. In the example just mentioned, the teacher might reprimand the children because they were not really serious about behaving properly in school. They, in turn, might attack others because they were so stupid. When the rejected displaced the urge to hurt to the wrong persons, they almost always presented some appearance of justification for their attack on these persons. The alleged justification seemed to have been needed so that, while they derived some satisfaction from hurting back at substitutes, they still managed to avoid the guilt and social disapproval that would have been theirs had their aggressions not been displaced.

It also seemed that, the closer the psychological *resemblance*, the greater the satisfaction from retaliation experienced by the hostile person in carrying out his aggression. For example, one person who had been rejected by his father had experienced—even before he had become conscious of the rejection—more satisfaction from lashing back hurtfully at another authority figure than from striking out at a non-authority figure. A child who had been rejected by his mother found it more satisfying to hit back verbally at a woman teacher than at a man teacher. More satisfaction seemed also to have been experienced by a rejected child in hurting his own brother rather than a stranger, because he was hurting back at the rejecting parent's child. Again, it was more satisfying for a parent who had been a rejected person to hurt his own child rather than a stranger, apparently because the hurting was in the same parent-child relationship in which the original hurt had been given even though the roles had been reversed.

Other studies also have found that abusing parents almost always had been abused and neglected themselves when they were young (21, 182, 197). This may throw some explanatory light on the fact that abused children appear in the emergency rooms of U.S. hospitals with lacerations, punctures, bruises, broken bones, and/or cigarette, cigar, and other burns. They have been nearly suffocated, half-drowned, poisoned, or beaten with a belt buckle, hammer, or other instrument. Statistics indicate that the injuries of twelve to twenty-five percent of these children are *nonaccidental* (147). Most of these children are under three years of age and the abuse is perpetrated largely by their mothers. Their parents' backgrounds show a pattern of having been reared in a traumatic manner, of feeling rejection, of being isolated and distrustful, and of having a poor self-image (21, 147)

The rejected who reported that they indulged in child abuse had to reckon with guilt and social disapprovals. By contrast, those who furiously pounded their pillows or some other *thing* found it less satisfying than pounding another person, but were almost wholly free of guilt as well as of social disapproval. When they imagined that they were raining blows on some specific person, they got more satisfaction but also experienced some guilt.

Finally, it seemed that all displacement of aggression, inasmuch as it was short of the mark of hurting back at the true culprit, left some dissatisfaction. It appeared, moreover, that the less the psychological resemblance between the substitute victim in displaced aggression and the real culprit, the less the satisfaction derived. Accordingly, the rejected who confined their displacement of aggression to inanimate things seemed to receive relatively little satisfaction, though they felt very little if any guilt. The dissatisfaction that remained did not weaken or gradually disappear. Instead, it appeared to remain in a cumulative, personal reservoir of negative feelings closely tied to inclinations to hurt back. This reservoir remained intensely dynamic and was never far below the surface of consciousness. Also, nearly every aggression against an inanimate thing appeared to be a displaced hostility whose true target—even though unrecognized by the aggressor—was one or more persons.

Aggression springing out of hostility against rejecting parents was displaced onto *self*, especially where parental acceptance came with the price-tag of the child's renunciation of all aggression toward them. Wolberg also found this to be the case (212). Where this was their experience, the rejected involved usually failed to see that the aggression was being displaced from their parents to themselves. In fact, at times they were conscious of neither the hostility involved nor the aggression taking place. This seemed to be the case in a number of self-defeating, self-sabotaging behaviors that frustrated the rejected.

Again, there was an awareness in some rejected of such hostility and aggression which they ascribed to sources other than parental rejection. One woman remarked, "I engaged in a real sexual orgy in order to destroy myself." She acknowledged that she had been contemplating suicide, as well. She maintains that she doesn't want to be bad— she wants to be good. However, she has the urge to destroy herself, because it is unacceptable to her that she has been living only for her children. She insists that she has to live for herself. As for her feelings about herself—she loathes herself.

A few rejected who had feelings of revulsion and hatred for themselves were not aware that they were directing aggression against themselves. One man, who despises himself, has found that the promotions in his business firm which he greatly desires are inevitably and repeatedly blocked by some stupid blunder of his each time that he knows he is being considered for advancement. Utterly baffled by these blunders, he remarked: "It looks as though I just can't win."

Infrequently, the rejected were conscious of directing the expressions of hostility they felt against their parents toward *others* who were recognized by them as stand-ins for their parents. Although she feels terrible about doing it, one woman deeply hurts her own child both physically and verbally. She recognizes clearly that she is doing to her child exactly what her mother did to her, and she acknowledges openly that she shouldn't be taking it out on her child. Nevertheless, she continues to do so. Implicitly, she knows she is thus getting even with her mother.

Aggressive behaviors which were recognized by the rejected as neither aggressions nor as having any relationship to hostility were also displaced to other persons or to themselves. One woman, who more than once remarked that God had gifted her with a mind and tongue that could be lethal in personal encounters, has by her speech almost destroyed many persons she has met. She has no hostility whatever, she explained, and her hurting words just seem to slip out. She mentioned that it's all right because she always apologizes afterwards.

In summary, it would seem that anger, hostility, and aggression were stimulated in the rejected by the very fact of their rejection. In dealing with these responses, all of the rejected appeared to have experienced, at some level, both anger and the inclination to hostility. In terms of coping with these two emotions, their records ranged all the way from no consent whatever to full consent, even when it was postponed. Their aggressions—which were but the externalizations of their hostile impulses—ranged over the same panoply of human responses. Accordingly, some rejected were indeed dangerous people who were in need of professional help, while others—for the time being, at least—were in adequate control of their destructive urges.

8
Scientific Considerations

Should the data which have been presented in this book, together with their offered explanations, be regarded as scientific? Although my anticipation is that at least the initial reaction of a number of psychologists will be to question the correctness of such a position, I believe that these data *should* be regarded as scientific. Accordingly, against the background of a brief review of the history of scientific psychology and the meaning ascribed to scientific method in psychology, I will endeavor to present a justification for that position.

It is generally recognized that the science of psychology owes a great debt to its illustrious forerunners, particularly those of the nineteenth century. Among others, Ernst Heinrich Weber and Gustav Theodor Fechner pioneered what is today known as the area of psychophysics (i.e., the relationships between stimuli and sensations). Hermann von Helmholtz published his findings on sight and hearing. Johannes Müller, regarded as the father of experimental physiology, published also on psychology. These men were regarded as scientists by their contemporaries.

The founding of scientific psychology came somewhat later, and is usually officially ascribed to Wilhelm Wundt, who in 1879 established at the University of Leipzig the first psychology laboratory in the world. Wundt instituted the *science* of psychology for the precise purpose of systematically and rigorously studying man's conscious contents. Almost from that day, psychologists have been in general agreement with regard to his basic twofold position that (a) psychology should declare its independence from philosophy, under whose auspices it had functioned until that time, and (b) it should be a science.

When psychology severed its connection with philosophy, it became a *natural* science instead of modeling itself on some other scientific pattern. It is this structuring of psychology on a *natural* science model that has been the crux of the disagreements through the years regarding what constitutes "scientific" psychology.

When Wundt and his coworkers determined that psychology should be a science, they were in no position to choose critically from among different scientific models the one best suited to the specific needs of their new discipline. They had to abide within a *natural science* model. In no other way could psychology have received recognition *as a science* by the scientists of that time (13, 170). The scientific paradigm was well-known. They simply accepted the contemporary model of a *natural* science with the physical science laboratory experiment as its basic method.

The natural science of Wundt's day stressed radical empiricism, quantification, and the application of mathematics to data. It was against the background, then, of the methods, techniques, and instruments of the contemporary natural sciences that Wundt undertook the scientific study of man. This consideration could help to explain his preoccupation with reducing conscious contents to "basic elements." While he viewed the object of psychology as the introspective analysis of the contents of immediate experience, he identified the "elements" thus studied as sensations and feelings. In examining these sensations and feelings, he made considerable use of Fechner's psychophysical methods. Wundt's preoccupation with natural science helps to explain his studies on "reaction time," in which he endeavored to measure the reaction times of the psychological phenomena of apperception, cognition, association, discrimination, and choice (22).

Such was scientific psychology's beginning. Thereafter, aside from their consensus on its independence and scientific nature, psychologists have found little about the makeup of psychology on which to agree. Since its founding, at least eight "schools" of scientific psychology have been identified. These "schools," with approximate dates of their chronological appearance, were: structuralism (1879); psychoanalysis (1895); functionalism (1896); hormic psychology (1908); gestalt psychology (1912); classical behaviorism (1913); Skinnerian behaviorism (c. 1938); and third force psychologies, i.e., phenomenological, existential, and humanistic (c. 1958).

The significant point here is that no two of these "schools" agreed regarding either the proper subject matter or methods of scientific psychology. Late in his life, Wundt was to confess his keen disappointment that, "as a coherent science, experimental psychology still awaits the foundations" (214). Consequently, what constituted authentic scientific findings in psychology was in contention almost from the beginning of the science.

Over the years, some psychologists found this conflictual atmosphere disturbing enough to search for common grounds in psychology. Unfortunately, not one of these psychologists notably succeeded in his attempt to unify psychology as a science. It seems instructive, nevertheless, to note precisely where such concerned psychologists were hoping to discover the key to some kind of scientific unity in their discipline. Implicit in their proposals for unifying scientific psychology are some stimulating reflections on the strengths and weaknesses of psychology *as a science*. It boils down to their thinking about what constitutes the key problems with the "scientific" in psychology. Following are solutions to the basic problems in scientific psychology which were proposed by some of these scholars.

Wilhelm Dilthey tried to show that the science of psychology could be thoroughly rigorous and systematic in a way that would be manifestly different from that of a natural science. He urged psychologists to renounce their methodological exclusivity so as to allow for the introduction of other scientific models, as well. In making this suggestion, Dilthey was in no way opting for a nonscientific psychology whose findings were drawn from literature. In fact, when his critics accused him of thus abandoning the science of psychology, he explicitly denied any such intention. What he wanted, he explained, was a genuine *science* of psychology which would put an end to the then-current methodological monopoly in psychology (157).

Brentano endeavored to bring unity to scientific psychology. To accomplish this unity, he combined the psychologies of his day into a single discipline. This discipline was genuinely empirical, but not exclusively experimental. Brentano's method was organized around psychic acts. His scientific data were "psychic phenomena," by which he meant particular manifestations of consciousness. Making a careful distinction between perception and observation, he argued that mental experience can only be perceived, while reality can be both perceived and observed. However, the mind's view of reality focuses on *perception* rather than on observation. Thus, he gave the stress to *experience* in contradistinction to behavior. Since his was an "act" psychology in which acts were psychic processes, some experimentally-minded psychologists of his time considered his system suspiciously close to logic, and thus to philosophy, from which psychologists were still struggling to free themselves (128).

Fernberger reviewed, with some skepticism, the previous attempts to unify scientific psychology. He concluded that any endeavor to unite all "schools" of psychology into a single science must be regarded as naive. Such a unification would presuppose at least a common denominator, which he felt to be nonexistent. The most he thought he could accomplish was to outline fully *two* separate and distinct *sciences* of psychology. The practical advantage of such an approach was that every psychological "school" could be adequately accommodated within either the "science of behavior" or the "science of consciousness" (55). Fearon, for somewhat analogous reasons, also advocated two distinct sciences of psychology (53). It seems significant that both men felt they had to renounce all hope of ever being able to combine all psychologies into a single science.

Calkins, who in 1891 had founded the first psychology laboratory at Wellesley, was deeply grieved by the persisting disunity in scientific psychology. In her address to the Ninth International Congress of Psychology at New Haven in 1929, she labeled the divisions within psychology as "one of the scandals of contemporary science" (128, p. 371). Not content merely to protest against this disunity, she produced her own plan to combine into one scientific discipline the four contemporary psychological "schools" of behaviorism, gestalt psychology, introspectionism, and self-psychology. Her effort, however, seemed to have little effect on the psychologists of her day, who continued to sharpen rather than lessen their differences about the content of scientific psychology (33).

Heidbreder also strove to bring some element of unity to the science of psychology. After she had finished her well-known account of the seven "schools" of psychology, she sought a way to unify them. She thought she detected fundamental similarities in that all "schools" were directed toward the same class of facts. She based this belief on the grounds that differences in definition generally involve only differences in the selection of facts, not a denial of the facts themselves. It was her sincere but unrealistic expectation that this essential "sameness" of subject matter would constitute the principle of unity for the various "schools" of scientific psychology (79).

Woodworth approached the problem from another perspective. For him, its solution lay in defining the science of psychology so broadly that it would embrace *every* "school." Such a broad definition, however, by no means proved to be satisfactory to all psychologists (213).

Finally, Gardner Murphy proposed what he regarded as an eminently practical solution to the problem. He simply affirmed that, de facto, psychology was the scientific study of *both* experience and behavior. This would embrace the action "outside the skin," as well as that "beneath the skin." Nonetheless, as psychologists examined this respected eclectic's sincere effort, they found he had left the crucial issue still unresolved. Murphy had failed to explain *why* psychology *as science* ought to embrace both experience and behavior (132).

What of psychology today? In spite of persisting problems centering around its scientific unity, psychology in the United States has shown remarkable growth. Some fifty years ago, for instance, many universities in this country offered only a few courses in psychology. Today, it would be difficult to find a four-year American college or university which does not offer at least an undergraduate psychology major. Many also offer at least one graduate degree in psychology.

Inasmuch as growth normally connotes both organization and unity, and in light of its great growth, what is the current state of scientific psychology? How much agreement is there in the United States regarding its scientific contents and methods? Basically, there are two opposing groups of scientific psychologists: the natural science or behavioristic group, and the humanistic group.

Among contemporary American experimental psychologists, the most frequently found expression of this natural science approach to psychology is B. F. Skinner's "radical behaviorism." Skinner's conception limits the content of scientific psychology to quantified, observable behavior and confines its methods to those found within this same orientation (58). Skinner has characterized himself as a "radical behaviorist" and, when asked during the Rice University Symposium on Behaviorism and Phenomenology in 1963 why he thus labeled himself, he replied: "I am a radical behaviorist simply in the sense that I find no place in the formulation for anything that is mental" (42, p. 317). Psychologists embracing a natural science model, including Skinner's followers, seem reasonably well satisfied with a natural science conception of the assumptions, methods, and contents of psychology.

The smaller group of scientific psychologists is humanistically-oriented. Many of these psychologists seriously question—not in its *totality*, but in *certain of its aspects*—the scientific adequacy for *human* psychology of a number of the integral components of the natural science conception of psychology, including the radical behavioristic expression. I regard myself as belonging to this minority.

Thus, psychologists have continued to differ about what belongs to scientific psychology. Undisguised antagonism is repeatedly found in university psychology departments throughout America between the experimental psychologists, referred to as the "rat people," and the clinical psychologists, termed the "sloppy method" researchers. Both groups claim to be scientific. Nonetheless, their overt conflict is an ongoing source of embarrassment and shame to many members of the profession (187). In the one camp, behavioristic psychologists—as scientists—are opposed to having the "subjective" introduced into psychology. In the other, humanistic psychologists—as scientists— take the position that viewing consciousness and experience as irrelevant to a viable scientific psychology constitutes an evasion of academic and professional responsibility. The humanistic psychologists are convinced that behavioristic psychologists must answer for their failure to treat meaningful phenomena in a meaningful way (69). As the behaviorists view it, on the other hand, the humanists must be held responsible for adulterating the science of psychology. And so the differences continue.

Over the years such differences between the "behavioristic" and "humanistic" approaches have only sharpened. In this connection, Carl Rogers (a leading advocate of the humanistic approach) astonished psychologists in 1974 when he wrote that his one disappointment with Skinner was Skinner's refusal to permit the nine-hour confrontation which the two of them had in Duluth to be released. In Rogers' judgment, it was the deepest exploration in existence of the issues between them. He concluded: "After the meeting, Skinner refused his permission. I feel the profession was cheated" (163, p. 118). Shortly thereafter, Skinner replied that the quality of the recording was so bad that he did not consider it fair to offer the tapes for rental or sale. He said he would not want a transcription circulated without editing, and added he would not relish the prospect of editing his share of it (185). It is difficult to know what the real story is—perhaps we never will know—but, implicit in such an incident is the unmistakable point that conflictual issues persist between the two scientific positions represented by these psychologists (160).

Much of the trouble which has plagued scientific psychology seems to be due to its having so completely divorced itself from philosophy. Psychology did need to venture forth from the philosophical nest and establish itself as a discipline in its own right, but there seems to have been a matter of overkill. By this, I mean that psychologists over the years have adamantly refused to establish any relationship whatever with most areas of philosophy. The one exception has been that of the philosophy of science, which was not recognized as a separate discipline until the twentieth century and still appears to be viewed with suspicion by some psychologists (199). Eacker, referring to the radical separation between psychology and philosophy, remarked that from an originally almost exclusive preoccupation with philosophical problems psychologists have come to eschew almost all philosophical considerations (49).

While many psychologists have had no hesitation whatever in borrowing assumptions and methods from physiology, neurology, anatomy, chemistry, physics, mathematics, and sociology, they have persisted in their boycott against almost everything from philosophy. Philosophers of science have been able to help psychologists face some of their problems. Many contemporary psychologists seemingly have yet to recognize that the academic field of philosophy is precisely the discipline that is capable of enabling them to evaluate adequately their proper subject matter and the validity of their assumptions. They still do not see philosophy as the discipline, par excellence, concerned with adequate frames of reference. One of the results of their ostracism of philosophy is that many psychologists apparently have not questioned their position that the *only* way they can achieve their research goals is by utilizing the methods of the established natural sciences.

All scientists, of necessity, bring assumptions to their respective disciplines. Some natural science psychologists are seemingly unaware that certain of their assumptions are being repeatedly challenged. A few of these professional colleagues do not even appear to be aware that they are making assumptions. On the contrary, the impression they give on occasion is that they view their assumptions as scientific facts rather than as positions which they themselves have brought to their scientific pursuits.

What are the assumptions found in the natural science model of scientific psychology? Following are a few assumptions that are apparent in the literature:

Evolutionism—the particular conception of the theory of evolution which maintains that there is nothing whatever in the psychological makeup of man, such as his reasoning or loving ability, that is different *in kind* from what is found in animals lower on the taxonomic scale.

Positivism—the philosophical position that what cannot be grasped through the senses is unknowable.

Reductionism—the philosophical position that all mental events can be reduced to neurological events.

Quantification—the philosophical position that all data can and must be submitted to measurement and/or counting.

Determinism—the philosophical position that all phenomena are considered as necessary consequents of antecedents.

A few psychologists appear also to be making the assumption of an *"independent observer,"* one whose presence and behaviors are believed to have no significant effect on their psychological subjects (69).

Scientific psychology as regarded by a very few psychologists would appear to verge on "scientism." "Scientism"—sometimes lightly labeled "Science with a capital S"—refers to the assumption that science alone is capable of providing adequate explanations and answers to all the questions of human existence. Scientism, however, instead of being the essence of scientific illumination, happens to be a degenerative phenomenon, inasmuch as it endeavors to force science into the preposterous role of being both a philosophy and a theology. It strives to evaluate the reality and worth of *everything* that exists. Those psychologists who overvalue their own methodical ideas to the point of seeing them as constituting the *only* scientific approach appear to approximate scientism (194).

Over the years, psychology has borrowed much from physics, especially in regard to its assumptions. For a long time, the physical world was assumed to be inert and thus needed to be set in motion by some form of energy. Certain psychologists seem to have made the assumption that man is to be viewed in this way.

If man is seen as a static being who, nevertheless, happens to be almost constantly in action, how is his activity to be explained? What is it that moves or motivates human behavior? Of those who employ a natural science model of scientific psychology, the majority see environmental forces which pull people as the more important sources of human motivation. At the same time, they also see an importance— even though a lesser one—in drives, needs, and so on, which push people. A smaller number of psychologists who espouse a natural science model reverse this relative importance, in that they assign the more significant role to inner forces which push people (107). Kelly remarks succinctly: "There are the pitchfork theories on the one hand, the carrot theories on the other" (93, p. 50). The salient point is that both of these groups find no place in their account of human motivation for personal self-determination. That personal self-determination is nonexistent is, of course, an assumption.

A few researchers also make an assumption regarding the importance of research equipment. It is undeniable that suitable laboratory equipment is necessary for much psychological research. Occasionally, however, a few psychologists appear to exaggerate the value of research equipment with their working assumption that, on the whole, science and scientific equipment are practically interchangeable terms. They take the position that to be scientific one *must* employ a notable amount of modern, highly technical equipment.

For further clarification, let me expand a bit and comment on some of the assumptions customarily espoused in the natural science model of scientific psychology:

First, let's consider *determinism*. Some psychologists working in the area of behavior control maintain that the entirety of human behavior is as subject to natural laws as are other natural phenomena. As applied to contemporary human scientific psychology, what does this assumption of determinism mean (69)? It means that a man, regardless of how he might feel about the matter, is not the true initiator of his behavior. His role is that of recipient. He does not *act*; he only *reacts*. His behavior is controlled by forces other than himself, forces outside him and/or within him. Man is not a doer, but one to whom or within whom things are being done. In this conception, man himself is excluded from the determiners of his own behavior. He possesses no more ability to cause his own behavior than do animals to cause theirs. From this psychological vantage point, human responsibility and imputability become unscientific terms; they are mental constructs.

Does this assumption of determinism hold a man responsible for behavior that is itself already determined? Krasner, a prominent psychologist, explains:

> I would conceive of man clearly in the robot end of the continuum. That is, his behavior can be completely determined by outside stimuli. Even if man's behavior is determined by internal mediating events, such as awareness, or thinking, or anxiety, or insight, these events can be manipulated by outside stimuli, so that it is these stimuli which basically determine our behavior (98, p. 22).

Skinner also elucidates:

> In what we may call the prescientific view (and the word is not necessarily pejorative) a person's behavior is at least to some extent his own achievement. He is free to deliberate, decide, and act, possibly in original ways, and he is given credit for his successes and blamed for his failures. In the scientific view (and the word is not necessarily honorific) a person's behavior is determined by a genetic endowment traceable to the evolutionary history of the species and by the environmental circumstances to which as an individual he has been exposed (184, p. 101).

Hebb, a well-known physiologically-oriented psychologist, states succinctly: "I am a determinist. I assume that what I am and how I think are entirely the products of my heredity and my environment." Hebb adds: "But most behavior of man or monkey or ape is under a joint guidance of sense input and the immediately prior pattern of cortical activity; and the cortical component in that control is free will. The idea that free will means indeterminism is simply a misunderstanding" (78, p. 75). This, in my judgment, is indeed a surprising misunderstanding. The misunderstanding, however, would appear to me to be on the part of this eminent psychologist when he was engaged in a philosophical consideration. He seems to have confused *indeterminism*, the conception of the absence of causation, with self-determination, which is one kind of causation and in no way considered to be a kind of indeterminism.

Since the assumption of psychological determinism wholly rules out any investigation of the validity of experienced self-determination in people, some psychologists have found it almost a straitjacket in their research. Leona Tyler, for example, had for years weighed the fact that determinism was generally assumed to be a necessary working assumption for a science of psychology. In the light of her psychological findings from studies of human subjects, however, she concluded:

> If freedom is interpreted to mean that one can actually make choices and take responsibility for their consequences, then espousing freedom means giving up psychic determinism. . . . I think we would be better off if we opted for the assumption that an individual has at least limited freedom to choose his own course of action (201, p. 1027).

Next, let's consider the assumption of *reductionism*. As Hebb expresses it: "Mind, for scientific purposes, can be regarded only as the activity of the brain. And modern psychology takes completely for granted that behavior and neural function are perfectly correlated, that one is caused by the other" (77, p. xiv). In another publication, he completes the identification: "Mind, then, is the capacity for thought, and thought is the integrative activity of the brain" (78, p. 75). The assumption of reductionism seems to run clearly counter to my own findings.

Castell does an outstanding job of refuting this assumption by spelling out distinctions between behavior and neural function. To sharpen such distinctions, he uses the words *activity* and *process*, and exemplifies his position by applying his points to the behaviors of an astronomer engaged in studying the solar system. The "astronomizing" behavior of the astronomer is *activity*, while that of his brain and nervous system is *process* (34).

The astronomer's *activity* would include discovering:

—that in trying to acquire knowledge he is fallible, so he knows his attempt could wind up in ignorance or error.

—that his activity is purposive, in that it is trying to do something. This purposiveness implies desire and belief. His desire is to know the solar system; his belief is that if he goes about it in a certain way he will succeed in discovering:

—that it is experimental and tentative, so knowing what he wants does not automatically ensure his employment of the proper method.

—that it is reasoned, and so he tries to answer such questions as "Why this step?" "Why this conclusion?"

—that he is confronted with certain alternatives, and so must consider different hypotheses to explain what he observes.

—that he is responsible, which means he must "be able to answer for" what goes on there, instead of looking for some excuse or way out of it.

—that it is judgmental, so he must determine that A is B, or A is either A or B, and so forth.

—that it can and often does involve response to a challenge in order to test a hypothesis.

If the astronomer turned his attention to the *behavior of his brain and nervous system,* he would not discover it fallible, purposive, experimental and tentative, reasoned, with certain alternatives, responsible, judgmental, involving a challenge, and so on. Castell would tell him: "The behavior of your brain and nervous system is not activity; it is process. In that respect it differs from your behavior and resembles the happenings of the solar system" (34, p. 25). The assumption of reductionism, then, in my thinking and in that of others, is not a philosophically sound one.

The assumption of *quantification* is widespread. Some psychologists simply do not ask nonmeasurement questions. Almost every dissertation in psychology today includes a measurement phase. In fact, there are contemporary psychologists still quoting, with approval, Thorndike's well-known dictum: "Anything that exists, exists in some amount and can be measured." While this assumption makes for orderliness, precision, and neatness because it limits consideration solely to quantification, it also presents serious problems. It makes it unfeasible to study, in their entirety, areas which are currently recognized as belonging to scientific psychology. I refer to such largely nonquantified, nonmeasured areas as states of consciousness, language, thought, psycholinguistics, cognitive development, personality, attitudes, and others.

In this context, it is interesting to note the judgment of Fodor. He maintains that behaviorism, the most frequently encountered psychological expression of natural science, is but a special case of operationism, i.e., the philosophical position which defines concepts only in terms of events and operations which can be observed and possibly measured. It is his opinion that behaviorism accordingly ought to share in the discredit that has recently been attached to operationism. He states: "If this is correct, the ultimate argument against behaviorism (in view of its assumption of quantification) is simply that it seeks to prohibit, a priori, the employment of psychological explanations that may, in fact, be true" (58, p. 89).

What, then, is to be said regarding the evaluation of the natural science model in scientific psychology? Its adequate appraisal belongs to the philosophy of science rather than to one of the sciences. Any difficulty that I might have with the particular scientific techniques, findings, or validity of findings of any psychologist would be a difficulty with him *as a scientist*. However, the positions that a psychologist *must* make *only* certain specific assumptions and *must* confine his scientific observations to quantifiable, nonmental observations are philosophical positions. In questioning another psychologist about them, I am questioning him, not as a scientist, but *as a philosopher* of science. Skinner fully agrees with this view. "Behaviorism, with an accent on the last syllable," he says, "is not the scientific study of behavior but a philosophy of science concerned with the subject matter and methods of psychology" (183, p. 951).

When seen in this perspective, I fault the natural science approach in psychology, including the currently prevalent "radical behavioristic" version, primarily as a philosophy of science rather than as a science. As a science, in fact, radical behaviorism has been an effective instrument for obtaining scientific findings, even though—in my judgment—these have been unduly restricted because of excessively limited methodology and content. The question, however, of whether the method and content of psychology should be so limited is a philosophical one, and not, as such, a scientific one.

I believe, as does Maslow, that the conflicts which have repeatedly arisen between method and the proper subject matter of scientific psychology—namely, man's full panoply of behaviors—have been too frequently resolved in favor of method (117). Others agree. Koch is of the opinion that the commitment of many scientific psychologists to their idea of a science has been stronger than their commitment to its proper subject matter—man. She sees the adamant commitment of a researcher solely to the use of this method as a very high price to pay for methodological exactness (96). Murray Levine concludes that, in our search for methodological purity, we have frequently lost sight of the substance of the psychological problems (102).

A number of the problems some natural science psychologists deal with rigorously are regarded by other psychologists as neatly and cleanly done, but largely irrelevant. I am in agreement that much of the prevalent scientific psychology, with its limiting methodology, lacks the means for treating numerous relevant areas in adequate fashion (7, 115, 170). Rogers accuses a number of these psychologists of allowing the world of psychological science to be reduced to behavior observed, sounds emitted, marks scratched on paper, and so forth (160). This calls to mind the remark Hebb attributes to Reg Bromily that "What's not worth doing is not worth doing well" (78).

In any event, it seems inescapable that many contemporary psychologists have failed to consider seriously that current statistical methods and conceptions of experimental design, ideal as they are for some research, may not be suitable for investigating other significant psychological problems. While the natural science conception of psychology undeniably has precision, its precision is simply not suited to the study of many relevant and unequivocally human phenomena. To me, it appears to lack especially the type of precision needed for adequately investigating areas of man's *integrated* functioning, such as language, thought, and personality development (69). Its very adherence, in fact, to its own type of precision has dictated that it either disregard, exclude, or distort such unequivocally human phenomena as the price for its inclusion among the natural sciences.

It is understandable why a number of psychologists today find themselves on the horns of a dilemma. They choose to assign priority to meeting the current criteria of their science at the price of neglecting man *as a person;* or they give priority to essential *human* characteristics and relegate the natural science standards to a position of secondary importance. The latter option, of course, leaves them exposed to the charge of being unscientific (69), a charge which many of them feel is unjustified.

Contemporary psychologists who use the natural science model have logically focused on man-as-object rather than man-as-person. In effect, this has largely confined their study of man to that of another organism. The viewing of such a scientific frame of reference as *the* scientific frame of reference seldom appears to be seen by them as in any way detrimental (69). Sanford, for one, thinks that among the consequences of contemporary psychologists' commitment to the natural science model must be listed the charge that many contemporary psychologists lack sensitivity to human experience (170). Equally disconcerting is the remark of the late eminent social scientist, Margaret Mead, that for a psychologist, the determination to be scientific has come almost exclusively to mean being impersonal or even inhuman (125). Another costly consequence is denoted in Giorgi's reflection that, if psychology continues to shut out all scientific ideals other than those of a natural science, it may miss making its most significant contribution as a science (69).

In view of the foregoing considerations, I could not justify a scientific study of man based on a natural science model. Nonetheless, I recognize that other psychologists remain adamant in their commitment solely to quantified behavior and purity of corresponding methods. In this context, Fodor suggests a jarring consideration for all of us. He points out the possibility that scientific psychology may be used to serve, not scientific needs, but rather the personal psychological needs of the scientist himself. For a scientist, science may become a defense, a security system, a means of avoiding anxiety and the upsetting problems of life. It can even become one way of avoiding life itself, a means of self-cloistering, "a kind of Chinese Wall against innovation, creativeness, revolution, even against new truth itself if it becomes too upsetting" (58). Fodor's point seems to be that we psychologists, of all people, should remain alert to the danger that a scientist can come to find in his science a refuge from reality instead of an aspect of reality.

At any rate, let me take one step further my objections to having to confine all psychological findings to a natural science model. Considerations of the adequate psychological study of man inevitably give rise to the nature of psychological differences found between men and animals. Do men and animals differ only *in degree*, quantitatively, or do they differ also *in kind*, qualitatively? If differences *in kind* do exist, they are of the utmost importance to psychology. Indeed, given differences in kind, psychologists could consistently disregard such data in their scientific investigations only by being untrue to their science. They would be failing to examine actual areas of their scientific discipline. Yet I see no way that the investigation of such differences could be accommodated within a natural science model.

This matter of "difference in degree" and "difference in kind" needs clarification. How are they distinguished? Two things can be said to differ *in degree* when one of them has more of a given characteristic which they both possess. For example, a bloodhound and a man both possess the sense of smell. However, they differ *in degree* in this regard because, although a bloodhound has a much more highly developed sense of smell, the man also can smell. On the other hand, two things can be said to differ *in kind* when one of them possesses a defining characteristic which is not possessed at all by the other. For example, a bloodhound has a sense of smell, whereas a tree has no sense of smell whatever.

Accordingly, when dealing with a difference *in kind*, one does not correctly speak of "more" or "less" regarding that which is different—a bloodhound does not have more of a sense of smell than a tree. However, where there is a difference *in degree*, it is always at least theoretically possible to find an in-between position. For example, one might hope to find an animal with a sense of smell less keen than a bloodhound's but more keen than a man's. Only where there is a difference *in kind* does the law of excluded-middle hold. For example, there is no possible position midway between a bloodhound's sense of smell and a tree's total lack of it.

Nevertheless, it should be recognized that there is such a thing as an "apparent difference in kind," which in reality is only an *enormous* difference *in degree*. Such a difference could be found where a characteristic possessed by one of them is almost immeasurably greater than that possessed by the other. An eagle's ability to fly, for example, is so far superior to a barnyard chicken's that the difference appears to be one *in kind*. (I am using "flying" in the sense of the ability to move the body through the air by using the body's wings.) The barnyard chicken, though it cannot soar above the mountain crags as does the eagle, can at least get airborne for a few seconds. In reality, then, this enormous difference between the flying ability of the two is a difference *in degree* only, because both can fly.

To my knowledge no reputable psychologists have seriously questioned the position that men and animals differ psychologically *in degree* in a great number of areas. The critical psychological point here is whether men also differ *in kind* from the animals.

A number of contemporary psychologists take the position that men differ *in degree only* from animals. Some of them appear to hold this position for two reasons. They assume, first of all, that the postulate of "developmental continuity" is correct. By the term "developmental continuity," psychologists refer to the position that, inasmuch as men have evolved, all of their psychological behaviors, whether internal or external, are also to be found in animals lower on the taxonomical scale. It is readily conceded that a number of human behaviors are to be found in lower animals in an almost immeasurably lesser degree and complexity. Nevertheless, their presence is claimed and so the difference in these behaviors between men and animals is merely an enormous one of *degree*. Such a position seems implicit in an assumption of some American psychologists. They assume that the "laws of learning" which were originally derived from animal experimentations are capable of explaining all human learning. The generalization of such laws to all human learning has been seriously questioned by Seligman (178).

By "developmental discontinuity," on the other hand, psychologists refer to the position that men, who have evolved, also show some kinds of behaviors not found at all in the lower animals. This, of course, is not to deny that in many of their behaviors, such as sensory experiences, men differ also *in degree* from the lower animals. Differences *in degree* are viewed as quantitative only, while differences *in kind* are qualitative.

Erich Fromm sees man as having been torn away from nature in the course of evolution. As a result of his having thus been separated, he has been left isolated from nature. *As man,* he has needs which are distinctly human—needs which the animals do not have at all. Fromm's five needs: relatedness, transcendence, rootedness, identity, and frame of reference are exclusively *human* needs; the behaviors employed to fulfill these needs are also exclusively human. These needs and their corresponding behaviors are simply not found in the animal world. In fact, the content of Fromm's well-known book *The Art of Loving* is *exclusively human.* The behaviors which it treats are found only in people (64).

Abraham Maslow's hierarchical arrangement of five human needs is as follows: physiological, safety, belonging, achieving, and self-actualization. These are arranged hierarchically from those needs which humans share with animals to those which are properly and exclusively human. The self-actualized person's real values, which he calls "metaneeds" (e.g., truth, beauty, honesty, goodness, and so forth), are simply nonexistent in the animal world. He maintains that here we are unmistakably dealing with behaviors and experiences that differ *in kind* from those in animals (117).

The insistence that, in order to hold a position of "developmental discontinuity" a psychologist must first explain how such qualitatively different behaviors evolved, is not a scientifically reasonable one. Scientists recognize the existence of many phenomena, including those they are unable to explain. Physicists have not explained electricity; however, they do not, for that reason, deny its existence. Psychologists who hold the position of "developmental discontinuity" do not begin with explanations, but rather with accurate observations of man. Through scientific observations, they find in men behaviors which they do not find at all in the lower animals. For these scientists, scientific observation is the starting point for scientific explanation, not its end result.

Some of the psychologists subscribing to "developmental continuity," on the other hand, regard the postulate as crucial to their particular working hypothesis of evolution. For them, this postulate is every bit as applicable to men as to all other vital organisms. Hence, an acknowledgment of psychological differences *in kind* between men and animals would imply, for them, a contradiction of their theory of evolution. Heidbreder seemed to have this problem. She wrote:

> Man, thus placed in the phylogenetic and evolutionary series, was exposed to the revealing light of comparative psychology, and as a conse-

quence psychology was freed from the idea that human beings constitute a unique and special case in the order of nature. . . . Experiments . . . adapting the methods of animal psychology to the examination of human thought, have repeatedly revealed the large amount of
"typically animal" trial and error in human thinking under these conditions, and have repeatedly emphasized similarities rather than differences between human and animal performances (79, p. 417).

For some psychologists, Lloyd Morgan's canon is at issue here. His
now-familiar canon said that we may not interpret an action as the
outcome of the exercise of a higher psychical faculty, if it can be interpreted as the outcome of the exercise of one which stands lower in the
psychological scale (130). This canon can readily be interpreted as making it difficult to attribute specifically human characteristics to animals.
On the other hand, it can be construed as supporting the view that all
human characteristics are simply different manifestations of characteristics found in animals. Some American psychologists appear to be
applying this canon in concluding that there are *no* psychological differences *in kind* between men and animals.

To those contemporary scientific psychologists, however, who maintain that there *are* psychological differences *in kind* between men and
animals, the insufficiency of psychological methods designed exclusively for quantified, observable phenomena is unmistakable. Such differences *in kind* can neither be perceived nor understood by investigators who restrict all data to externally observable behaviors (5).

In the interest of clarifying further the types of differences between
men and animals, I will comment briefly on just one psychological area
that I regard as showing differences *in kind*, namely, that of human
language. I do not intend this as a *demonstration* or *proof* of such psychological differences *in kind*. Indeed, to undertake such a demonstration would be out of context here—and it would require a complete
volume in its own right. Rather, my purpose here is simply to clarify,
by such an example, what I regard as one of those psychological differences *in kind*.

Full recognition is given to the excellent research being done on
communication in animals, particularly with dolphins and with the
learning of sign and symbol communication by chimps. Experiments
with the chimpanzees named Washoe, Mojo, and Sara, for instance,
have shown that they have achieved what has been termed the Stage I
rudiments of language. This stage includes signs for classes of objects,
agents, and actions; generalizing the words "more" and "probably";
and signaling the names of objects not physically present.

The point at issue is: Do such behaviors constitute even the barest rudiments of human language capacity? In a child, these Stage I meanings express his interactions with the sensory-motor world. He does not distinguish singular numbers from plural numbers, present events from past events, completed actions from those not completed, definite objects from indefinite class instances, nor has he any of the "fine tuning" of meanings that he will develop in Stage II. There is no evidence that chimpanzees can go beyond the child's performances in Stage I. The unmistakable point is that it seems highly probable that children at Stage I do not yet have human language (30).

Chomsky maintains that any methodology suitable for animal experimentation is clearly inadequate for the study of complex psychological phenomena in the area of man's linguistic abilities (36). Implications of the uniquely human characteristics of language abound in statements by authorities on human language. Kagan, recognized as preeminent in this field, remarks that it is not yet clear how the child acquires grammar so early and how he comes to be able to generate so many new sentences he has never heard before (90).

Robins, a British authority, states:

> There is a legitimate controversy, however, over the nature and extent of the positive contribution that the human brain brings to the activity of grammar construction, the activity by which the child develops an indefinite creative competence from the finite data that make up his actual experience of the language. Creativity is what must be stressed as the product of first-language acquisition. By far the greatest number of all the sentences anyone hears and utters during his lifetime are new; that is, they have not occurred before in his personal experience. But individuals find no difficulty at all in understanding, at once, almost everything they hear, nor, for the most part, in producing sentences to suit the requirement of every situation. This very ease of creativity in man's linguistic competence makes it hard to realize its extent (158, p. 657).

If, in fact, there are differences *in kind* in the area of human language (such as I have endeavored to exemplify here), then many contemporary psychologists have seriously failed to recognize and study them.

Every scientist should occasionally reflect that there is a need to examine the propriety of allowing fashionable assumptions or postulates to dictate a priori restrictions on research. This is particularly the case where research seeks to elucidate the shadowy areas of the psychology of the human person.

In summary, then, it is my judgment—as well as that of other psychologists—that the natural science model of psychology, while able to yield precise, objective, and reliable findings, is too limited and sterile to serve adequately its proper goal, which is the scientific study of man's behavior (118).

Psychologists searching for new scientific models are driven back to the basic concern for authentic scientific method. All seem to be in agreement that the touchstone of scientific psychology is genuine scientific method. Knowledge which has been obtained through *scientific method* may rightly be called "scientific," and no other knowledge may be so termed (69). What is "scientific method"? Bridgman states concisely that the scientific method, as far as it is a method, is nothing more than one's doing one's damnedest with one's mind, no holds barred (28). Despite this almost flip—though incisive—observation, it must be openly acknowledged that philosophers of science have simply failed to reach a consensus regarding the definition of "scientific method." Caws explains the failure this way:

> The term "scientific method". . . can only refer to the lowest common denominator of a range of methods devised to cope with problems as diverse as classifying stars and curing diseases. If such a lowest common denominator exists—that is, if some recognizable characteristics are shared by the extremes of the continuum of methods plausibly called "scientific"—it can amount to little more than fidelity to empirical evidence and simplicity of logical formulation, fidelity to the evidence taking precedence in cases of conflict (35, p. 339).

In view of such controversy among the philosophers of science, is the conclusion warranted that in psychology "scientific method" must be strictly confined to laboratory experimental methods? Are there no other channels for gathering psychological data? At times, as Hempel points out, scientific exploration involves nothing more than direct observation of the pertinent facts (82). Toulmin makes this point forcefully:

> . . . the facts in question may be discovered by using observational methods, i.e., by recording them as they occur naturally, without employing any special contrivances affecting their occurrences. This situation is, of course, the normal case in astronomy, in which the objects of study cannot be influenced or controlled (199, p. 382).

Are there any clear indications of *changes* in current scientific models for scientific psychology? In my own judgment and that of other psychologists, there are a number of such indications. First, there have been many proposals for changes—for instance, that psychology should be a human science (69), based on phenomena (58, 69, 160, 162,

194, 203), recognizing one's relationships to other persons (163), explaining all behavior (69, 146, 169, 203), studying man as a person (27,
69, 74, 118, 195), and innovative (48, 69, 118, 173).

Indications of needed changes are implicit in Rogers' challenge:

> I have raised the question whether psychology will remain a narrow
> technological fragment of a science, tied to an outdated philosophical
> conception of itself, clinging to a security blanket of observable behavior
> only; or whether it can possibly become a truly broad and creative sci-
> ence, rooted in subjective vision, open to all aspects of the human con-
> dition, worthy of the name of a mature science (162, p. 387).

One of the most incisive summary statements I have encountered of
a proposed scientific model for psychology is the following one by
Giorgi:

> To be scientific, according to criteria that emerge from the way science is
> practiced, psychology must deal with the experiential-behavioral rela-
> tionships of man in a detailed way and it must arrive at intersubjectively
> valid truth among a group of men who are qualified to judge the data
> and facts arrived at. . . . To be objective, or accurate, in our terminol-
> ogy, the psychologist must be able to arrive at intersubjectively valid
> knowledge; he must be able to assume a specifiable attitude toward his
> phenomena; and he must be open to himself, others and the world in
> such a way that he allows what is present to him to be the way it
> presents itself. To be empirical, psychology must be based upon phe-
> nomena that are given in experience. To be human, it must have as its
> subject matter the human person and he must be approached within a
> framework of reference that is also human, i.e., one that does not do
> violence to the phenomenon of man as a person. . . . But the project
> itself is not less empirical, objective, scientific, or psychological than
> psychology conceived along natural scientific lines. It simply reflects a
> different conception of those terms (69, pp. 224–25).

Has action been taken on any of the suggested changes? Some
writers have taken the optimistic position that a good number of
psychologists have already begun to carry out some of the suggested
changes. After Allport had reviewed the literature on the development of new scientific methods in psychology, he concluded that all
these and many more signs indicate the growing dependence of modern theories upon a model that is none the less scientific for being
humane (7).

Leona Tyler discerned signs of change in the attitudes of many psychologists toward both research and practice. She saw these shifts in

attitude as the beginnings of the fulfillment of her hopes for a psychology that will contribute in its own unique way to the progress of mankind. In fact, she felt that psychologists have already clearly begun, through such shifts in attitude, to increase their individual and collective understanding of human nature (201). Day, reflecting on the Rice University Symposium on Behaviorism and Phenomenology, concluded that we are moving toward an effective reconciliation of these two conflicting psychological positions (42).

After finding his research efforts repeatedly frustrated by current psychological methods, Maslow explained his own innovations as follows:

> In a word I had either to give up my questions or else to invent new ways of answering them. I preferred the latter course. And so also do many psychologists who choose to work as best they can with important problems (problem-centering), rather than restricting themselves to do only that which they can do elegantly with the techniques already available (method-centering) (118, p. 16).

Ernest Hilgard thinks that the changes psychology has already made are significant. After citing a number of innovations which he found in the literature, he concluded: "Finally, and perhaps most important from an experimenter's point of view, the maturity of psychology beyond a strident behaviorism now permits more direct interest in awareness, attentive processes, sleep, dreams and other 'subjective' phenomena" (83, p. 568).

In 1972, Segal and Lachman published their review of the changes that had already taken place in psychology. They contrasted these changes with what had previously held sway in psychology. This is how they summed it up:

> All told, it is not difficult to understand the optimism of the period and the reasons why intellects of the highest order were seduced by S–R behaviorism. Indeed some of the best of them attempted to apply the neobehavioristic prescriptions to the study of complex behaviors such as attitudes, verbal behavior, concept formation, language, and thinking, e.g., Gibson, 1940; Hovland, Janis and Kelly, 1953; Miller and Dollard, 1941; Osgood, 1953; Skinner, 1975 (177, p. 50).

Dember, having found evidences up to 1974 of changes in the specific area of motivation, wrote:

> The most striking development—significant enough to be termed revolutionary—is that psychology has gone cognitive, and so has motiva-

tion. Indeed, part of the impetus of general theory and research toward cognition was provided by dissatisfaction among motivation theorists with the prevailing (S–R) behavioristic model that had characterized American psychology for several decades (44, p. 161).

I include myself among those sympathetic to persons introducing changes in the scientific models for psychological research, and count myself among those participating in such changes. In retrospect, I am reminded of Erik Erikson's remark that "the clinician can learn of the true nature of man only in the attempt to do something *for* and *with* him" (50, p. 80).

Now let me explain the *method* that I employed in gathering the data reported in this book. To begin with, during the period of nearly thirty years of clinical practice, the hundreds of people who came to me did not approach me as subjects for psychological study. Instead, they contacted me, a Jesuit-priest psychologist, in the hope of receiving help with their problems and solace for their hurts. My purpose in dealing with them was not to study them. Instead, it was to try to give them psychological help. Nonetheless, a number of these clients later on spontaneously freed me to use whatever I had learned from them in any way that I might judge beneficial to others.

The clinical method I employed, and in which I had been professionally trained, is one of the recognized methods in psychotherapy. It is called "Client-Centered Therapy" or "Client-Centered Counseling" (hereafter referred to as C.C.C.). Formerly termed "non-directive," the method was introduced to psychotherapy by Carl Rogers.

My role in using C.C.C. was to strive, as far as possible, to *see* and *understand* the behaviors and experiences being described to me by each client and their meanings as he came to interpret and then report them to me. I functioned most efficiently in that role if and when a psychological climate spontaneously occurred in which a person felt sufficiently safe to share with me his desires, disappointments, anxieties, fears, beliefs, personal meanings, goals, thoughts, convictions— in effect, the entire gamut of experiences which he chose to reveal.

My continuing effort was to understand these experiences and behaviors *from the point of view* of the person who was relating them to me. My remarks were intended to verify whether I was understanding what he was telling me and, if so, to indicate that to him. When I was not clear about what the person was telling me, I would ask what he meant. I endeavored to focus my attention on discerning as clearly as possible what he was describing to me.

I tried to leave each person wholly free to speak or remain silent and, when he chose to speak, to tell me only what he wanted. In no way did I seek to guide or direct the conversation or to interrupt, comfort, reassure, or enlighten the client. I was satisfied just to try to grasp, as fully as possible, what the person was relating.

In any authentic interpersonal relationship of this nature, there is no way of completely ruling out every possible reinforcement—positive or negative—coming from the tone of voice, gestures, silences, and so on, of the clinician. Instead, what I am affirming of my own clinical performance is the absence from it of conscious, deliberate reinforcement of any kind. When, in spite of my intentions, the client felt that a response of mine was in fact leading him in a conversational direction he did not wish to go, he soon discovered that he was free to just change the subject without needing to fear that I would somehow drag him back to it.

Why such a clinical procedure should be regarded as psychotherapy does not belong to the subject matter of this book. Even though the procedure I am describing here is a form of psychotherapy, the point needs to be stressed that in this book I am not concerned about it *as* psychotherapy. Let me explain.

Though my original intention of giving psychological help persisted, something quite different also occurred. As I listened intently to hundreds of men and women relate to me their experiences and behaviors, I began to recognize striking, psychological patterns. These findings seemed to generalize to wider populations. For my own enlightenment during the course of those many years, I had often made notes of reported psychological experiences and behaviors which puzzled me. Later, I also jotted down the explanations for them which the clients, in the course of psychological counseling, uncovered and then communicated to me.

While the experiences and behaviors that any one client communicated to me were only those of that particular individual, some of them increasingly appeared to be verified in many persons. So it happened that what was intended by me as a method of therapy actually became also a scientific research window through which I was progressively being shown the crucial dynamics of personal experiences and behaviors. Thus, the C.C.C. method revealed to me a vista of experiences and behaviors which appeared to have common denominators.

These experiences and behaviors, as they were unfolded for me, manifested general psychological themes. Such themes were always expressed through the personal psychological variations of individual clients. *It is with these psychological "themes," as I found them in rejected persons, that I have been concerned in this book.*

So that the reader may have the opportunity to examine concretely this method of C.C.C. through which I observed the psychological experiences and behaviors of the rejected, I have incorporated into an appendix edited transcripts of two of my taped clinical sessions with one client who had been rejected by his parents. This particular client, when giving me permission to record the sessions and to use the materials in any way I saw fit, expressed the hope that they might some day be of some benefit to others. In my judgment, these transcripts give a fair sample of this scientific, naturalistic, observational method of C.C.C., as I employed it. With the exception of deletions of names of persons and places which I judged necessary to safeguard the identity of this rejected client, I have in no way altered the original content of the tapes.

During the many years of my clinical practice, there were occasions when my judgment dictated that I should discontinue the C.C.C. method with a particular client, and make use of a more directive method of psychotherapy. Whenever this happened, I did shift to another method. The psychological findings regarding the rejected that are reported in this volume, however, have been derived exclusively from my C.C.C. observations of what was being witnessed to me.

Through the method of C.C.C., I found that experiences and behaviors could be carefully observed phenomena. Here I wish to quote, with full personal agreement, two apropos remarks of Levine:

> We should be permitted to use our intelligence when engaged in rigorous confirmatory research. Accepting the notion of rigor, to my mind, does not inevitably imply that the phenomena of interest are necessarily brought into the laboratory or that confirmatory research is necessarily quantitative research. . . . Let me state that I am in no way following the model of a hypothetical-deductive, quantitative laboratory science, but rather reporting evidence for some theoretical considerations that seem to me to be stated better in terms of verbal concepts rather than in terms of precise mathematical equations (102, p. 668).

My position is that C.C.C. *can* be a form of scientific naturalistic observation. By naturalistic observation, I mean the investigation of phenomena in their naturally occurring life situations. There the phenomena, unarranged by any researcher, are investigated as they exist. Rausch agrees with the inclusion of clinical method under scientific naturalistic observation. He goes on to state that, inasmuch as the clinician is a naturalistic observer, he must be a disciplined observer if his observations are to be considered as scientific. After insisting that the *reports* of experiences and behavior as they happen in life can be legitimate sources of data, he continues:

> My emphasis has been on clinical psychology . . . as a method of investigation. Some have suggested that the method is appropriate for voyages of discovery but not for trials of proof. . . . I am convinced, however, that clinicians as well as non-clinicians need to recognize and accept the clinical approach as a naturalistic research method which, like other methods in science, demands training, caution and rigor, and is subject to error and limitations, but is nevertheless legitimate for scientific exploration, discovery and even verification (155, p. 144).

This context calls to mind Charles Darwin's account of his five-year voyage around the world, begun in 1831, in the ship *Beagle*. While on it, he made careful naturalistic observations of the geology and natural history of every place he visited. As he did so, his scientific theory emerged step by step. When the voyage ended, his scientific understanding was by no means complete. However, I doubt that anyone would seriously maintain that his investigation through naturalistic observation was not scientific observation (41).

Lorenz appears to be convinced that naturalistic observation can also be used for "trials of proof" of a hypothesis. He engages in laboratory studies in order to develop hypotheses about animal behavior which he then seeks to test in the natural environment (111).

It is my position that naturalistic observations, employing a clinical method such as C.C.C., can arrive at the reported psychological phenomena themselves. A clinician, using such a method, understands that often he cannot come to see experiences and behaviors as adequately as does the client reporting them. Nevertheless, he can ordinarily apprehend them and, particularly through an authentic, empathic sharing of the communications of the other person, comprehend a good deal of what the client is saying about even his intensely personal experiences and behaviors.

What are some of the problems with C.C.C. as an observation method? It is readily acknowledged that this scientific method of observing psychological events is peculiarly open to self-deception and misinterpretations. This concerns me as a person and also as a psychologist. Most psychologists, however, realize that they have never been free from real concern about how their own behaviors might interfere with the phenomena they are investigating (166, 167).

Scientific data cannot be derived unless a researcher somehow questions his phenomena, but this questioning requires that the researcher take a stance—and such a stance can have a decided effect on what he "finds." MacLeod exemplifies this point very well. He points out that a researcher in psychological learning must decide to ask either how long it takes to learn a task or how the learner experiences his task. He must make such a choice with the knowledge that he cannot be sure which of the two options is preferable in the situation. Moreover, the "method of serial anticipation" and the "reproductive method" are both recognized methods in researching verbal learning. Which should he use? What is his orientation? The method a researcher employs will depend on the approach he takes. If he takes the position that experiences parallel brain activities, he will normally tend to employ physiological methods; if he takes some other position, he will be inclined to choose one or more other methods (114).

C.C.C. cannot be said to avoid all presuppositions. Ackermann is convinced that psychological evidence appears firmly to support the contention that scientific observation is never free from presupposition. He openly takes the position that we can see only what we are prepared to believe that we can see (2).

Would this also be true for laboratory observation? As Rosenfeld and Baer have shown, it would be naive to assume that psychological experiments conducted within the confines of the laboratory are wholly free from possibilities of self-deception and misinterpretation (166). As valuable as psychological experiments can be, we must never forget two pertinent considerations with regard to them: (1) Experimental situations are *artificial* situations, since they exist in a way not found in nature, and (2) they are *human* artifacts, inasmuch as the experimenter selects the equipment, defines the variables, identifies the stimuli, and then collects, interprets, and writes up the data. In view of these two considerations, it would be simplistic to assume that the experimenter's impact on his human subjects is correctly limited solely to his perception of that impact (69).

Furthermore, every experimenter is aware that one or more uncontrolled, extraneous variables can be present and unrecognized in an experimental situation. An experimenter also knows that he can go astray on other scores. There is such a thing as a bad experiment. An experiment's worth depends on *how* it is conducted. The danger of going astray is not unique to such a scientific method of observation as C.C.C.; it is present also in experimentation, as well as in other methods. Accordingly, the acknowledgment that error could be associated with any given scientific method does not, of itself, make that specific method unscientific. Science always stands on the edge of error.

In the context of these considerations of potential inaccuracies of research findings, the additional point needs to be made that in human psychological research subjects must be presumed to possess sufficient motivation to cooperate in the research project. What is to be said about the motivation of the persons who furnished the data reported in this book? In my judgment, their motivation to reveal their inner experiences was amply provided by their need for help. Precisely because they were hurting, they were eager to talk and reveal themselves.

Because C.C.C. in its very nature places so much importance on *verbal reports*, two further relevant questions need to be raised here. First, were the rejected *honestly* communicating what they were experiencing? The sincerity, warmth, and feeling communicated cannot be conveyed in writing. Admittedly, there can be no infallible norm in this matter. An experienced researcher would, as did I, make prudential judgments about the honesty of each individual. These judgments were based, first of all, on such elements as observed consistencies and inconsistencies, gestures, facial expressions, tone of voice, silences, and so on. There were other elements, as well, such as peripheral impressions and perceptions. Even though I was not conscious of these at the time, I knew they were operative in formation of judgments regarding the honesty of an individual's communications. I would expect that every experienced clinician, after a sufficient number of sessions, would conclude that he must seriously question an occasional client's honesty in communication. Usually, as the sessions continue, a clinician feels increasingly comfortable regarding the client's honesty.

Second, were these rejected *accurately* communicating their experiences and behaviors? Besides the clinician's own judgment of the matter, there is in C.C.C. an additional check on accuracy of communication, one which an examination of the transcripts of the tapes in the appendix of this volume will bear out. I refer to the fact that, when a clinician's spontaneous responses show the rejected that their meaning is being grasped, very frequently they immediately confirm this awareness. The affirmations appear in such spontaneous responses as "yes," "yeah," "uh huh," and, while they do not appear on the transcripts, often by a nodding of the head or a confirming look or gesture.

In addition, the accuracy of communication may be indicated just by the fact that the rejected continue to pursue the development of their conversations without experiencing interruption. Thus, they are implicitly indicating their feeling that they are being understood. On the other hand, it frequently happens that, when the clinician's remarks show them they are not being understood, they stop to clarify or correct before continuing their accounts.

Lastly, I think it is necessary to ask two key questions relative to the findings reported herein. First, have they given an adequate ex-

pression to some of the proposed psychological innovations enumer-
ated? Now that the reader has finished the book, he will be able to
answer this question for himself. Meanwhile, in my opinion, the contents of this volume are in keeping with the following innovations
that were suggested:

The psychological study of man as a person should
—be a *human* science.
—be based on the *phenomena* themselves.
—be a systematic explanation of human *experience.*
—have the human person as the *frame of reference.*
—take into account the *social* dimension of man.
—assume man's capacity for *self-determination.*
—emphasize the *qualitative* aspects of the phenomena.
—accept the fact that *verbal reports* of subjects can be scientific.
—employ a *descriptive* approach.

Second, it is now feasible to present the reader with a more meaningful answer to the initial question of whether these reported findings
should be regarded as authentic *scientific* findings in psychology. My
position is that they should be regarded as such, inasmuch as they
have been derived through a method which, in my opinion, warrants
inclusion under scientific naturalistic observation—a scientific method.
My basis for regarding C.C.C. as a method of scientific naturalistic
observation is that it reasonably fulfills the following scientific requirements for such a method, as they are subscribed to by many scientists:

—fulfillment of the *goal* of science: to observe, describe, and
endeavor to make the phenomena intelligible.
—*empirical:* drawn from observational evidence.
—*objective:* the reported data are capable of being tested by
checking against the findings from other researchers using similar
and different research methods.
—the experience of the observing person as its source: the researcher carefully observing the psychological phenomena (here,
through the method of C.C.C., as these phenomena are communicated to him, especially through verbal expressions).
—the hypotheses must be replicable: presented in such a way
that they are capable of being tested by other researchers employing similar methods.

Finally, I anticipate that, whereas a number of psychologists will
agree with my conclusions, others will take issue with them. I fully
respect the right of others to hold different positions. By the same
token, I assume they will respect my position. That position is now
clear to the reader: along with a number of my professional colleagues,

I maintain that personal experiences and behaviors—together with their meanings and lawful, orderly relationships—when investigated by professionally trained persons through a scientific method of naturalistic observation such as Client-Centered Counseling, can be productive of authentic scientific findings.

Appendix:
Transcripts of Counseling Sessions

The following edited transcripts were made from tapes of two counseling sessions that were held one week apart during a client's second year of counseling. The tapings took place in my office at Gonzaga University. The tapes were made and the transcripts are included here with the full knowledge and consent of the client.

The client was a rejected man in his late twenties, married, with young children; he was a teacher. The names of his wife, school, employer, colleagues, and friends have all been deleted in order to safeguard anonymity.

The transcripts have been edited for clarity to the extent of omitting some irrelevant comments, repetitions, and sounds; for example, "In my job, ah, my job, I find that . . . ah . . ." would appear in these transcripts as "In my job, I find that. . . ." Inasmuch as the tapes of the sessions were transcribed verbatim, and editing *changes* in content were minimal, the grammar often does not appear in correct form. In all other respects, these transcripts provide an accurate representation of the Client-Centered Counseling method in operation. [Note: In the transcripts, C indicates client and T indicates therapist.]

At times, it is difficult to ascertain the meaning of some of the client's remarks and my responses (i.e., exactly what was being said), since the facial expressions, gestures, tonal qualities, etc., which were integral parts of the original conversations are missing. However, the client's responses indicate that during the counseling sessions we must have understood each other.

Though only two sessions are reproduced here, there are evidences of psychological growth taking place in this client. The reader should find the transcripts rich in points covered in this book, and I am of the opinion that the reader who studies them carefully will reap worthwhile information.

First Session

C: It was a compulsion on my part last week to inform you that classes had been going very, very well.

T: You had to get it out, hm?

C: Yeah, I think it's really true that I've become very much involved in it. I mean it takes possession of me entirely, and I can, as I say, be working on a concept, an idea, that I will bring in or use—wholly consumes me—a lot of feeling, racing of the heart, etcetera. It's just—it means so much to me that it frightens me. As I become clearly conscious of it, as I step back and————.

T: It's surprisingly really important in your experience in that way, hm?

C: Yeah. It's not that I object to being that involved in the process; it's just that I object to being involved in it, for my own sake. So I think the current status is that it boils down to the fact, who will be served, really? Whether it is me and, as I say, this pervasive need for success and adulation, etcetera— whether it will be that or it will be, basically, Christ's goals.

T: Who is it for, hm?

C: Yeah, as I say, it's—I won't say frightening, because it doesn't frighten me, but it seems to pretty much resolve itself there now—I mean, as I see things.

T: It's disconcerting to you to find so much of you in it, which runs counter to what you would really like it to be.

C: Yeah, yeah—especially, I think, when I can see that this is the real me. I mean I can even step back and view this and not change it one iota. I mean it is—this is where my heart is, and the past and what could have explained this and been the cause of that—these things have very little meaning for me—as I see them now.

T: And now, rather than having real concern about causation in this thing, it's taken the aspect of "This is you, the needing you."

C: And, as you said that, I say I don't really care where this comes from, because long since have I seen a lot of the behavior that it would've been easy to damn my parents for. I see not only the same tendencies, but the same overmanifestation of them in my own actions. I say, the affixing of blame in all these things—I seriously couldn't care less.

T: So what you might ascribe it to simply doesn't matter.

C: Maybe I'm being difficult on myself, but I don't feel that, either. I mean it just seems to me to be the last word on folly to be so concerned about ferreting these things out, when actually, as I say, there's so much of me, right now, that is involved in it—even when I'm aware of it—that it seems to me right there is a pretty good place to start.

T: Sort of the frank acceptance of the realization that "this—this is me, never mind about anybody else. This is the way I am."

C: And not any defensive way, because I have more positive feelings, I think, toward my parents, etcetera, than I have ever had.

T: So it's more realistic, rather than————.

C: As I see the whole thing, perhaps—I see the whole thing as very humorous. I mean that these are the problems people face, and then—and me—we don't do very well with them [laugh] really. And this is kind of funny.

T: You can almost look at this in a detached sort of way so that you can see the humor in it.

C: Yeah, I think it does induce kind of a faint smile when you are very incisive with what has happened to you in the past, etcetera, and then you look at your own behavior now and look at the behavior of those who, on the basis of other actions—who shouldn't fall into these errors and respond the same way to the same challenges—as I say, it loses a lot of its meaning for you.

T: Almost seems like a type of fiddling to go looking for these origins—.

C: That's right.

T: It seems much more true to the factual picture here to say, "O.K., this is—it's almost funny. This is the way I operate, this is the way I feel, and this is, therefore, the starting point of doing anything."

C: So as I say, the real conflict is right here, because as you were saying—. Then I practically vetoed—not vetoed, but dismissed—everything you said, because I was waiting to get my line in, straining at the camel and—rather, straining at the gnat and swallowing the camel, etcetera. This is my real here-and-now problem.

T: Impatiently waiting for me to stop making words so you could get on with it, hm?

C: Yeah—so I can summarize this very concisely, and let you know that, "Gosh, why didn't I listen to him in the first place?" And you wouldn't have to have wasted this much time. I mean this is my real—the real problem, and I suspect there's an awful lot being missed in what other people have to give as a function of it. I mean just as I've missed so much.

T: That maybe you're not looking, you're not listening———?

C: Yeah—you can't afford to—I think my religious conflict now regarding what I should do, what I ought to be doing—I think this is a real one. Before there were so many confounding conflicts.

T: Symptomatic more than—this seems to you much more basic.

C: Yeah, basic, yeah! I know—I think I know I should go all the way, in a sense. But I also know that, as the world judges, I would be excused for not doing this.

T: What you ought to do is clear.

C: Uh-huh. I won't say it's clear, but I'll say that, if I wanted it to be clear, I think that it would be obvious.

T: And to the extent that you would need to fall short of what you thought you ought to do, this would be justifiable; and people, in ordinary estimation, would say that it was.

C: I can conjure words like "prudence" and "state in life," etcetera—I mean all these things that I could use; but it's funny—I know and I know that I know.

T: These—you'd be using these words.

C: I hope this isn't war-like speech, but every moral theologian in the world could tell me to be less wild-eyed and accept what I am, etcetera. In other words, I'm not wanting for justification—if I needed it. I'm not sure, really, just what does obstruct me, now. For instance, we have some friends here— I've mentioned them to you—the gal's name—convert—the kids. Several of the kids have had—what is it called?—cystic fibrosis, and she's a convert, etcetera. They don't have a clothes dryer, and we were talking about getting them one. And my brother had a very excellent job with some [type of business] firm and quit and started his own [field of business] down in [city named]; they're having a rough time getting started. We could help them, etcetera. Well, I mean, we don't have money—we have $200 saved for the [expenditure]. And I know perfectly well that I could seek out advice on these points and be told, "No, you must be prudent, this is your state in life. Even if you don't have to pay for the [expenditure], you should save that money—it's earmarked for a specific purpose which is consistent with your state in life here," etcetera. I mean these things don't have meaning for me.

T: You're aware of the fact that, in this as in so many things, if you were to go to a moral theologian, you're sure they would cover any retreat from these difficulties that you wanted—would cover you perfectly. And yet you know that you'd be using them. You know what you ought to do, and going to a theologian would be running for cover—to get away from the painful, the sacrificial———.

C: Yeah—I mean, I have determined within myself that this running around—the very act of it would not have meaning for me, really.

T: No matter that they would say, it wouldn't be effective for you.

C: I mean I just hear a resounding voice, see, that says, "When your brother was in need, what did you do?" And you can throw in the breeze statements like, "Well, I was—this is for [expenditure]." But the thing that really disturbs me about myself now is that I still lack—I can see it. It's funny, of all the things I can see humor in—I can see it in everything and in anything—this I don't see humor in.

T: There's nothing comical or funny—nothing painlessly incongruous about this at all.

C: I get so very wrought up about almost any issue now, if I think that it relates somehow.

T: If you see a relevancy———.

C: Yeah, for instance, this "Communism on the Map" film, now. [Wife's first name] and I both can become so worked up about it, and she'll finally say, "Well, we better actually do something and not. . . ." Gad! As I say, it's the fear—concern for guarding self, etcetera—that holds me back always, it would seem. For instance, the issue—more obvious issue—over this film is: Is it entirely factual? Is it true that Communism has advanced the way that it has? Well, if it is partially factual, the one thing that is obvious must be that the abuses that Communism seeks to correct must be pretty flagrant if it is getting the reception that Communism is, according to this film. So I think you could view Communism as a symptom, then, and the people who are putting this film on, of course, do not want that. They want you to go off and fight

Communism, as such. It's put out by some Protestant college—a small Protestant college—ultraconservative group, etcetera, and apparently their intention is somehow to lump any kind of movement that aims at broader welfare legislation, etcetera, under Communism, which would make the thing, as far as our successfully combating this, almost impossible. And, as I say, I get so worked up about these, and I'm going to try to express what I think will be the best way to fight Communism with the greatest hope of success. As I say, the only place I'm blocked, now, seems to be in this type of thing. I guard myself for fear that I'll be looked upon with disfavour.

T: Almost a form of human respect.

C: Well, anyway, the same with—I seem to be able to explain what's taking place now more accurately on the basis of this battle. I mean, this urge to—feeling that I ought to be in the forefront as far as Christ's will here, etcetera, and then the obvious straining for self-respect and respect from others——.

T: With the resultant failure in yourself of not coming up to your own expectations for you.

C: Uh-huh—in reality they are mine. I do see them though as Christ's, really; but it's not real clear, because there are times—the more that I sit and think of it all, the more I wonder whether the analysis I have just gone through isn't a little superficial, really. I mean—as I say, I can get worked up over it. I don't know how important it is, really, that a nation call itself Christian if it doesn't act in this way. As I say, I see the big problem as blocking the advance of Communism in various lands, and then—I just wonder if that's not a very superficial way to view this.

T: With possibly affording at least a means of justifiably looking away from the real things—something almost of the red herring?

C: You mean it takes the heat off me, so to speak?

T: As you look at this thing, it almost seems—if I understand you—that from your point of view here there's an awful lot of people feeling worked up about this erroneous solution that is being offered, called Communism—and with this concern about this solution, being so erroneous, people are managing to stay away from the things that are desperately clutched at as the solution for—in other words, the tremendous evils that are there.

C: I'm not real sure that we're on the same——.

T: I may have lost you there. All right——.

C: As I say—I mean, you come to realize that any political order which forces man to be human toward his fellow man is rather dismal commentary on human nature as it sits now, and you realize that the final change isn't one of government, etcetera—men's hearts—this kind of takes the drive out of the whole thing.

T: Reform is individual reform—sanctification—it's not international. So it makes all this pother look pretty sad?

C: Uh-huh, but I still think—as I say—the compulsion is still there to act, but I'm not sure how or——. If it were to be just personal action—I mean, within

the confines of my daily contacts (I'm constrained to use the word just there)—
I feel as if this is not sufficiently potent. That's strange, too, because there's an
awful lot to be done there, really.

T: But somehow or other, the urgency experienced is to set fire on the earth,
and this is not setting fire.

C: At times I think you entertain the possibility of whether guilt in the
everyday failures doesn't kind of stimulate this need for some grandiose expiation by personally leading the charge against Communism.

T: Some heroics—some great—some really————.

C: Telling————.

T: Notable—more to take care of Christ's needs. I mean it almost seems as
though you're fiddling while Rome burns—while men burn. And all the flubs
in your fiddling, all the sour notes that you hit, would be all taken care of all at
once by this, the grand act, that would be yours—as you would do something
that really would be worthwhile, to you.

C: I really am unable to give myself benefits of the doubt or even to look at
myself in a way here which says, "Well, now, maybe some of the stuff you
said is b.s. and maybe it's all not true, and there's just no latitude for imperfec-
tion—there's no acceptance, really. The fact that well, maybe this is what you
are trying, generally, etcetera; and maybe you haven't expressed this perfectly
and maybe it hasn't been faultlessly honest."

T: This—these reflections don't help, to you. The experience in the drive is:
Whole hog or no pork chop. And you look around at these tidbits you're
thinking about and concerned with and drawing—dealing with, and you get
no boost from them whatever.

C: The feeling is, quite simply, that I just don't like myself. I can't stand to
hear myself talk—I can't stand to—I don't know. Everything seems to me to be
incomplete, faltering, bungled—nothing.

T: As you experience it, [client's first name], there is a very profound dislike
of you which carries over in dislike, and in terms of dubiousness, about anything that comes from you; and everything—if you do it, it isn't really worthwhile—it isn't. It bears the mark of unacceptability.

C: Uh-huh, and I think that is largely because I could do it. Somewhere, I
have accepted the notion that the issue isn't really whether I can do any of
these very ponderous tasks; the issue isn't whether or not I will be successful
at them. The issue is, Why haven't I been? It's quite strange. I never really
questioned the fact that, if I would only work myself to the point, then these
things could be done—and I wasted all of this time and, really, there's nothing
to be commended.

T: The very blame which you put on yourself for not—implicitly, very
strongly, says, "You could if you would have." So you never questioned the
"could have."

C: There's no acceptance of limitations. I mean—Zola wrote and is dead and
the world is still in turmoil. Pope Leo X spent some time here—we have

problems yet. I don't see myself as potentially limited the way Pope Leo X was, and————.

T: This is the fact of the matter.

C: It seems that way. I mean what—of course, it is perfectly ludicrous for someone to—I was going to say, it's ludicrous for *me* to say that, who can do nothing, but————.

T: It is, and it isn't; and "it isn't" is very real.

C: I mean, I can laugh at it now.

T: When you get it out and put it out in words—state it this way—it even strikes you as funny, and yet that which you're putting out in words is very real.

C: Uh-huh, and it's so real that while you were saying that now I was thinking I have a few paragraphs that I'm cranking out now, and I have them partially carved. I don't know, as you were saying that I was saying, "Now, let's see, how am I going to finish this? How am I going to tie it up so that the tide will be changed against————

T: While I was talking, this was an interruption. In a sense that didn't really mean it would be interruption. I didn't really distract you, in other words, from the ————.

C: Me.

T: Yes, from what you were doing.

C: This is me, yeah. My, but it is easy to become mired. I think that you would almost chuckle if you were to listen to your opening statements about 25 minutes later or 40 minutes later. This is some more, probably, of the taking a whack at myself for being such an ass, really. Coming here and saying, "Well, now, of course, I think—Harumpf—problem has resolved itself down to this point and this point, and it is quite clear that the decision must be made," and then 40 minutes later, while you're stumbling around the old ruse—it's funny.

T: You can see yourself going back and listening to those first remarks and saying, inside yourself, "Come off it!"

C: Yeah, if I deal with something a sufficient time, it'll get gummed up. I know—it's so strange. You can say those things, and you believe them in a sense, and then in another sense, why, I can say "Come off it" then, too.

T: In a very true sense, it's water off your back—doesn't get you. You seem to be operating at different strata, and this is the one stratum that doesn't touch you, that which is here at the other strata—stratum, we should say————.

C: Oh, gad—I think one thing is, and I shudder to make a positive statement, increasingly clear to me; but I can understand why I don't ever get anything done—why I don't ever follow it through. I mean, whether it is successful or not, I can see why I don't ever follow it through—how some part of me must've been threatened—when you see that the general tone of what is going on is that I am pushing a little too hard, trying to do a little more than I probably should, and there was a question that part of me wanted to ask and it was, "Well, should I wallow in this?—didn't all of the saints, etcetera, have to make this choice that they were going to go at this totally? Would you rather that I just accept the status quo? And not seek a———."

T: And be bogged down in a (quotation) "damnable mediocrity," yeah———.

C: It does appear obvious, I think, that I, in almost every sense—I do shunt back and forth between at least two possible ways to behave.

T: Vacillation is the pattern.

C: Yeah, geez, I don't like myself. I expect that you have very negative feelings about me, now, and that you're very bored with this.

T: You feel it almost has to be that way, really.

C: Yeah, I feel that you really—in a very real way—that you can't stand me—I mean, literally. That is a very unpleasant———.

T: That, really, [client's first name], I have to practice charity?—to act as if this were not so, but deep down———.

C: I don't think it's so deep. I mean, as a matter of fact, I think the tolerance is quite thin, really. I'm not saying it's going to break out. I'm saying it's quite thin.

T: So, really, it looks to you—now, am I ahead of you?—as though I am sharing your feeling toward you.

C: Uh-huh, uh-huh—and of everything we have said, this is real.

T: You're leveling now—all the way through?

C: Uh-huh. I mean, this is something that we both feel, in spite of all of the verbal accord, etcetera—there's now rapport like we enjoy here that—gosh, I don't know what it is. It's just that I think—literally, I think I repel people.

T: So, in this particular situation, [client's name], you cannot—deep down, you cannot subscribe to the fact that I accept you. You can't—as you say, you can't—because this would, if you want, be an impossibility. There's no acceptability in you. If you say this is something you feel—that you have this effect on people—because this is the way you are, you can't believe—no matter what else may or may not be—that I would be an exception to this. You just can't.

C: Somewhere, I think, this has been converted into a feeling—maybe it has—that there's some niggardliness involved on the part of others, really. It's funny, when I was letting some of that feeling out, that I should falter there— that it's not necessarily true, but it's the way that they force me to act. I don't know how protective that is, but I get the feeling that people don't want to acknowledge me—that I'm too insistent for them, or too much a terrier or something.

T: You make them uncomfortable.

C: Uh-huh, yeah. I get the feeling they would like to ignore me if they could, but that's where the terrier, as I say, will not be denied. And that's when I finally provoke feelings of disgust.

T: If you were to let them have, let's say, their way and act on their natural preference, they would turn—they would choose to look the other way, but you're not going to let them. You crowd them. You push them, and you make them—if you want—you make them take a position, and they eat their words or eat their attitudes.

C: I bother them actively now.

T: You press them.

C: I'm almost willing to draw them into controversy on any score, because somehow or other I am strong in this setting and they aren't. I don't even see what it is—it's almost as if I've got nothing to lose and, because I've got nothing to lose, I'm invincible.

T: You hold—you force their attention, to begin with. They can't disregard you and, besides that, it's almost as though you are contesting them in your bailiwick rather than theirs. You're at home, and you know the terrain.

C: I wouldn't say that so much, because—as I say—I don't care necessarily what the fight—what the dispute—involves. I'm going to win and I know it and they know it, and————.

T: The dispute is the important thing, the subject matter isn't. It's an area in which you best them—both of you know it.

C: It's funny—I've never seen it fail. In the [academic subject named] class, [student's name] told me—we were involved in some controversy, and I am not—there is a certain amount of bragging here—but he was telling me that he was over at lunch and a couple of the kids stayed afterwards. I think I have told you this. The rest of the class was eating there and waiting to see how they had done, and [student's name] said a kid said he'd come up to the table and cut me down; and I've noticed in class, too—there are times when they'll just entirely give up. I mean, they'll shake their heads and say, "You can't beat him." Now, these things come to me without thought—no effort, nothing—and I don't care who they are. As I say, I've been here eight solid years, now, and [wife's first name] was just telling me the other day she's noticed this since I first met her. Kids used to come up to the apartment and we'd talk about philosophy, religion, etcetera. In that setting, I would not fear—as I say, I'm not bragging, but I think I have yet to be bested at this. It can be a personal, "ad hominem" type thing or, as I say, it can range any place and I don't have the vaguest idea where it is going, and I don't—At that time, I am without fear.

T: You almost, in a natural way, glory in it. You can almost feel sorry for them. You've got them dead to rights, and no matter where they go, you've got them, and they know you've got them.

C: Uh-huh. There's a kid in my class [class identified]—he's a malcontent—and we were discussing the concept of freedom with supervision and what a fine line that is, etcetera, etcetera—how careful you must be if you're going to judge a hospital policy, predicated on freedom with supervision. And I brought up when they were teen-agers, and the father says, "Take the car"; and they look in the rearview mirror and there is dad following them. This is freedom with supervision—does this constitute freedom? And, as I say, I squashed this kid—oh, maybe seven or eight times—and he's just burned, and so he pipes up, "What kind of father did you have?" Of course, the class got quiet because they really thought that they had me. And I waited the right time and I said, "I had one with two cars." And, of course, the kid was squashed. And this was his big, big chance to finally cut me down. As I say, at a time like that, I don't ever think—there's no active thought to the process—that is all, really.

T: You mean that it's spontaneous—you come up with the right thing, you know it, so you never give it a second thought. You have no fear about it at all—it's just a matter of when and how—but this kid's dead in the water. He's belly up, whether he knows it or not. He knows it only so far, but you know that he is.

C: It's very strange—here. I mean, I think he thought he really had me—this was something personal, very hard to answer—and had I responded on a personal basis about my father and what he meant, etcetera—but to treat the whole issue with such utter disdain just ruined the whole thing for him.

T: Collapsed right around his ears.

C: At that time, I am infinitely calm, etcetera, but just now—telling it here—I find I get all physically————.

T: [unclear] . . . of it in this situation.

C: I don't think it's here so much as I want to show you that you don't have to worry about me. I'm not going to embarrass you with any lack of acuteness in me and in the classroom. So, here, telling it to you, it wasn't the same—it's not the same thing, here, being judged more————.

T: This is a radically different situation.

C: Yeah. I'm sure my father always eschewed that—to express oneself would be to embarrass him. It was too fraught with danger—that you would try this—and he was muzzling me constantly. It made him uncomfortable.

T: This threatened him.

C: Just being physically present in a group made him—if it would've been possible for him, I think, to have vanished into thin air at that time, that would've been the action of choice. I told you about the time—and it means something to me, I don't know why—when we were taking our trip to California. I was talking to him, and the waitress came up. He kicked me under the table and said, "Shh." He didn't want my talking when the waitress came up to the table—he'd much rather have us sitting there—and I was just astonished. I wasn't really, but I mean—what could I possibly do? What could I possibly say—to this gal? We'd never see her—five hours from now we'd be 300 miles from here. Some diner————.

T: It baffled you completely that—why should he be concerned about this?

C: And so much so to the point that it didn't matter whether he cut me off, just so this faceless gal who he'd never see didn't find out how pitifully inadequate this conversation would be. Eating in a diner was fraught with danger.

T: You could be overheard.

C: I could be overheard. If I were feeble-minded or something like this [laugh], I mean, I could see why he'd want to throw the black shroud over me and————.

T: So that he wouldn't be embarrassed. The rest of them wouldn't know and be mortified—than to explain this away, some way.

C: I mean he came in with me—and that in itself was sacrifice enough—you don't have to push him here and expect him to listen to me talk, too, while the other————.

T: Almost the feeling that it was enough in his mind, if you want, to expose himself to the danger of appearing with you.

C: The horrible waste—that's all that I think of. [Number of] children, a family life that spans 30 years, with those kind of—under those pressures and strains—gad, that's an awful waste. When, really, the family itself could've been a self-contained unit.

T: Could've been, but for————.

Second Session

C: Anyway, as I said, it's been a real hectic day—I told you that Bill was the one who was supposed to have called you—he's been in my office two or three hours.

T: Bill who?

C: [Last name]

T: Yeah, I see what you mean.

C: Well, it worked out. He wrote a paper on—he departed from the paper I asked him to write, which is fine—it didn't bother me, really, except that he wrote on Existential Psychoanalysis. It didn't make too much sense, really. College delusions. He just whacks at Freud, etcetera; he thinks these boys have done a much better job. This was fine, too, so I've been asking him why. In class they've been going over it, you know, and I figure I'll put him on the hot seat and, anyway, this morning he made no—wasn't even coherent, didn't make the slightest logic. You just could not follow him—a lot of terminology—got into the sticky substance. Sartre mentions—it was pretty apparent, really not done well. So he wanted to see me about it to drive it home—I mean, to clear it up—and when I left him now, I think I threw him off stride plenty, as he said he never thought of it that way, first time he'd ever thought of it that way, etcetera.

T: A little shattering, hm?

C: Yeah, he has to go home and think it over. So I got my status back, which I was trying—as I was saying, I was talking to [teacher's name]. Apparently, he's never lost, really—this is the way he is. If you're the slightest bit paranoid, he'll really unnerve you with his—just the way he acts, really. So, anyway, that went on and that was something to do with being pooped.

T: Taxing, hm?

C: Yeah. I really do wonder why it is that what I understand, logically—the things that I can tell myself, which can serve as a balm, kind of—that these are only people, and to perform for them, feel compelled to, and to be disturbed if you feel you haven't done a good job, doesn't make sense when you're dealing with the same order of being. What difference does this make? When you're talking about God or something, I can see why you'd be very concerned and very anxious.

T: Why this should be disturbing.

C: But the feeling is certainly there—I mean, the feelings are absolutely immune to what amounts to an intellectual conviction, really.

T: As if compartmentalized—air-tight compartments, really.

C: And it's not only that, because, when I'm out of the setting, I can really feel that if I could just be set back in the threatening setting right now I could handle it—times when the conviction does sweep down, I think, into the past. Of course, I'm not sure whether the conviction's causing that feeling of strength or whether something else does, and then you kind of verbalize this, I don't know————.

T: At any rate, in the anticipated and the imagined, you can actually get one to ramify the other. In the actual, you don't experience this penetration.

C: The time factor is important here. If the performance is an imminent thing, then it's not quite so easy to have this feeling of strength. As a matter of fact, it cannot be done; but if you can kid yourself at times that it is not something that you must do in 5 or 10 minutes————.

T: Time is the buffer, and the less time, the thinner the protection.

C: Uh-huh. For example, yesterday I was invited to this Education luncheon they have—they have a luncheon over in the hall every so often. And that was a dreadful experience, if I may use that—in walking over with [teacher's name], who was also going—with a lot of feeling of being anxious, and motor inability to stop shaking. And then I went to the faculty meeting and, in bygone days, that would have stimulated much the same feelings. But I had completely forgotten it, really. I was walking down and [teacher's name] grabs me and says, "Come on, it's time to go up." And my reaction to that was different. Walking up the stairs, I wondered to myself, "What is dissimilar here? Why aren't the feelings just the same as they were yesterday?" The externals were much the same, except for one important difference—I thought I would be called upon to say a few words to the Education luncheon and I was right, and I didn't expect this.

T: So this was safer in that regard.

C: So it seems like the time factor might have something to do with it, and my own expectations.

T: There was an element of surprise—I mean, as far as time here. An element of surprise where you were told, "This thing is on the pan right now," so you didn't have to sweat it out over a period of time.

C: No, but I had received it passively. Now, I say I'm not sure—there are two variables that I can see, really.

T: Yeah, and the reaction was different. This one was emotionally right, inside, and the other one was most unpleasant to you.

C: It's not debilitating, really. It's hard to say how it's changed—I still like to run, just turn my back on the whole thing—and I think there's still as much bodily involvement, too, but something's different here. When I look for the area of difference it———

T: Where you didn't quite—the thing that you notice here in this. It does not produce a progressive weakness in you, as I understand. In other words, not debilitating in that sense.

C: Yeah. Now, see, what I have done is jump over to something else here. I'm talking about even the anxious feelings which preceded and went along with the Education luncheon—even that kind of feeling is less than it would have been, I think, two or three years in the past; but when I try to find out where these changes———.

T: The fact that you're aware without having explanation—this does not take the same tone that it used to?

C: Yeah, I'm really perplexed when I try to see why, because I'd still just as soon run.

T: So it still seems as threatening, a———.

C: But somehow I know that it's different. But as I told—tick off the only areas that are conscious to me, it isn't different.

T: So you can't really find a satisfying explanation for the difference?

C: I'm not trying very hard—it's almost as if I know it's different, but I don't want it to be different, and I'm not going to bestir myself looking for the reasons why.

T: Something in you is not in favor of this.

C: Uh-huh [laugh], yeah—one would say that—kind of "look for yourself, if you want to." It's not helping me any. I mean, it just tells me that it's an involved, gigantic effort, and I just get tired. I mean I don't bother looking———.

T: Are you saying that the knowledge—the experiential, let's say, evidence that you have of your additional strength in terms that you can cope with now—is, itself, in some way or other threatening? From the fact that you can, to the fact that maybe there will be some kind of demand or obligation arise from that? Or am I ahead of you———?

C: You're not ahead of me theoretically, but you're ahead of me at the feeling level. It's funny———. Yesterday—it's not funny, but I noted the fact that some of the other people there were very reticent to speak, and a couple of them almost looked as if they were praying that they wouldn't be noticed. If it weren't for the backs of chairs, they would've gone off them; and I noticed one fellow next to me who's been there a long, long time—when you would ask him something, he wanted to get out of it. His speech was very clipped and abrupt, and when he was through, you knew he was through and don't look further. And I noticed someone else who seemed to be—at least by their behavior—seemed to be very uncomfortable throughout the whole business.

T: To the extent that they were actually showing, physically, indications of the desire to get out—both their speech and other behavior—inasmuch as the situation———.

C: There were three or four times when [the Assistant Principal] would throw something out, was obviously looking for nibbles, and it got downright embarrassing three or four times.

T: No takers?

C: None at all—very rigid atmosphere, and I just thought: "Well, now, why is it that the obvious message doesn't change you? I mean, why can't you see that, if there are others who are faltering at the start, you should be able to. By the very fact that they are having trouble doing this, this should give you a measure of strength—'See what I can do, when you even can't do it'?"

T: Over and above the fact that the company should be reassuring—you really had company in this experience—even go beyond that and show that in this discomfort, which you were sharing with all of them, a show of strength— which they couldn't actually call up at that time. This type of thing, hm?

C: Yeah, and I did speak up once during the course of—and once even when he turned—he had finished with me. I had just finished, and I could've just as well kept my mouth shut and————.

T: So this was beyond the call of the occasion.

C: Uh-huh. And if I were interested in being safe, I was safe, but I wasn't sure that I was safe, because I wanted to do a better job—really to be sure, just in case the first one hadn't been a sufficient number of large words and very involved sentence structures, etcetera. I wanted to kind of get this back, even though I don't know what I was getting back.

T: Let's put a little guarantee on it—throw in the clincher in the end. So, as you look at it, this additional, let's say, courage to go beyond what was re- quired by the whole situation—this, you don't know—you can't decide your- self whether this was something that was understandable, principally in terms of an urge to do, to perform, to achieve, to accomplish, in a situation like that, or whether it was primarily the need to, let's say, correct and clinch what you'd already said—in other words, to cover, in case there was anything that was [unclear] or loophole in what you'd said.

C: I'm trying to see how this relates to behavior on his part after I'd finished. He looked aside now for someone else and is going to talk about something else or—something, I don't know. And I started talking again and forced him back—his face, his head was forced back to listen. He was very gracious about it.

T: But you made an effort to capture his attention. In reality, you don't know exactly why, as he pulled away, you pulled him back.

C: It's a horrible inability to get involved in a topic, as such. To me, the topic is nothing more than a vehicle—it has no meaning in itself, really, except as it can be turned and distorted someway to my end.

T: It's almost a competitive area.

C: I'm not the least bit sincere in this topic. I mean what I say, and what I might really feel about—well, at that time, I'm not even equipped to know what I really feel.

T: As though you can't afford to make the topic the first consideration. These others things are there, and the topic takes second place down the line. You're taking care of your needs first, through the medium of topic discussion————.

C: I wonder if they are my needs, insofar as I say I don't know what my needs are, as far as really—if I were to say, "Oh, come on, what do you really feel about it?" I'm sure, if I sat there and pondered, what I would say might be entirely different from what I had just said. It's all social stimulus value what I say, and it doesn't—as far as being honestly involved in the topics, it's anything but that. Now, whether this is because I'm so anxious at that time that I can't even catch my real feelings, with so much disorganization at that time—that I have to take what I can get. This, maybe.

T: This could be. You honestly don't know, yourself, what it is that you're pursuing—let's say, endeavoring to achieve, to get out of this—and why.

C: It would seem on the surface that the best probability for getting something I would want to get from it would be to look at my real feelings and give them up—[laugh] give them up! I mean, express them. I mean, if you have any confidence in yourself whatsoever, it only makes sense that the best thing you could do for yourself, at that time, would be what you honestly think, unless you have a suppressed premise that you are an absolute ass, really.

T: So in a way it strikes you as peculiar. Logic would seem to demand this—and yet, if that's what logic demands, logic simply is not yet apparent here.

C: For a second during that stressful time—yet it seems that shorter periods of time separate my being able to look at this thing in that light, and even after I've just finished, than there would've been in the past. At least, I can still be in that setting and see what a farce this is, really.

T: [unclear] . . . freedom experienced here which was not before—freedom in the sense that you're not bound, attention-wise, completely to this thing—that it still has the first position, but it's not monopolistic, as it was.

C: Yeah—this thing seems to be sidling up a little bit closer each time—kind of muscling in. I'm thinking that this whole thing is silly, that you'll never know, really.

T: A doubt that—probable doubt on the value of this entire operation.

C: I can't do it. It's a futile enterprise because of the person I happen to be, really.

T: The doubt moves back onto your competency and your feeling of confidence; and these, in turn—you feel—on your evaluation of yourself; and—logic here—you should look at what I am; therefore, how could I possibly do much about this?

C: I say, I couldn't really be honest—I couldn't really be—I don't know————.

T: Is honesty a luxury that you can't afford to use in this type of situation?

C: It's funny—all kinds of words come up—I couldn't really be honest, couldn't really be pure, good, clean—just a whole series of—kind of a blanket combination.

T: All so many different, you might say, operational aspects of the me, hm?

C: Yeah, still emanating from the same source, as you say. When I go back to what I've said, I'm just thinking how much of that is really true, how much of that is worthwhile—this is distinctly mine; it's no show—almost as if, when I do get down to the real me, my real feelings, the show is to be preferred.

T: Bad as it is, it's almost insufferable to be what would be the you, just the you, expressing yourself as you.

C: Yeah, yes—as if a negative wave of feeling—like I want to kick myself.

T: Almost a concomitant of the feeling you have about you and your worth.

C: I hate myself—I want to make fun of myself—to shut me up, kind of. It's strange—I'd like to see me in the center of all forms of physical violence and, even as I'm talking now, I want to zip myself up—kind of.

T: To the despicable aspect of the me, which, if it cannot somehow or other be disposed of at least can be concealed.

C: For what I said when I first started, what I just said, and what I'm saying now—these things are all lamentable, really, and I shouldn't have said them. I'm assuming that I'm something that I am not—I mean, that I would presume to sit here and waste your time and waste tape and waste typing time when there are garbage disposal units around. It seems like a real travesty.

T: Inside you're crying "sham"—the presently unshakable conviction that, deep down, you're not worthy of any of these things—that you're flying under false colors—that the real you simply does not come up to any of these things—that the real you isn't worthy of being noticed, recognized, attended to, let alone cared about.

C: It hurts if this happens. I am embarrassed by it.

T: As though, in a way, you're aware of an unbecoming exposure—is that it?—as though you stepped in the way?

C: Uh-huh. I feel a desire to change the setting, somehow. That's too—change the psychological setting by causing some kind of a fight, really—getting out of here physically.

T: Do something to make it different—make it otherwise.

C: It's not anything that frightens me, really—the difference between fear and anger.

T: You're irked, close to furious, but not frightened.

C: Uh-huh. I'm trying to understand—how my embarrassment from exposure here makes me angry toward you.

T: You don't understand why you should be so angry, let alone angry at me.

C: I had something, but it's gone. It's impossible to express, except that—I feel now that—I mean, I can't deny your reaction, or lack of it, but I can mistrust————.

T: Keep your fingers crossed—you know, you can see what appears to be—but as far as trusting, let's say, as I understand the continuing acceptance and the trustworthiness in every sense, you still have a big question mark.

C: Uh-huh. At some place there, I'm not sure, the anger itself went out. Now, I think all people are basically stupid and ridiculous, petty and mean, and I'm not one [laugh]—one action I could tie it to.

T: But you notice this is the shift.

C: It started with me, it seemed like—then I could see others the same way—almost as if they'd done something to me and I don't know what.

T: You feel as if they must have, is that it?

C: I feel as if they're no better than I am.

T: And at that level, you're a mere mortal—you've got a lot of company—and rather than your standing off, different from them, now you see yourself as—you feel, in a way, they're your peers.

C: I mean, I don't have to strive, really. I don't know—I'd have to be embarrassed by them maybe or threatened by them, but that only comes when I can be hostile.

T: You need it?

C: Yeah, I cannot be threatened if I'm hostile—I mean, if that's how they are—I don't know. In order to see them that way, in order to deal with them or accept them or———. Now what you started to say was what I was feeling, but when I started to say it, it got fogged over.

T: They have to be the "bad guys" in order for you to have this experience?

C: I think so—in order not to be threatened or pressed by them or exploited by them.

T: The only way to keep them from being a danger to you?

C: They have no control over me or power.

T: It's the one way you can be free of their domination, or actually their power to hurt you.

C: Uh-huh. That is it, there—my whole perception of them changes. All I have is an image of the hall out there, [name of principal] and the people walking around, and that I can see them in a real negative, sarcastic way—I can laugh at them then.

T: And you find you must cast them in that role in order to feel safe?

C: In order to be mad, rather than afraid; and if I have to choose, I'll get mad—it doesn't hurt as much.

T: So between the two, of being threatened by them or angry at them, the less painful is being angry at them. And in order to be angry at them, you have to see them as angering, infuriating in what they are doing and in what they are.

C: This is complicated by the fact that, if you could express it and remain independent, fine. But you depend on them to eat, so that's a horrible problem.

T: In some ways, you can't be completely free—no matter which way you choose, you are still aware of the fact that they do have the power.

C: I see them capitalizing on this.

T: They're in the driver's seat———.

C: And using it.

T: Exploiting you? Taking advantage?

C: Yeah. If I could only be independent—if I only had at my fingertips—if I had at my behest all the resources that I need, then I could see them any way I damn please.

T: If you could only work this thing out so you'd in no sense whatsoever be obligated, then you'd be free to tell them to go to hell—then you'd be free to look at them anyway you wanted. You wouldn't have to tell them to go to hell.

C: Uh-huh—well, the consequence of saying that wouldn't bother me.

T: Are you saying, [client's first name], that the consequences of that would, in one sense at least, be sort of a relief?

C: If I—if the conditions I set up were satisfied, yeah, and I didn't have to worry about————.

T: You doing your share.

C: A relief—I guess so. I'd say it would be revenge, and a relief because of that.

T: It would be satisfaction from the ability to hurt back?

C: As I see it now, of course, I only stand to be hurt by what I might say, and they can go around with their faces and a job and ignore me, really, and I've got to suffer that lack of focus, lack of concern. It could be worse. It could be—out.

T: They can—they're in a position to ignore you.

C: And to know they are doing it.

T: And to do it when [unclear].

C: And not have to answer for it. Kind of stoic, but I can't help believing that they're not getting some satisfaction out of it. They know what they are doing—or he knows.

T: There's something, you suspect, gratifying about the fact that————.

C: That I'm cornered.

T: That you're cornered, and that they're culpable, really.

C: I should see it as an oversight, maybe, but I don't feel that that's the explanation for it—it's devious; it's calculated.

T: It's too deliberate.

C: They enjoy walking by without having to [unclear]—not having to acknowledge.

T: Satisfying to them that they know, and let you know, that you don't exist as far as they are concerned.

C: They don't have to be troubled.

References

1. Abraham, K. "A Short Study of the Development of the Libido, Viewed in the Light of Mental Disorders" [1924]. In *Selected Papers on Psycho-Analysis*. London: Hogarth Press, 1927.
2. Ackermann, R. *The Philosophy of Science*. New York: Pegasus, 1970.
3. Adler, A. *The Neurotic Constitution*. New York: Moffatt, Yard, 1917.
4. Adler, A. *The Practice and Theory of Individual Psychology*. London: Kegan Paul, 1924.
5. Adler, M. *The Difference of Man and The Difference It Makes*. New York: Holt, Rinehart & Winston, 1968.
6. Adorno, T. W.; Frenkel–Brunswik, E.; Levinson, D. J.; and Sanford, R. N. *The Authoritarian Personality*. New York: Harper, 1950.
7. Allport, G. W. "Scientific Models and Human Morals." *Psychological Review*, 54 (1947):182–92.
8. Allport, G. W. *Becoming: Basic Considerations for a Psychology of Personality*. New Haven: Yale University Press, 1955.
9. Allport, G. W. *The Nature of Prejudice*. New York: Doubleday, 1958.
10. Ausubel, D. *Ego Development and the Personality Disorders*. New York: Grune & Stratton, 1952.
11. Ausubel, D. *Theory and Problems of Child Development*. New York: Grune & Stratton, 1958.
12. Ax, A. "The Physiological Differentiation Between Fear and Anger in Humans." *Psychosomatic Medicine*, 15 (1953): 433–42.
13. Bakan, D. "The Mystery-Mastery Complex in Contemporary Psychology." *American Psychologist*, 20 (1965): 186–91.
14. Bandura, A. *Aggression: A Social Learning Analysis*. Englewood Cliffs, N.J.: Prentice–Hall, 1973.
15. Becker, E. *The Denial of Death*. New York: Free Press, 1973.
16. Becker, W.; Peterson, D.; Hellmer, L.; Shoemaker, D.; and Quay, H. "Factors in Parental Behavior and Personality as Related to Problem Behavior in Children." *Journal of Consulting Psychology*, 23 (1959): 107–18.
17. Becker, W.; Peterson, D.; Luris, Z.; Shoemaker, D.; and Hellmer, L. "Relations of Factors Derived from Parent Interview Ratings to Behavior Problems of Five-Year-Olds." *Child Development*, 33 (1962): 509–35.
18. Berkowitz, L. *Aggression: A Social Psychological Analysis*. New York: McGraw–Hill, 1962.
19. Bibring, E. "The Mechanism of Depression." In *The Meaning of Despair*, edited by W. Gaylen. New York: Science House, 1968.
20. Block, J. "Personality Characteristics Associated with Fathers' Attitudes Toward Child-rearing." *Child Development*, 26 (1955): 41–48.

21. Blumberg, M. "Psychopathology of the Abusing Parent." *American Journal of Psychotherapy,* 28 (January 1974): 21–29.

22. Boring, E. *A History of Experimental Psychology.* 2nd ed. New York: Appleton–Century–Crofts, 1950.

23. Bowlby, J. *Maternal Care and Mental Health.* New York: Schocken, 1966.

24. Bowlby, J. "Some Pathological Processes Set in Train by Early Mother-Child Separation." *British Journal of Psychiatry: The Journal of Mental Science,* 99 (1954): 265–72.

25. Bowlby, J. "Separation Anxiety." *International Journal of Psychoanalysis,* 41 (1960): 89–113.

26. Bowlby, J.; et al. "The Effects of Mother-Child Separation: A Follow-up Study." *British Journal of Medical Psychology,* 29 (1956): 211–43.

27. Brandt, L. "American Psychology." *American Psychologist,* 25 (December 1970): 1091–93.

28. Bridgman, P. *The Way Things Are.* Cambridge: Harvard University Press, 1959.

29. Brown, N. *Life Against Death: The Psychoanalytic Meaning of History.* New York: Viking, 1959.

30. Brown, R.; and Hernstein, R. *Psychology.* Boston: Little, Brown, 1975.

31. Burchinal, D.; Hawkes, G.; and Gardner, B. "The Relationship Between Parental Acceptance and Adjustment of Children." *Child Development,* 28 (1957): 65–77.

32. Buss, A. *The Psychology of Aggression.* New York: Wiley, 1961.

33. Calkins, M. "Common Ground in Contemporary Psychology." In *9th International Congress of Psychology: Proceedings and Papers,* pp. 108–9. Princeton, N.J.: Psychological Review Co., 1930.

34. Castell, E. *The Self in Philosophy.* New York: Macmillan, 1965.

35. Caws, P. "Scientific Method." In *The Encyclopedia of Philosophy,* Vol. 7, pp. 339–43. New York: Macmillan and Free Press, 1967.

36. Chomsky, N. *Psychology and Ideology Cognition,* Vol. 1. New York: Mouton, 1973.

37. Chorost, S. B. "Parental Child-Rearing Attitudes and Their Correlates in Adolescent Hostility." *Genetic Psychology Monographs,* 66 (1962): 49–90.

38. Christie, R.; and Jahoda, M., eds. *Studies in the Scope and Method of the Authoritarian Personality.* Glencoe, Ill.: Free Press, 1954.

39. Coopersmith, S. "The Relationship Between Self-Esteem and Perceptual Constancy." *Journal of Abnormal Psychology,* 88 (1964): 217–21.

40. Coopersmith, S. *The Antecedents of Self-Esteem.* San Francisco: W. H. Freeman, 1967.

41. Darwin, C. *The Voyage of the Beagle.* New York: Bantam Books, 1972.

42. Day, W. F. "Radical Behaviorism in Reconciliation with Phenomenology." *Journal of the Experimental Analysis of Behavior,* 12 (March 1969): 315–28.

43. DeForest, I. "The Self-Dedication of the Psychoneurotic Sufferer to Hostile Protest and Revenge." *Psychiatric Quarterly,* 24 (1950): 706–15.

44. Dember, W. N. "Motivation and the Cognitive Revolution." *American Psychologist,* 29 (March 1974): 161–68.

45. Despert, J. L. *The Emotionally Disturbed Child.* New York: Doubleday, Anchor Books, 1970.

46. Dollard, J.; Doob, L.; Miller, N.; Mowrer, O.; and Sears, R. *Frustration and Aggression.* New Haven: Yale University Press, 1939.

47. Dollard, J.; and Miller, N. *Personality and Psychotherapy.* New York: McGraw–Hill, 1950.

48. Dreyfus, H. L.; and Dreyfus, F. A. "Translator's Introduction." In *Sense and Nonsense,* by M. Merleau–Ponty. Evanston: Northwestern University Press, 1964.

49. Eacker, J. M. "On Some Elementary Philosophical Problems of Psychology." *American Psychologist,* 27 (1972): 553–65.

50. Erikson, E. H. *Insight and Responsibility.* New York: Norton, 1964.
51. Estes, H. C.; Haglett, C. H.; and Johnson, A. M. "Separation Anxiety." *American Journal of Psychotherapy,* 10 (1956): 682–95.
52. Evoy, J. J.; and O'Keefe, M. *The Man and the Woman, Psychology of Human Love.* New York: Sheed & Ward, 1968.
53. Fearon, A. D. *The Two Sciences of Psychology.* Englewood Cliffs, N.J.: Prentice–Hall, 1937.
54. Fenichel, O. "Depression and Mania." In *The Meaning of Despair,* edited by U. Gaylin. New York: Science House, 1968.
55. Fernberger, S. W. "Behavior-vs-Introspective Psychology." In *Readings in Psychology,* edited by C. E. Skinner, pp. 36–38. New York: Holt, Rinehart & Winston, 1935.
56. Feshbach, S. "Aggression." In *Carmichael's Manual of Child Psychology,* Vol. 2, edited by P. H. Mussen, pp. 159–259. New York: Wiley, 1970.
57. Figge, M. "Some Factors in the Etiology of Maternal Rejection." *Smith College Studies in Social Work,* 2 (March 1932): 237–60.
58. Fodor, J. K. *Psychological Explanation: An Introduction to the Philosophy of Psychology.* New York: Random House, 1968.
59. Freud, A. *The Ego and the Mechanisms of Defense.* New York: International Universities Press, 1946.
60. Freud, A.; and Burlingham, D. *Infants Without Families.* New York: International Universities Press, 1944.
61. Freud, S. *Inhibitions, Symptoms, and Anxiety,* Vol. 20 of *The Complete Psychological Works of Sigmund Freud.* London: Hogarth Press and the Institute of Psychoanalysis, 1959.
62. Freud, S. *The Complete Psychological Works of Sigmund Freud.* 23 vols. London: Hogarth Press and the Institute of Psychoanalysis, 1966.
63. Fromm, E. "Selfishness and Self-Love." *Psychiatry,* 2 (1939): 507–23.
64. Fromm, E. *The Art of Loving.* New York: Harper & Row, 1956.
65. Funkenstein, D. N. "The Physiology of Fear and Anger." *Scientific American,* 192 (1955): 74–80.
66. Galdston, R. "Observations on Children Who Have Been Physically Abused and Their Parents." *American Journal of Psychiatry,* 122 (1965): 440–43.
67. Gallagher, J. J. "Rejecting Parents?" *Exceptional Children,* 22 (1956): 273–94.
68. Gecas, V.; Calonico, J.; and Thomas, D. "The Development of Self-Concept in the Child: Mirror Theory Versus Model Theory." *Journal of Social Psychology,* 92 (February 1974): 67–76.
69. Giorgi, A. *Psychology as a Human Science.* New York: Harper & Row, 1970.
70. Goldstein, K. *The Organism.* New York: American Book Co., 1939.
71. Goodstein, L. D.; and Rowley, V. N. "A Further Study of M.M.P.I. Differences Between Parents of Disturbed and Nondisturbed Children." *Journal of Consulting Psychology,* 25 (1961): 460.
72. Gottesman, S. "Hereditability of Personality." *Psychological Monographs,* 77 (1963): 572.
73. Guex, G. *La Névrose d'Abandon.* Paris: Presses Universitaires de France, 1950.
74. Gurwitsch, A. *Studies in Phenomenological Psychology.* Evanston: Northwestern University Press, 1966.
75. Hamilton, V. "Effect of Maternal Attitude on Development of Logical Operations." *Perceptual and Motor Skills,* 33 (August 1971): 63–69.
76. Hawkes, G. R. "The Child in the Family." *Marriage and Family Living,* 19 (February 1957): 46–51.

77. Hebb, D. O. *The Organization of Behavior*. New York: Wiley, 1961.
78. Hebb, D. O. "What Psychology Is About." *American Psychologist*, 29 (February 1974): 71–79.
79. Heidbreder, E. *Seven Psychologies*. New York: Appleton–Century–Crofts, 1933.
80. Heidegger, M. *Being and Time*. New York: Harper & Row, 1962.
81. Helper, M. "Parental Evaluations of Children and Children's Self-Evaluations." *Journal of Abnormal and Social Psychology*, 56 (1958): 190–94.
82. Hempel, C. G. *Aspects of Scientific Explanation*. New York: Free Press, 1965.
83. Hilgard, E. "Hypnotic Phenomena; The Struggle for Scientific Acceptance." *American Scientist*, 59 (September–October 1971): 567–77.
84. Horney, K. "Maternal Conflicts." *American Journal of Orthopsychiatry*, 3 (October 1933): 455–63.
85. Horney, K. *Our Inner Conflicts*. New York: Norton, 1945.
86. Jacobson, E. "The Effect of Disappointment on Ego and Superego Formation in Normal and Depressive Development." *Psychoanalytic Review*, 33 (1946): 129–47.
87. Jones, E. *Papers on Psychoanalysis*. New York: William Wood and Co., 1923.
88. Jourard, S.; and Remy, R. "Perceived Parental Attitudes, the Self, and Security." *Journal of Counseling Psychology*, 19 (1955): 364–66.
89. Kagan, J. "Socialization of Aggression and the Perception of Parents in Fantasy." *Child Development*, 29 (1958): 311–20.
90. Kagan, J. "Human Behavior, Development of." In *Encyclopaedia Britannica*, 15th ed.; *Macropaedia*, Vol. 10. Chicago: Encyclopaedia Britannica, Inc., 1974.
91. Kagan, J.; Hosken, B.; and Watson, S. "The Child's Symbolic Conceptualization of the Parents." *Child Development*, 32 (1961): 625–36.
92. Kearsley, M.; Snider, M.; Richie, R.; Crawford, J.; and Talbot, N. "Study of Relations Between Psychologic Environment and Child Behavior." *American Journal of Diseases of Children*, 104 (1962): 12–20.
93. Kelly, G. "Man's Construction of His Alternatives." In *Assessment of Human Motives*, edited by G. Lindsey. New York: Grove Press, 1960.
94. Kempe, H.; and Helfer, R. *The Battered Child*. Chicago: University of Chicago Press, 1974.
95. Knight, E. "A Descriptive Comparison of Markedly Aggressive and Submissive Children." Unpublished master's thesis, Smith College School for Social Work, 1933.
96. Koch, M. "Anxiety in Preschool Children From Broken Homes." *Merrell-Palmer Quarterly*, 7 (1961): 225–31.
97. Kockelmans, J. *Phenomenology and Physical Science*. Pittsburgh: Duquesne University Press, 1966.
98. Krasner, L. "The Behavior Scientist and Social Responsibility: No Place to Hide." *Journal of Social Issues*, 21, 2 (1965): 9–30.
99. Kris, E. *Psychoanalytic Explorations in Art*. New York: International Universities Press, 1952.
100. Leakey, R. L.; and Lewin, R. "Is It Our Culture, Not Our Genes, That Makes Us Killers?" *Smithsonian* (November 1977): 56–67.
101. Lee, P.; and Kenworthy, M. *Mental Hygiene and Social Work*. Boston: The Commonwealth Fund, 1929.
102. Levine, M. "Scientific Method and the Adversary Model." *American Psychologist*, 29 (September 1974): 661–77.
103. Levy, D. "A Method of Integrating Physical and Psychiatric Examination, with Special Studies of Body Interest, Overprotection, Response to Growth and Sex Differences." *American Journal of Psychology*, 9 (July 1929): 121–94.

104. Levy, D. "Primary Affect Hunger." *American Journal of Psychiatry*, 94 (1937): 643–52.
105. Levy, D. *Maternal Overprotection*. New York: Columbia University Press, 1943.
106. Lewis, H. "Unsatisfactory Parents and Psychological Disorder in Their Children." *Eugenics Review*, 47 (1955): 153–62.
107. Liebert, R.; and Spiegler, N. *Personality: Strategies for the Study of Man*. Rev. ed. Homewood, Ill.: Dorsey Press, 1974.
108. Liverant, S. "M.M.P.I. Differences Between Parents of Disturbed and Nondisturbed Children." *Journal of Consulting Psychology*, 23 (1959): 256–60.
109. Loeb, J.; and Price, J. "Mother and Child Characteristics Related to Parental Marital Status in Child Guidance Cases." *Journal of Consulting Psychology*, 30 (1966): 112–17.
110. Lomas, J. "On Maternal Symbiotic Depression." *Psychoanalytic Review*, 43 (1956): 423–31.
111. Lorenz, K. *On Aggression*. New York: Harcourt, Brace & World, 1966.
112. Lundin, R. *Personality: A Behavioral Analysis*. 2nd ed. New York: Macmillan, 1974.
113. Maccoby, E. "Attachment and Dependence." In *Manual of Child Psychology*, edited by P. H. Mussen. New York: Wiley, 1969.
114. MacLeod, R. "Phenomenology." *International Encyclopaedia of the Social Sciences*, 12 (1964): 68–72.
115. MacLeod, R. "The Teaching of Psychology and the Psychology We Teach." *American Psychologist*, 20 (1965): 344–52.
116. Marcuse, H. *Eros and Civilization: A Philosophical Inquiry into Freud*. Boston: Beacon Press, 1966.
117. Maslow, A. *Motivation and Personality*. New York: Harper & Row, 1954.
118. Maslow, A. *The Psychology of Science: A Reconnaissance*. New York: Harper & Row, 1966.
119. Maslow, A. *Motivation and Personality*. 2nd ed. New York: Harper & Row, 1970.
120. Maslow, A.; and Mittelmann, B. *Principles of Abnormal Psychology: The Dynamics of Psychic Illness*. New York: Harper, 1941.
121. Masserman, J. *Principles of Dynamic Psychiatry*. Philadelphia: W. B. Saunders, 1946.
122. May, R. *The Meaning of Anxiety*. New York: Ronald Press, 1950.
123. McDonald, R. "Intrafamilial Conflict and Emotional Disturbance." *Journal of Genetic Psychology*, 101 (1962): 201–8.
124. McNeil, E., ed. *The Nature of Human Conflict*. Englewood Cliffs, N.J.: Prentice–Hall, 1965.
125. Mead, M. *Anthropology: A Human Science*. New York: Van Nostrand, 1964.
126. Meerloo, J. "The Father Cuts the Cord." *American Journal of Psychotherapy*, 10 (1956): 471–80.
127. Michalak, J. "City Life in Primers." *New York Herald Tribune*, January 26, 1965.
128. Misiak, H.; and Sexton, V. *History of Psychology*. New York: Grune & Stratton, 1966.
129. Mitchell, J. "Self-Family Perceptions Related to Self-Acceptance, Manifest Anxiety and Neuroticism." *Journal of Educational Research*, 56 (January 1963): 236–42.
130. Morgan, C. L. "Comparative and Genetic Psychology." *Psychological Review*, 12 (1905): 78–97.
131. Mowrer, O. *Learning Theory and Personality Dynamics*. New York: Ronald Press, 1950.
132. Murphy, G. *A Briefer General Psychology*. New York: Harper & Row, 1935.
133. Murphy, G. *Personality: A Biosocial Approach to Origins and Structure*. New York: Harper & Row, 1947.
134. Mussen, P.; Conger, J.; and Kagan, J. *Child Development and Personality*. 4th ed. New York: Harper & Row, 1974.

135. Mussen, P.; Young, H.; Gaddini, R.; and Morante, L. "The Influence of Father-Son Relationships on Adolescent Personality and Attitudes." *Journal of Child Psychology and Psychiatry and Allied Disciplines*, 4 (1963): 3–16.

136. *National Survey of Children*. Conducted by Temple University's Institute for Survey Research—a sample of 2,208 children of grammar school age, and their parents, were interviewed. Published in March 1977.

137. Newbauer, P. B. *Children in Collectives: Child-Raising Aims and Practices in the Kibbutz.* Springfield, Ill.: Charles C. Thomas, 1965.

138. Newell, H. W. "Psychodynamics of Maternal Rejection." *American Journal of Orthopsychiatry*, 4 (1934): 387–401.

139. Newell, H. W. "A Further Study of Maternal Rejection." *American Journal of Orthopsychiatry*, 6 (1936): 576–89.

140. Newell, H. W., quoted in P. M. Symonds. "A Study of Parental Acceptance and Rejection." *American Journal of Orthopsychiatry*, 8 (1938): 679–88.

141. Odier, C. *Anxiety and Magic Thinking.* New York: International Universities Press, 1956.

142. Ostow, M. "Parents' Hostility to Their Children." *The Israel Annals of Psychiatry and Related Disciplines*, 8, 1 (April 1970): 3–21.

143. Pearson, G. H. J. "The Psychosexual Development of the Child." *Mental Hygiene*, 15 (October 1931): 685–713.

144. Pease, D.; and Gardner, D. "Research on the Effects of Noncontinuous Mothering." *Child Development*, 29, 1 (March 1958): 141–48.

145. Pemberton, D. A.; and Benady, D. R. "Consciously Rejected Children." *British Journal of Psychiatry*, 123 (1973): 575–78.

146. Pervin, L. A. "Existentialism, Psychology, and Psychotherapy." *American Psychologist*, 15 (1960): 305–9.

147. Phillips, D. C. *The Abused Child Primer.* Seattle: Washington State Medical Association, 1974.

148. Porter, B. M. "The Relationship Between Marital Adjustment and Parental Acceptance of Children." *Journal of Home Economics*, 47 (1955): 157–64.

149. Rabin, A. B. "The Maternal Deprivation Hypothesis Revisited." *The Israel Annals of Psychiatry and Related DIsciplines*, 1 (October 1963): 189–200.

150. Rado, S. "The Problem of Melancholia." In *The Meaning of Despair*, edited by W. Gaylen. New York: Science House, 1968.

151. Rado, S. "Psychodynamics of Depression from the Etiologic Point of View." In *The Meaning of Despair,* edited by W. Gaylen. New York: Science House, 1968.

152. Rank, O. *Psychology and the Soul.* Philadelphia: University of Pennsylvania Press, 1950.

153. Rank, O. *Modern Education: A Critique of Its Fundamental Ideas.* New York: Agathon Press, 1968.

154. Ransford, H. E. "Isolation, Powerlessness and Violence: A Study of Attitudes and Participation in the Watts Riot." *American Journal of Sociology*, 73 (1968): 581–91.

155. Rausch, H. L.; and Williams, E. P., eds. *Naturalistic Viewpoints in Psychological Research.* New York: Holt, Rinehart & Winston, 1969.

156. Rheingold, J. C. *The Mother, Anxiety and Death: The Catastrophic Death Complex.* Boston: Little, Brown, 1967.

157. Rickman, H. P., ed. *Meaning in History.* London: G. Allen, 1961.

158. Robins, R. H. "Language." In *Encyclopaedia Britannica*, 15th ed., Vol. 10. Chicago: Encyclopaedia Britannica, Inc., 1974.

159. Rogers, C. R. *On Becoming a Person.* Boston: Houghton Mifflin, 1961.

160. Rogers, C. R. "Toward a Science of the Person." In *Behaviorism and Phenomenology*, edited by T. W. Wann. Chicago: University of Chicago Press, 1964.
161. Rogers, C. R. "Psychotherapy Today, or Where Do We Go From Here?" In *Psychotherapy Research*, edited by G. E. Stollok, B. G. Guerney, Jr., and Meyer Rothberg. Chicago: Rand McNally, 1966.
162. Rogers, C. R. "Some New Challenges." *American Psychologist*, 28 (May 1973): 379–87.
163. Rogers, C. R. "In Retrospect: Forty-six Years." *American Psychologist*, 29 (February 1974): 115–23.
164. Rogers, C. R.; and Dymond, R., eds. *Psychotherapy and Personality Change: Co-ordinated Studies in the Client-Centered Approach*. Chicago: University of Chicago Press, 1954.
165. Rosenberg, M. "Parental Interest and Children's Self-Conceptions." *Sociometry*, 26 (1963): 35–49.
166. Rosenfeld, H. M.; and Baer, D. M. "Unbiased and Unnoticed Verbal Conditioning: The Double Agent Robot Procedure." *Journal of the Experimental Analysis of Behavior*, 1 (July 1970): 99–107.
167. Rosenthal, R. *Experimenter Effects in Behavioral Research*. New York: Appleton–Century–Crofts, 1966.
168. Roudinesco, J. "Severe Maternal Deprivation and Personality Development in Early Childhood." *Understanding the Child*, 21 (1952): 104–8.
169. Royce, J. *Man and Meaning*. New York: McGraw–Hill, 1969.
170. Sanford, F. *Psychology: A Scientific Study of Man*. 2nd ed. Belmont, Calif.: Wadsworth, 1965.
171. Sappenfield, B. R. *Personality Dynamics*. New York: Knopf, 1954.
172. Sarason, E.; and Sarason, B. "Dynamics and Morality of Violence and Aggression—Some Psychological Considerations." In *Readings in Abnormal Psychology*, compiled and edited by E. Sarason and B. Sarason, pp. 340–51. New York: Appleton–Century–Crofts, 1972.
173. Sartre, J. P. *Sketch for a Theory of the Emotions*. Translated by P. Mairet. London: Methuen, 1962.
174. Schachter, S.; and Singer, J. "Cognitive, Social and Physiological Determinants of Emotional State." *Psychological Review*, 69 (September 1962): 379–99.
175. Schulman, R.; Shoemaker, D.; and Moelis, I. "Laboratory Measurement of Parental Behavior." *Journal of Consulting Psychology*, 26 (1962): 109–14.
176. Sears, R. R. "Relation of Early Socialization Experiences to Aggression in Middle Childhood." *Journal of Abnormal and Social Psychology*, 63 (1961): 466–92.
177. Segal, E. M.; and Lachman, R. "Complex Behavior or Higher Mental Process: Is There a Paradigm Shift?" *American Psychologist*, 27 (January 1972): 46–55.
178. Seligman, M. E. "On the Generality of the Laws of Learning." *Psychological Review*, 77 (1970): 406–18.
179. Seligman, M. E. *Helplessness—On Depression, Development and Death*. San Francisco: W. H. Freeman, 1975.
180. Serot, N.; and Teevan, R. "Perception of the Parent-Child Relationship and Its Relation to Child Adjustment." *Child Development*, 32 (1961): 373–78.
181. Shoben, E. J., Jr. "The Assessment of Parental Attitudes in Relation to Child Adjustment." *Genetic Psychology Monographs*, 39 (1949): 101–48.
182. Silver, L. B.; Dublin, C. C.; and Lourie, R. S. "Does Violence Breed Violence? Contributions from a Study of the Child Abuse Syndrome." *American Journal of Psychiatry*, 126 (1969): 404–7.

183. Skinner, B. F. "The Restatement of the Philosophy of Behaviorism." *Science,* 140, 31 (May 1963): 951.

184. Skinner, B. F. *Beyond Freedom and Dignity.* New York: Knopf, 1971.

185. Skinner, B. F. "Comment on Rogers." *American Psychologist,* 29 (August 1974): 640.

186. Soddy, K. "The Unwanted Child." *Journal of Family Welfare,* 11 (1964): 39–52.

187. Sonnemann, D. *Existence and Therapy.* New York: Grune & Stratton, 1954.

188. Spielberger, C. D. *Anxiety,* Vol. 1. New York: Academic Press, 1972.

189. Spitz, R. A. "Hospitalism: An Inquiry into the Genesis of Psychiatric Conditions in Early Childhood." *Psychoanalytic Studies of the Child,* 1 (1945): 53–74.

190. Spitz, R. A. "The Role of Ecological Factors in Emotional Development in Infancy." *Child Development,* 20 (1949): 145–55.

191. Spitz, R. A. "Environment Versus Race: Environment as an Etiological Factor in Psychiatric Disturbances in Infancy." In *Psychoanalysis and Culture,* edited by G. W. Wilbur and W. Muensterberger, pp. 32–41. New York: International Universities Press, 1951.

192. Spitz, R. A. "The Psychogenic Diseases in Infancy." *Psychoanalytic Studies of the Child,* 6 (1951): 255–75.

193. Spitz, R. A.; and Wolf, K. M. "Anaclitic Depression: An Inquiry into the Genesis of Psychiatric Conditions in Early Childhood." *Psychoanalytic Studies of the Child,* 2 (1946): 313–42.

194. Strasser, S. *Phenomenology and the Human Sciences.* Pittsburgh: Duquesne University Press, 1963.

195. Straus, E. *The Primary World of the Senses.* Glencoe, Ill.: Free Press, 1963.

196. Symonds, P. M. "A Study of Parental Acceptance and Rejection." *American Journal of Orthopsychiatry,* 8 (1938): 679–88.

197. *Time.* "Battered Child Syndrome." Vol. 80, No. 3 (1962), p. 60.

198. Toffler, A. *Future Shock.* New York: Bantam Books, 1970.

199. Toulmin, S. E. "Philosophy of Science." In *Encyclopaedia Britannica,* 15th ed.; *Macropaedia,* Vol. 16, pp. 375–93. Chicago: Encyclopaedia Britannica, Inc., 1974.

200. Turner, M. B. *Philosophy and the Science of Behavior.* New York: Appleton–Century–Crofts, 1967.

201. Tyler, L. E. "Design for a Hopeful Psychology." *American Psychologist,* 28 (December 1973): 1021–29.

202. Ulrich, R.; Stachnik, T.; and Mabry, J., eds. *Control of Human Behavior.* Glenview, Ill.: Scott, Foresman, 1966.

203. Van Laer, P. H. *Philosophy of Science,* Part 1. Pittsburgh: Duquesne University Press, 1966.

204 Vogel, E. F. "The Marital Relationship of Parents of Emotionally Disturbed Children: Polarization and Isolation." *Psychiatry,* 23 (1960): 1–12.

205. Wahl, C. W. "The Fear of Death." In *The Meaning of Death,* edited by H. Feifel. New York: McGraw–Hill, 1959.

206. Warren, H. C. *Dictionary of Psychology.* New York: Houghton Mifflin, 1934.

207. Wertham, F. "Battered Children and Baffled Adults." *Bulletin of the New York Academy of Medicine,* 48 (1972): 887–98.

208. White, R. W. *The Abnormal Personality: A Textbook.* New York: Ronald Press, 1948.

209. Winder, C. L.; and Rau, L. "Parental Attitudes Associated with Social Deviance in Pre-Adolescent Boys." *Journal of Abnormal and Social Psychology,* 64 (1962): 418–24.

210. Witkin, H.; Lewis, H. B.; Hertzman, M.; Machover, K.; Meissner, P. B.; and Wapner, S. *Personality Through Perception.* New York: Harper, 1954.

211. Witmer, H. L. "Studies in Maternal Over-Protection and Rejection." *Smith College Studies in Social Work*, 2 (March 1932): 181–87.
212. Wolberg, L. R. "The Character Structure of the Rejected Child." *Nervous Child*, 3 (1944): 74–88.
213. Woodworth, R. S. *Contemporary Schools of Psychology*. New York: Ronald Press, 1931.
214. Wundt, W. "Contributions to the Theory of Sensory Perception." In *Classics in Psychology*, edited by T. Shipley, pp. 51–78. New York: Philosophical Library, 1961.
215. Wylie, R. *The Self-Concept*. Lincoln: University of Nebraska Press, 1961.
216. Yarrow, L. "Maternal Deprivation: Toward an Empirical and Conceptual Re-evaluation." *Psychological Bulletin*, 58 (1961): 459–90.
217. Zilboorg, G. "Fear of Death." *Psychoanalytic Quarterly*, 12 (1943): 465–75.

Index